Activities for Developing Mathematical Thinking:

Exploring, Inventing, and Discovering Mathematics

Joseph G. R. Martinez
University of New Mexico

Nancy C. Martinez
University of New Mexico

PEARSON

Merrill
Prentice Hall

Upper Saddle River, New Jersey
Columbus, Ohio

Library of Congress Cataloging-in-Publication Data

Martinez, Joseph G. R.,
  Activities for developing mathematical thinking : exploring, inventing, and discovering
mathematics / Joseph G.R. Martinez, Nancy C. Martinez.
    p. cm.
  ISBN 0-13-098742-5
  1. Mathematics—Study and teaching (Elementary)—United States. 2. Mathematics—Study
and teaching (Middle school)—United States. 3. Mathematical ability in children—United States.
4. Cognition in children. I. Martinez, Nancy C. (Nancy Conrad) II. Title.
  QA135.6.M366 2007
  372.7—dc22   2006043687

Vice President and Executive Publisher: Jeffery W. Johnston
Senior Editor: Linda Ashe Bishop
Associate Editor: Meredith Sarver
Senior Production Editor: Mary M. Irvin
Design Coordinator: Diane C. Lorenzo
Senior Editorial Assistant: Laura Weaver
Cover Designer: Candace Rowley
Cover Image: Fotosearch
Production Manager: Pamela D. Bennett
Director of Marketing: David Gesell
Marketing Manager: Darcy Betts Prybella
Marketing Coordinator: Brian Mounts

This book was set in Garamond by Carlisle Publishing Services. It was printed and bound by
R. R. Donnelley & Sons Company. The cover was printed by Coral Graphics.

Pearson Education Ltd.   Pearson Education Australia PTY, Limited
Pearson Education Singapore, Pte. Ltd.   Pearson Education North Asia Ltd.
Pearson Education Canada, Ltd.   Pearson Educación de Mexico, S.A. de C.V.
Pearson Education—Japan   Pearson Education Malaysia, Pte. Ltd.

10 9 8 7 6 5 4 3 2
ISBN: 0-13-098742-5

Contents

Worksheets and Handouts

The following worksheets and handouts are to be used with various activities in this text. All worksheets and handouts are on the accompanying CD-ROM and can be printed out for activity use.

Numbers Log

Graphing Coins

Coin Bingo Card

Calculator Worksheet

Race Cards for 250-Mile Race

Base-10 Blocks Worksheet

Chinese Stick Numbers

Multiplication/Division Facts Worksheet

Chinese Stick Numbers II

Bug Worksheet

Building Shapes Worksheet: Polygons

Building Shapes Worksheet: Three Dimensions

Frieze Patterns

Timing Log Sheet

Measuring Circles to Find Pi

Tessellations Worksheet

Polygons and Angles Worksheet

M&Ms Worksheet 1

M&Ms Worksheet 2

Apple Pictograph Worksheet

McDonald's Farm Worksheet

T-Chart Worksheet

Tally Sheet for 1 Coin, 10 Tosses

Tally Sheet for 2 Coins, 30 Tosses

Tally Sheet for 2 Coins, 40 Tosses

Tally Sheets for 30 Tosses of Dice

Fractions Worksheet

Fractions with Counters Worksheet

Fractions with Shapes

Musical Notes and Fractions Worksheet

Planning a Party Worksheet

Graph and Pie Chart Worksheet

Numbers at the Zoo Worksheet

Counting Sheets

M&Ms Count & Crunch

Ratio-Worksheet 1

Ratio Worksheet 2

Make Your Own Manipulatives

The following math manipulatives are on the accompanying CD-ROM and can be printed out for activity use.

Fraction Strips

Fraction Squares

Fraction Circles

Pattern Shapes

Tangrams

Tangram Puzzles

Tangram Solutions

Geoboard

Base-10 Blocks

Counters

Decimal Squares

Multiplication Arrays

Polygon Cutouts

Blackline Masters

Modified Cartesian Coordinate Grid

Geoboard Dot Paper

One-Centimeter Grid Paper

Triangular Grid Paper

Teaching Forms

Classroom Observation Form

Portfolio Checklist Form

Learning/Teaching Plan Form

Inquiry-Based Lesson Plan Form

Introduction

How students learn and teachers teach mathematics is changing. The traditional mathematics class emphasized memorizing procedures and facts and applying standard algorithms. Reformed mathematics instruction is active rather than passive, with an emphasis on inquiry and process. Finding multiple pathways to multiple solutions is encouraged rather than discouraged, and developing mathematical thinking is as important a result of problem solving as correct solutions.

In the classroom, these changes are resulting in a different classroom dynamic as well as different student and teacher behaviors. The traditional mathematics classroom was quiet and orderly. Teachers lectured. Students worked alone. Achievement was measured by the number of correct answers on tests and exercises.

A reformed mathematics classroom functions more like a learning laboratory. Teachers pose questions and provide support for a process of inquiry. Students collaborate. They model mathematical situations, formulate and test hypotheses, and propose and justify solutions. Learning tools might include traditional ones (rulers or meter sticks, compasses, protractors) but also mathematics manipulatives such as base-10 blocks, tangram pieces, geoboards, and fraction or algebra tiles. Students use computers to find background for concepts or examples of similar mathematical situations and to explore ideas in interactive tasks that let them approach problem solving from a variety of perspectives. They work to construct mind tools—strategies and mental processes for making sense of mathematics—and to develop mathematical thinking. In effect, students become math-scientists—active, systematic inquirers who seek to explore, invent, and discover mathematics.

The mathematics activities collected here provide directions, contexts, and goals for the inquiry process. They emphasize hands-on learning and an inductive rather than deductive approach to mathematics. That is, the starting point is questions, not answers. Students build and construct answers for themselves.

Asking Questions: Teaching Mathematics As Inquiry

From a traditional perspective, beginning lessons with questions rather than answers may seem to turn the learning process upside down. Because traditional instruction defined teacher-student roles as conveyor and receiver of knowledge, most classes began with the end. That is, the concept, algorithm to be learned, or facts to be memorized were explained and illustrated with examples first; then students applied the information in exercises. Questions in this type of class were primarily the means for assessing students' performance, and for the most part these were questions with set answers: What is the formula for ____? How do we solve for x in problem ____? What is the correct answer to problem ____?

Teaching mathematics as inquiry follows a different pattern and calls for different types of thinking. Teachers still teach—that is, the teacher continues to play an important role; however, instead of being an oracle of knowledge, the teacher is a guide to knowledge. Instead of providing the answers, the teacher constructs learning environments and pathways—contexts and questions that will lead students toward discovering their own answers and meanings.

A basic premise of inquiry-based mathematics teaching is the idea that students can and should discover mathematics for themselves. In his article "Never Say Anything a Kid Can Say!" Steven C. Reinhart (2000) emphasizes the need for students to develop and explain their own answers. He writes that for students "to ever really learn mathematics, they . . . have to do the explaining, and I, the listening" (478). In other words, instead of providing all of the answers and explanations—acting, in effect, as an oracle of mathematical knowledge—the teacher guides students through a learning process that is inductive rather than deductive.

This process starts with questions that generate hypotheses to be investigated. The method is scientific and also creative. Students investigate mathematical situations, and they construct or create the mental structures needed to formulate and understand for themselves mathematical concepts.

Key components of a successful inquiry-based activity include the following:

- A series of questions that connect and engage students;
- A meaningful context or problem that challenges and demands critical thinking;
- Tools and materials, both virtual and actual, to allow hands-on or active investigations.

Effectively implemented, inquiry-based mathematics instruction involves students with "real questions to stretch their critical thinking" and helps them understand concepts and relationships at a deeper, more intrinsic level. These activities can also

> Help students see connections between classroom learning and the world outside the classroom; motivate them to use the skills already learned and to see the need for new skills; and engage them in constructing meaningful concepts and, eventually, generalizations. (Herrera and Roempler, 2004, 2)

Overall, inquiry-based activities allow teachers to move beyond telling and explaining to showing and discovering. In the classroom, inquiry means that students use statistical tools to find patterns in weather data or design studies of their own about "the average amount of time commercials take during a one-hour broadcast" (Herrera and Roempler 2004, 1). Or it means finding math in the real world and using mathematical concepts and thinking to develop problem-solving strategies for handling money or creating a work of art based on tessellating polygons.

To ensure that students stay on track during the activities, teachers can guide and shape the process with questions and tasks that focus efforts and match investigations to specific problem-solving goals.

Guiding Inquiry: Exploring, Inventing, Discovering Mathematics

Some discovery-learning enthusiasts would prefer to give students open-ended tasks that allow them to range through and explore mathematical concepts freely, without the restraints of specific time limits and learning objectives. The realities of teaching mathematics in the 21st century make this freewheeling type of mathematics study almost a practical impossibility. Although discovery and inquiry may be synonymous with good teaching, both for mathematics and science, testing requirements and social as well as curricular demands restrict students' and teachers' time. Accordingly, "time dedicated to the

inquiry process—observing, explaining the observations, and arriving at a generalization—can be difficult to justify. . . ." (Herrera and Roempler 2004, 3).

To balance the demands of good teaching with the demands of society and curriculums, teachers can use a process of guided inquiry. Investigation is still the method, but the parameters of the investigation are more closely defined. Questions are carefully designed to promote a steady but not scripted progress from investigating a mathematical situation to organizing, interpreting, and understanding the findings.

An effective pedagogical strategy can structure students' inquiries toward specific curriculum goals. Based on the work of Anton E. Lawson and John W. Renner and applied to mathematics concept learning, our strategy organizes the inquiry process into three stages (Lawson and Renner 1975; Martinez 1988, 2001):

Stage 1: **Explore** the concepts.
Stage 2: **Invent** or construct mental structures and tools to deal with the concepts.
Stage 3: **Discover** ways to understand, connect, apply, and extend the concepts.

In the classroom, this strategy allows teachers to focus tightly or broadly, to end or extend the investigative process, and to match learning objectives to the performance and assessment goals of a variety of mathematics curriculums.

Applied in this book, *Activities for Developing Mathematical Thinking*, the explore-invent-discover strategy structures and guides mathematics investigations. Study begins with questions that engage students, set a context, and help focus the inquiry process. Students work first to understand and relate to the mathematical situations. They **explore** relationships and meanings with hands-on methods and manipulatives that let them model and visualize mathematical situations and, in effect, experience them directly. As students work, they **invent** and test problem-solving strategies and even construct their own procedures and algorithms. And through the process of investigating, students **discover** the meanings implicit in mathematical situations and learn to extend, connect, and apply their discoveries.

Using the Activities in the Classroom

The activities described here help students develop their mathematical thinking skills by guiding them through the explore-invent-discover learning process. Each activity includes recommended grade levels and NCTM process and content standards. Activities begin with concepts to be explored, materials needed, and questions teachers might ask to prompt the learning process. Descriptions of what teachers will do (when appropriate) and what students will do are followed by discussions of approaches students might take toward understanding or solving problems, strategies they might invent or construct, and outcomes or discoveries they might make. Many activities conclude with specific suggestions for extending study.

Icons that appear at the onset of each activity identify the mathematical focus of each activity.

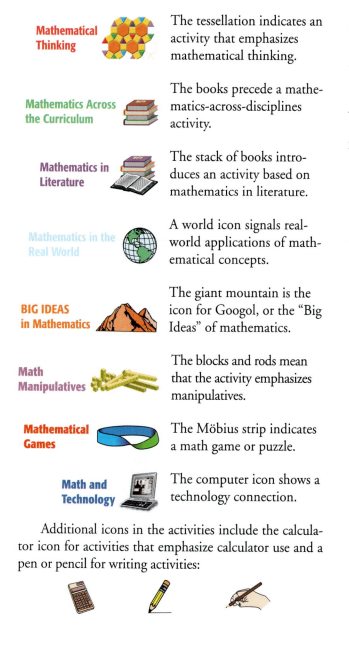

Mathematical Thinking

The tessellation indicates an activity that emphasizes mathematical thinking.

Mathematics Across the Curriculum

The books precede a mathematics-across-disciplines activity.

Mathematics in Literature

The stack of books introduces an activity based on mathematics in literature.

Mathematics in the Real World

A world icon signals real-world applications of mathematical concepts.

BIG IDEAS in Mathematics

The giant mountain is the icon for Googol, or the "Big Ideas" of mathematics.

Math Manipulatives

The blocks and rods mean that the activity emphasizes manipulatives.

Mathematical Games

The Möbius strip indicates a math game or puzzle.

Math and Technology

The computer icon shows a technology connection.

Additional icons in the activities include the calculator icon for activities that emphasize calculator use and a pen or pencil for writing activities:

Activity CD-ROM

Materials for many of the activities in this text indicate the use of accompanying worksheets and handouts. Some activities reference the use of math manipulatives. The activity worksheets and math manipulatives are located on the CD-ROM that is located in the back of the text.

References

Herrera, Teresa, and Kimberly S. Roempler. "Classroom Resources for Inquiry and Problem Solving." *ENCFocus Features* (2004): http://www.enc.org/features/focus/archive.

Lawson, Anton E., and John W. Renner. "Piagetian Theory and Biology Teaching." *American Biology Teacher* 37 (September 1975): 336–43.

Martinez, Joseph G. R. "Exploring, Inventing, and Discovering Mathematics: A Pedagogical Response to the TIMSS." *Mathematics Teaching in the Middle School* 7 (October 2001): 114–19.

———"Helping Students Understand Factors and Terms." *Mathematics Teacher* 81 (December 1988): 747–51.

Reinhart, Steven C. "Never Say Anything a Kid Can Say!" *Mathematics Teaching in the Middle School* 5 (2000): 478–82.

Understanding Numbers

1 Finding the Numbers in Your Life

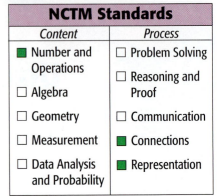

Grade Levels PreK–8

NCTM Standards	
Content	*Process*
■ Number and Operations	☐ Problem Solving
☐ Algebra	☐ Reasoning and Proof
☐ Geometry	☐ Communication
☐ Measurement	■ Connections
☐ Data Analysis and Probability	■ Representation

Overview

Numbers are all around us. They help us organize our days, describe where we live, connect with others, budget our income, and measure our worlds. As students discover the numbers in their lives, they also discover the important role numbers play in helping people make sense of the worlds they live in—of their personal worlds of home and school and of the bigger worlds of their communities and society.

Activity

What ideas or concepts will students explore?

- "Life" or personal numbers
- Numbers in society
- Numbers as organizers
- Data collection
- Frequency counting
- Classifying

What materials will you need?

drawing paper • construction paper • colored markers • crayons • rulers • compasses • log sheets (See "Numbers Log" in the Worksheets & Handouts section of the CD-ROM that accompanies this text, or make your own)

What questions could you ask?

What do numbers say about you?
What numbers are important to you?
What numbers do you like or not like?
Can you describe yourself with numbers?
Can you describe yourself with mathematical ideas?

What will students do?

Numbers Self-Portrait (Grades PreK–2) Draw a picture of yourself. Then label different parts of the picture with words and numbers. For example, label fingers and give the number of fingers. Label feet and give shoe size or length. Label and count buttons, pockets, hair braids, freckles.

Numbers Idea Web (Grades K–8) Draw an idea web with you in the center. Then, in circles like balloons, write the important numbers in your life. You might include your age, your address, your phone number, the number of people in your family, and any other numbers that are important to you.

Are any numbers important for more than one reason? For example, 7 might be important because you are 7 years old and because you have 7 cousins or 7 guinea pigs. Draw more balloons to show the different ways in which a number is important to you. Use straight lines to connect numbers to you in the center or to other balloons.

Explain the numbers map to your classmates.

Numbers Graph (Grades 4–8) Keep a record of what you do for 2 to 3 days. Put your activities in categories, such as eating, playing, studying, doing chores.

Make a log sheet with the activities at the top and lines between the activities. Whenever you do something, put a mark under the activity on your log sheet.

At the end of the period, count the marks in each category. Draw a bar graph with a numbered scale on the left and your categories at the bottom.

What do these numbers say about you? Write a brief description.

*What strategies might students **invent** or construct?*

Students might start by making a list of all the numbers that have meaning to them—their age, the number of people in their families, their address, important phone numbers such as 911. They might represent what they find with charts, drawings, collages, life lines with important dates marked, photo albums with pictures of the people or things represented by various numbers.

*What insights, connections, or applications might students **discover**?*

- Numbers are everywhere.
- Numbers can describe people and places.
- Society uses numbers to organize cities, time, events.
- Frequency counting is an important skill in data collection.
- Idea webbing can help organize and make sense of a variety of seemingly unrelated facts.
- Numbers can be distinctive and personal instead of abstract and impersonal.

2 Making Numbers Books

Grade Levels PreK–2

NCTM Standards	
Content	*Process*
■ Number and Operations	☐ Problem Solving
☐ Algebra	☐ Reasoning and Proof
☐ Geometry	■ Communication
☐ Measurement	☐ Connections
☐ Data Analysis and Probability	■ Representation

Overview

Understanding what numbers mean is a first step to thinking with numbers. Exploring and representing the many meanings possible for each digit show students that numbers have many uses and need to be interpreted in contexts.

Activity

What ideas or concepts will students *explore*?

- Using numbers to interpret the real world
- Counting forward and/or backward
- Making connections between numbers, objects, incidents, places, self

What materials will you need?

construction paper • yarn • scissors • glue • crayons, colored pencils, or markers

What questions could you ask?

What is your favorite number? Why?
How many digits are there?
How do we make numbers when we run out of digits?
How many different ways can you think of to use each digit?

What will students do?

Use construction paper and yarn to make a book with a cover and sheets for pages. Design a cover with numbers and related drawings. Choose a number theme—7 days of the week, favorite numbers, counting 1 to 10 or 10 to 1. Devote a page of the book to each number in the theme. Use drawings, cutouts, pictures, words, or mathematical sentences to show the meanings and relationships of each number.

What strategies might students *invent* or construct?

Students might draw webs with each number at the middle and related ideas or things radiating on lines. They could make collages of objects, images, and ideas related to each number. They might combine drawings and text with a sentence and picture for each number.

What insights, connections, or applications might students ***discover****?*

- Numbers have meaning as points in a sequence.
- Numbers have meaning individually.
- Numbers help describe who we are, what we look like, where we live.
- Numbers help organize our lives, what we do, and when we do it.
- Numbers help us describe the world around us.

3 How Tall Is My Dino?*

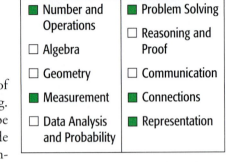

**BIG IDEAS
in Mathematics**

Grade Levels K–3

NCTM Standards	
Content	*Process*
■ Number and Operations	■ Problem Solving
□ Algebra	□ Reasoning and Proof
□ Geometry	□ Communication
■ Measurement	■ Connections
□ Data Analysis and Probability	■ Representation

Overview

Understanding the concept of size begins with comparing. What is tall, taller, tallest can be explained by putting objects side by side and placing them in increasing or decreasing order, or we can use a standard and numbers for expressing size relationships. Using a nonstandard unit for measuring, such as paper clips or blocks, is a good starting point for introducing students to standards of measurement. The big idea here is that students can identify a unit of measurement and then use counting and numbers to describe the size of an object.

Activity

*What ideas or concepts will students **explore**?*

- Size, relationships, comparisons
- Using comparative terms such as tall, taller, tallest; short, shorter, shortest; big, bigger, biggest
- Reading and writing numerals
- One-to-one correspondence in counting
- Connecting number to quantity
- Measurement with a standard

What materials will you need?

drawing paper • pictures/books of different types of dinosaurs • centimeter cubes or blocks • crayons and markers • rulers or meter sticks • string • masking tape

What questions could you ask?

Which real dinosaur was the tallest? The longest? The heaviest?
Why were some dinosaurs so big?
Were there any small dinosaurs?
What happened to the dinosaurs?
Among the dinosaurs you have drawn, whose is tallest, shortest, longest, skinniest, widest, and so forth? How do you know?

---

*Adapted from an activity taught by Bernadetta Crawford

What will students do?

Look at pictures of different kinds of dinosaurs, such as apatosaurus, stegosaurus, and tyrannosaurus rex, Note the long neck of the apatosaurus, the short neck and stumpy legs of the stegosaurus, and the upright posture and carnivorous teeth of the T. Rex. Talk about their sizes, weights, habits, and habitats.

Working individually or in small groups, draw a tall dinosaur and a short dinosaur. You might model your drawings on specific dinosaurs or make up dinosaur-like creatures.

Measure the dinosaurs with centimeter cubes and draw a tower of cubes next to the dinosaurs. (Younger children can put a dot in each cube of height and count the cubes. Older students can use metric and English measures and use string to create comparative measurements.)

What strategies might students _invent_ or construct?

To connect numbers and measurements, some children will count and label the measuring units one at a time. Others will work with blocks of units and count by 2s or 5s and so forth. Developing models of size, such as lengths of string, to compare and measure serves as a helpful reference point for checking and establishing the meaning of number values and the appropriateness of the comparisons.

What insights, connections, or applications might students _discover_?

- Measuring means assigning numbers to quantities.
- Whatever the measuring standard, the higher the number, the taller, longer, bigger, and so forth the object measured is; the smaller the number, the shorter, smaller, and so forth the object measured is.
- Measuring size can incorporate several steps.

What extensions can you make?

Ask "How big was a real dinosaur?" Have older students look for information about size—weight, length, height—in reference books or on the Internet. They can present their findings visually with drawings and in written form or oral reports. Also ask students to "show" how long a 75-foot apatosaurus would be by using string comparisons and measuring 75 feet of school hallway or gym space.

4 Counting with Cheerios*

Mathematics in Literature

Overview

Grade Levels PreK–2

NCTM Standards	
Content	*Process*
■ Number and Operations	☐ Problem Solving
☐ Algebra	☐ Reasoning and Proof
☐ Geometry	■ Communication
☐ Measurement	■ Connections
☐ Data Analysis and Probability	■ Representation

Counting for many young students means reciting the number sequence. To tie counting to objects requires them to connect numbers to objects in a sequence and to understand the concept of total. This activity puts counting within the context of a story and uses Cheerios as manipulatives to model the counting process.

Activity

What ideas or concepts will students explore?
- Connecting number words and numerals
- Ordering and counting objects, images
- Counting by 10
- Number sequence to 100

What materials do you need? Barbara Barbieri McGrath, *The Cheerios Counting Book*. (New York: Scholastic 1998) • Cheerios cereal • Styrofoam cups

What questions could you ask? [Line up 1, 2, 3, 4, 5, 6, 7, 8, 9, 10 Cheerios on a tabletop.] How many Cheerios do I have?
[Hold up a handful of Cheerios.] How many Cheerios do you think I have in my hand?
[Put the handful of Cheerios on the table.] How many Cheerios are there? How close was your guess?

What will students do? Take a cup of Cheerios. Be sure you have a flat surface to work on and plenty of room. Listen as your teacher reads *The Cheerios Counting Book* one page at a time showing the pages. When the book shifts from individual numbers to decades, stop and discuss the way the number sequence is grouped by 10s.

Represent the numbers on each page with Cheerios. Show numbers from 1–20 individually. Then rearrange the first 20 Cheerios in groups of 10 and keep adding 10 at a time until you reach 100.

---

*Adapted from an activity taught by Deborah Kahler

*What strategies might students **invent** or construct?*

Students might duplicate the arrangements of Cheerios that they see on the pages, or they could devise their own patterns and figures.

*What insights, connections, or applications might the students **discover**?*

- Grouping makes counting large numbers easier.
- There are 10 groups of 10 in 100.
- There are 20 groups of 5 in 100.
- The total is the last number named in counting.

What extensions can you make?

Point out and discuss the arrangement and number of the fruit counters printed around the edge of the book pages. Have the students draw fruit or other objects to represent selected numbers. After the students have made 10 groupings of 10, have them count the Cheerios remaining in their cups. You might group and count first by 5s, then by 10s.

5 Graphing with Candy Hearts, Jellybeans, or Gumdrops*

Math Manipulatives

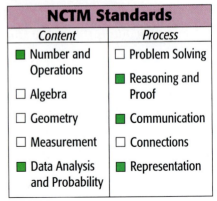

Grade Levels K–2

NCTM Standards	
Content	*Process*
■ Number and Operations	☐ Problem Solving
☐ Algebra	■ Reasoning and Proof
☐ Geometry	■ Communication
☐ Measurement	☐ Connections
■ Data Analysis and Probability	■ Representation

Overview

Edible manipulatives such as candy hearts, jellybeans, or gumdrops help engage students and keep them on task. Colored candies also add visual and tactile dimensions to the activity and help underscore the relationship of the counted candies and the colored bars on the graphs.

Activity

*What ideas or concepts will students **explore**?*

- Counting
- Classifying
- More, less, same
- One-to-one correspondence

What materials will you need?

plastic baggies with Valentine conversation hearts, gumdrops, or jellybeans • large-block graph paper • small Styrofoam cups • crayons to match colors of candy

What will you do?

Show students the bags of candies to catch their attention. When they ask if they can eat some, you might say, "Yes, but not these and not now." The hearts they are working with will be too dirty to eat. Later, when everyone has completed the activity, you might hand out some candies to be eaten. Be sure to have some nonsugar candies for those not allowed to eat sugar. To introduce the activity, show students the candies and a sample graph that you made, and ask questions about colors, height of the bars in the graph, and so forth.

What questions could you ask?

How many colors of candies are there?
When you close your eyes, how many colors do you remember?
How many colors are used in the graph?
Which bar in the graph is tallest? Shortest? Are any the same?
What does the height of the bars in the graph mean?
Which color do you have the most, least, or same of?
Who in the class has the most, least, or same of each color?
How many more or less do you have of each color?
If everyone has 20 candies, why do the graphs look different?

---

*Adapted from an activity taught by Deborah Kahler

What will students do?

Gather your materials: a cup with 20 candies and supplies for graphing. Working in small groups, sort the candies by color and then write the colors across the bottom of a sheet of graph paper. Draw and color bars to show the distribution.

What strategies might students *invent* or construct?

To decide how tall to make each bar in their graphs, students might put a candy in each square, or they might count the candies in each group and count the number of squares.

What insights, connections, or applications might students *discover*?

- Using one block for one heart results in a graph picture of the numbers.
- Graphs can be used to compare numbers of things.
- A graph can bring together information collected by counting, classifying, or measuring.

6 The Revolving Jar

Grade Levels 2–6

NCTM Standards	
Content	*Process*
■ Number and Operations	■ Problem Solving
☐ Algebra	■ Reasoning and Proof
■ Geometry	☐ Communication
■ Measurement	☐ Connections
☐ Data Analysis and Probability	☐ Representation

Overview

Developing estimation strategies to tell "how many" combines several areas of mathematical content. Students will be estimating numbers as well as dealing with volume, space, and a variety of regular and irregular geometric shapes. Calculations might involve counting and multiplying. The estimation jar in the title of this activity is revolving because students take turns filling it and setting estimation tasks for their classmates.

Activity

What ideas or concepts will students *explore*?

- Estimating
- Volume
- Spatial relationships
- Counting in context

What materials will you need?

quart or pint jar • objects to fill jar (Goldfish crackers, peanut M&Ms, pretzels, gumballs, pennies, small pebbles, grains of rice or beans, and so forth) • diagrams for an overhead projector: squares and circles filled with squares, circles, and triangles • large box and small boxes of various sizes • log paper, • pens or pencils

What questions could you ask?

How many bite-sized candy bars do you think would fit in a quart jar? A pint jar?
Would these jars hold more pretzels or more Goldfish? How do you know?
How many different ways can you think of to find out how many objects are in a container?
How would the shape of the container affect the total?
How would the shape of the contents affect the total?

What will you do?

Fill the jar, counting the items as you go. Talk about volume and space—how many squares, circles, and triangles you can squeeze into a two-dimensional square or circle, how many more might be squeezed into a three-dimensional square (a cube) or a globe. Illustrate with overhead diagrams and boxes. Discuss how different shapes leave empty spaces in the big box and reduce the number of small boxes it can hold.

What will students do?

Examine the filled jar carefully; make an estimate of the number of items in the jar; and then enter the date, the container and its items, and your estimate on the log sheet.

What will you do?

When all of the students have made an estimate, put ranges of numbers on the board. Have everyone stand up. As you cross off different ranges, those whose estimates fell within those ranges can sit down. Give the jar to the student whose estimate is closest and, if appropriate, ask the student to share the contents with her or his classmates.

What strategies might students *invent* or construct?

Some students might count all of the objects and then guess the number of objects they cannot see. Others might count by layers, bottom layer first, and then duplicate all the way to the top. Older students might multiply the number in one layer by the number of layers.

What will students do?

If your estimate was closest, you "win" the jar. Take it home and fill it with something different for a repeat of the estimation activity the following week.

Record the winning estimate in your logs so that you can discuss and reflect on your estimation strategies periodically.

What extensions can you make?

Vary the shape of the container and the type of activity content. For example, bring to class a bag of ladybugs, the kind sold at nurseries for release in a garden. Have the students develop strategies for estimating the number of ladybugs in the bag. Later in the schoolyard or a nearby park, you can show the students how to release the ladybugs in a shady, green area with plenty of water and connect the estimation activity with an environmental science lesson.

What insights, connections, or applications might students *discover*?

- Volume can be related to number by using counting to measure contents—that is, the jar may be 20 Goldfish high, 10 Goldfish wide, and 12 Goldfish long.
- The shape of objects affects the number of them that a container will hold.
- Practice helps us develop a feeling for how much a container will hold so that we can sense what number is too much or not enough.

7 Walking on the Googol Side

Grade Levels 1–3

NCTM Standards	
Content	*Process*
■ Number and Operations	■ Problem Solving
☐ Algebra	☐ Reasoning and Proof
☐ Geometry	■ Communication
☐ Measurement	■ Connections
☐ Data Analysis and Probability	■ Representation

Overview

To develop number sense, students need to connect numbers and real things; however, it can be difficult to make big numbers seem real and meaningful. A good place to start is the googol. Children love the story of the mathematician who asked a child to name the number written in numerals as 1 with 100 zeros. Knowing that a child named the googol and the googolplex makes the numbers seem more accessible. The googol story helps them think about and visualize the googol and prepares them to learn some important things about big numbers.

Activity

What ideas or concepts will students explore?
- Large numbers
- Connections between words and numerals
- History of numbers

What materials will you need?
The story "Is the Googol Too Big?" (printed at the end of this activity) • drawing paper • markers or crayons • ruler, punch-out circles, or compass

What questions could you ask?
What are the biggest numbers you know?
What is a million? A billion? A trillion?
How would you write these numbers in words or numerals?
Why do we need big numbers? Or *do* we need big numbers?

What will students do?
Listen as your teacher reads the googol story aloud. When she or he reads the last sentence, think about and discuss how to answer "Can you help the Googol?"

Then make a googol name map. Write *googol* in the center of a piece of paper and draw a circle around the word. Then write down other words and ideas related to the googol, drawing circles and lines to show how your thoughts progress.

Next, name a big number. Not all big numbers have been named. Find out the meaning of big numbers like a million, a billion, and a googolplex. Except for the googol and the googolplex, numbers above vigintillion (one with 63 zeros) have not been named. Identify and write an unnamed big number and give it a name.

Write the Googol's name. Find as many ways to write the Googol's name as you can. You might use words, numbers, numbers mixed with words, pictures, manipulatives, or the computer.

Draw the Googol. What do you think the Googol looks like? In the story its face is a number 1 and its body winds around the classroom. Do you think it looks like a caterpillar? Would it have hands and feet and wear clothes and a hat?

Write a story. If the Googol came to your school, what would it do? Is there room for the Googol in your classroom, in the hallway, on the playground, in the cafeteria? What would happen if there were a fire drill or an assembly while the Googol was visiting? Write a story and draw pictures to show what might happen.

*What strategies might students **invent** or construct?*

Some will try to understand big numbers by writing them out but will soon discover how difficult it is to write and keep track of that many zeros. Some will try to make comparisons—"A million is like_____" or "A googol is like_____ ." Older students might look for information on the Internet about astronomical distances and the numbers needed to represent them.

*What insights, connections, or applications might students **discover**?*

- Some numbers are so big that it is easier to write them down with words rather than numerals.
- Numbers can have names just as people or objects have names.
- We need large numbers when we talk about quantities like the distances between the stars or the mass of planets and stars.
- There may be many ways to represent one idea.

Is the Googol too big?

Mrs. Garcia's fourth-grade class was happy. Today for math, Mrs. Garcia had promised a visit from an old friend, the Googol.

The last time the children had seen the Googol, they had been in second grade; it had come to class to learn how to write its name and make a name map. It had learned how to write 1 with 100 zeros and how to spell its name with letters. It had learned about the mathematician Dr. Kasner; his nephew had given the Googol its name.*

But today the Googol had a problem.

"The other numbers have been teasing the Googol," said Mrs. Garcia. "They say nobody uses it. Its name is silly, not at all like other numbers, and it's too big."

"That's mean," said Chloe.

"Yeah," agreed Royce.

Tomas nodded and shrugged. "But it is kind of big."

"Yeah," Royce agreed with him too. "It could hardly fit in here." He turned in a circle and stretched his arms wide. "You can't hug a Googol."

Some of the children laughed.

"That is so mean," Chloe told them.

"It's not our fault," complained Loretta. She felt bad that she had laughed. "What can we do about it? The Googol is just the Googol, a really big number. We can't change that."

"We can't change it," said Mrs. Garcia, "but maybe we can help the Googol to feel better about itself. Let's see if we can put the Googol's problem in the form of some questions and then look for the answers. Can anyone think of a question?"

"What's a Googol used for?" suggested Kim.

"What's good about the Googol's name?" asked Jose.

"Is the Googol really big?" added Royce, who was having second thoughts about his earlier comments. "Are there any bigger numbers?"

Mrs. Garcia wrote the questions on the white board. Then working in small groups or alone, the children searched for answers. They looked up *googol* on the Internet and in the encyclopedia. In the math/science corner, they experimented with different ways to represent a googol—writing it out on a single sheet of paper, writing the number 1 and 100 zeros on separate Post-It notes and putting them on a long string that stretched across the classroom.

Finally it was time for the Googol's visit. The door to the classroom opened wide. First came the head, which looked like a giant 1. Then came the body, a long, long, long line of zeros. The Googol turned right as it came through the door and made a circle around the room until the last zero was inside.

"Hello, Googol!" cried the children.

"H'lo," the Googol replied. It tried to smile but still looked sad.

"It's time for some answers." said Mrs. Garcia. "What did you find to help the Googol?"

Chloe raised her hand. Her group had been looking for ways to use the Googol.

"The Googol is an important number," she said. "Dr. Kasner used it to help us understand the idea of infinity. The total number of particles in the universe is less than a Googol, but a Googol is still smaller than infinity."

"A lot of things are named for the Googol," added Tomas. "The *Wikipedia* encyclopedia says that the Internet search engine Google was named for the Googol, but they got the spelling wrong."

"Googol," said Jose, "is a really great name. Other big numbers have horrible names, like 1 with 60 zeros is a novemdecillion." He stumbled over the pronunciation. "I can't even say it. One with 99 zeros is even worse." He went to the white board and carefully copied the word *duotrigintillion*. "Googol is a lot easier to say, and I like it better."

"The Googol isn't really that big," said Royce. "We can write it on just one piece of paper. But there isn't enough paper and ink in the universe to write a googolplex. And you really *can* hug the Googol! Group hug, everyone!"

The Googol felt much better, especially after the group hug, but it wanted to hear more. Is there more? What can you add to help the Googol feel better about itself?

For a story about the Googol's first visit, see Martinez, Nancy, and Joseph Martinez, "Introducing Big Numbers: A Walk on the Googol Side." Lollipops, 103 (2001):13–24.

8 Up, Down, All Around—Show Me with Calculators

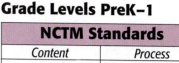

NCTM Standards	
Content	*Process*
■ Number and Operations	■ Problem Solving
☐ Algebra	☐ Reasoning and Proof
☐ Geometry	☐ Communication
☐ Measurement	☐ Connections
☐ Data Analysis and Probability	■ Representation

Overview

Calculators are important tools for learning about numbers. Learning how to use the calculator, how to represent number ideas and operations, and how to interpret the results begins with the basic skills of operating and reading the calculator.

Activity

What ideas or concepts will students explore?

- Identifying and representing number ideas on the calculator
- Doing addition and subtraction with + and − keys
- Understanding the role played by the symbol = in calculations
- Using the calculator to explore more, less, same

What materials will you need?

individual calculators • large charts or overhead diagrams with labeled keys and examples of addition and subtraction

What questions could you ask?

What does it mean "to calculate"?
Why is a calculator called a calculator?
When might it be helpful to have a calculator handy?
Are there some calculations you do not need a calculator for?
Which is faster—adding on the calculator or on paper? On the calculator or in your head? Why? Does it depend on how many numbers you are adding? Explain.

What will students do?

Listen as the teacher explains that the calculator is a tool to help you work with numbers. Watch as the teacher demonstrates the use of different keys. Following along on individual calculators, practice turning the calculators on and off; entering one-digit, two-digit, and three-digit numbers. Discover what happens when you use the +, −, and = keys and how *plus, minus,* and *equals* can be related to *more, less,* and *same.*

*What strategies might students **invent** or construct?*

To alternate number with action keys, some might find it easier to use the forefinger to hit number keys and another finger to hit action keys. Others might use thumbs and work two-handed.

*What insights, connections, or applications might students **discover**?*

- Calculators help keep track of long strings of numbers and operations.
- When you subtract more than you add, the calculator shows the result as a minus number.
- The calculator only shows one entry at a time, but it still remembers the ones you did before.

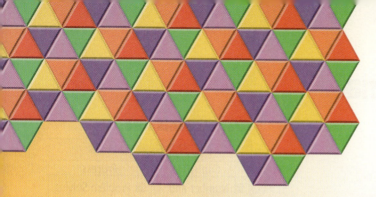

Understanding Number Systems and Place Value

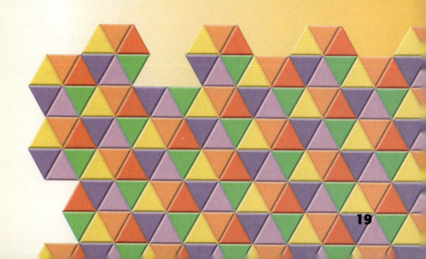

9 My Math Journal

Grade Levels K–8

NCTM Standards	
Content	*Process*
☑ Number and Operations	☑ Problem Solving
☐ Algebra	☑ Reasoning and Proof
☐ Geometry	☑ Communication
☐ Measurement	☑ Connections
☐ Data Analysis and Probability	☑ Representation

Overview

Creating a math journal not only helps students focus on their math work but also gives them a sense of ownership. Because the journals are personal creations, the work itself becomes more personal and therefore more personally meaningful. The root of the word *journal* is "day," and keeping a math journal should be a daily project. Students can use the journal to record and solve problems, to explain the problem-solving process, to reflect about learning mathematics, to explore attitudes about mathematics, and even to be creative—for example, to write math stories or to use math concepts in art.

Activity

What ideas or concepts will students explore?
- Developing a personal perspective on mathematics
- Representing math concepts with words, numbers, drawings
- Making math activities part of daily life

What materials will you need?
8 1/2″ × 11″ newsprint or other unlined paper • construction paper • crayons, colored pencils, markers • staple gun

What questions could you ask?
When you think about mathematics, what kinds of pictures or images do you see in your mind?
What does math mean to you personally?
What kinds of math do you do every day?
What do you think it means to keep a math journal?
Are there any math concepts that you need to write down so that you can be reminded of them when you work?
What kinds of things would you like to put in a math journal?

What will students do?
Fold several sheets of unlined paper in half. Fold construction paper to make a book cover slightly larger than the pages. Staple cover and sheets along fold. Design and color a cover, including your name and "My Math Journal" as well as math-related drawings or symbols.

Every day write a problem in your journal that the teacher puts on the chalkboard or shows with an overhead projector. Work out the problem and explain what you did, including any difficulty you may have had.

*What strategies might students **invent** or construct?*

After writing the problem in their journals, the students might use drawings to help them visualize the mathematical situation. They might write out a problem-solving approach or comment on the difficulty of the problem and on other problems or situations it brings to mind.

*What insights, connections, or applications might students **discover**?*

- Writing out problems helps us to focus and interpret.
- Showing a problem in a variety of ways makes it easier to understand and solve.
- Working math problems daily in a journal takes math out of textbooks and makes it seem more immediate and accessible.

10 How Much Money?*

Mathematics Across the Curriculum

Grade Levels K–1

NCTM Standards	
Content	*Process*
■ Number and Operations	☐ Problem Solving
☐ Algebra	■ Reasoning and Proof
☐ Geometry	☐ Communication
☐ Measurement	■ Connections
☐ Data Analysis and Probability	■ Representation

Overview

What is money? Answering that question involves a number of abstract concepts—some mathematical, such as the decimal or base-10 system on which our monetary system is based; some sociological, such as the ideas of value and exchanging money for things or services. Understanding and using our monetary system is an essential survival skill. Children can begin the process by learning to identify coins and discovering that the monetary value of the coins is related to the markings on the coins rather than an indication of their size. Representing the coins with drawings and graphs helps students develop mental images for the coins and reinforces classification of the different types. Playing Coin Bingo allows them to practice identification and to develop flexibility and facility in distinguishing the coins themselves and their different values.

Activity

*What ideas or concepts will students **explore**?*

- Names and number value of coins
- Money as quantities
- Quantities as units (5¢, 10¢, 25¢, and so forth)
- Representing quantities with graphs
- Equivalencies of coins and groups of coins

What materials will you need?

plastic bags with assortment of pennies, nickels, dimes, and quarters • sheets of graph paper with number values of coins written at the side (see "Graphing Coins" in the Worksheets & Handouts section of the CD-ROM that accompanies this text) • Bingo sheets with number values of coins written at random in boxes (see "Coin Bingo Card" in the Worksheets & Handouts section of the CD-ROM) • crayons or markers • drawing paper

What questions could you ask?

What is money?
How do you know how much each coin is worth?
Is there more than one way to show 5¢? A dime? A quarter? 15¢? 20¢?
What can you buy with a quarter? A dime?
How many pennies would you need to buy a 10-cent piece of mint candy?

---

*Adapted from activities taught by Maria Chavez and Carmen McKierney

What will you do?

Give each child a plastic bag with coins. (Using real money rather than cutout pictures or play money can make the activity more meaningful but also presents risks since children may not understand that they should not keep the coins.) Have the children look at both sides of the coins as they learn the names and number values. Guide the children to compare the coins for size, color, and value.

What will students do?

Identify the coins in the plastic bag. Give the name and value of each one. Then count the number of each type of coin. Use the graph paper to make a graph showing the number of each type of coin. Count off and color in boxes for the number of quarters, dimes, nickels, and pennies.

Draw and count the coins in the bags. Write the total number for each coin next to the drawing. Then show with drawings and numbers the various ways to make up totals using different coins.

What will you do?

Hand out Coin Bingo cards. Explain that the game involves putting a coin on the different boxes as the caller names them. The object of the game is to fill a straight line with coins.

What will students do?

As the teacher names each coin, identify the coin, and then put it on a space worth the appropriate value. When you make a line with coins, call, "Bingo."

What strategies might students _invent_ or construct?

They might convert each coin to pennies and count totals or begin with the largest coin and count up or down to find desired amounts.

What insights, connections, or applications might students _discover_?

- The size of the coin does not tell you its worth.
- Different combinations of coins can be used to arrive at the same amount.
- Graphs can be used to show numbers.
- The value of coins can be written as numerals and combined for totals.

11 How Big Am I? How Big Are You?*

Grade Levels K–3

NCTM Standards	
Content	*Process*
☑ Number and Operations	☑ Problem Solving
☐ Algebra	☐ Reasoning and Proof
☐ Geometry	☐ Communication
☑ Measurement	☑ Connections
☐ Data Analysis and Probability	☑ Representation

Overview

Understanding the different number systems involved in measuring size begins with making comparisons. The size of one thing is compared to the size of another: for example, the height of one student is compared to another. Comparisons might begin generally, looking for the tallest, shortest, and so forth, and then continue using a common nonstandard measuring device such as a length of string. In this activity students use the experience of measuring with string as preparation for measuring with tapes and other standard tools that represent size with standard numerical units.

Activity

*What ideas or concepts will students **explore**?*

- Measurement
- Relation, proportion
- More, less, same
- Using measuring tools
- Representing space with numbers
- Comparing size, number values

What materials will you need?

tape measures, rulers, yardsticks • string in various colors • pencils • Post-It notes • markers or crayons • drawing paper • scissors

What questions could you ask?

How many of you know how tall you are? Do you know how you were measured?

Have you ever used a ruler or a tape measure? What do you think we could use these tools for?

Who do you think might be the tallest, next tallest, and so on in your family? In this class? How could you find out for certain?

Do you know what size you wear in jeans, T-shirts, or shoes? What does it mean when you wear a particular size of something?

---

*Adapted from a lesson taught by Teresa Sandoval

What will students do?

In teams of two, use colored string to measure each other. Cut lengths of different colored string for height; length of arms, legs, and feet; and distance around head, wrist, and ankle. Use Post-It notes to label each length of string with name and measured part. Then with the measuring tools, figure out and write down the length of each piece of string in centimeters and inches (or inches and feet).

Draw a self-portrait, adding labels and measurements. If the drawings suggest other parts to be measured, you can do so and add those measurements to the picture.

What strategies might students *invent* or construct?

To get a straight measure of height, some might measure their partners against a straight wall or other object. When they run out of tape or ruler space, they might hold their space with a finger and go back to the beginning, counting on or adding to get the total. For comparisons, they can line up all of the string strips to find the tallest or go by the numbers.

What insights, connections, or applications might students *discover*?

- You can measure in centimeters or inches; the numbers will be different, but the length stays the same.
- Measurements affect the sizes you wear.
- It may take several lengths of a tape or ruler to measure one strip of string.

12 Exploring Place Value with Blocks

Grade Levels 2–5

NCTM Standards	
Content	*Process*
■ Number and Operations	■ Problem Solving
□ Algebra	■ Reasoning and Proof
□ Geometry	□ Communication
■ Measurement	■ Connections
□ Data Analysis and Probability	■ Representation

Overview

Because the concept of a base-10 number system is abstract, students need concrete ways to explore place value and face value. Two kinds of blocks—connecting cubes and base-10 blocks—let students model numbers and "see" how place value builds by 10 units, 10 tens, 10 hundreds, and so on. Students begin by building numbers with the manipulatives and then move on to representing the numbers with drawings and numerals.

Activity

What ideas or concepts will students *explore*?

- Grouping numbers
- Base-10 structuring
- Exchanging, trading, regrouping
- Equivalencies
- Place value and face value

What materials will you need?

connecting centimeter blocks • base-10 blocks, manufactured or cutouts (see "Pattern: Base-10 Blocks" in the Make Manipulatives section of the CD-ROM that accompanies this text) • pencils • paper • ruler

What questions could you ask?

How many numerals are there?
How many numbers are there?
How do we show numbers larger than 9?
How many 1s are there in 10? How many 10s in 100? How many 100s in 1,000?
What do we mean when we say we have a base-10 number system?
What is the place value of a number? The face value?

What will students do?

Building Block by Block Working in teams, use connecting centimeter blocks to create a number line from 1 to 20. Then rework the line so that no set of numbers has more than 10 in one connected unit.

Plastic connecting blocks (sometimes called Unifix cubes) can be combined for groups of 5 or 10 units.

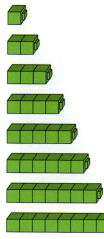

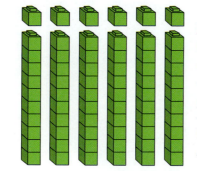

Think of a number from 1 to 20; build the number with blocks; then draw and write the number on a piece of paper. Do the same with numbers from 20 to 30, 30 to 50, and 50 to 100.

Show with blocks and then on paper several ways to make 5, 8, 10, 16, 22, 30.

Building by Tens In teams, explore the different base-10 block pieces. Use a centimeter ruler to measure units, rods, flats, and cubes. Draw around each piece; write the name and dimensions on a piece of paper. Then use the pieces to measure each other. How many units does it take to make a rod? How many rods to make a flat? How many flats to make a cube?

Building and Writing by Tens Working individually, build a number using one or more units and one or more rods. What is the number? Draw and write it on a piece of paper. Do the same with one or more units, one or more rods, and one or more flats. Can you do the same with a cube, no flats, one or more rods, and no units? How about one cube, two flats, three rods, and four units?

Trading Blocks for Blocks Work in groups of four. Divide the base-10 blocks so that each student starts with one kind of unit. Trade 10 units for a rod, 10 rods for a flat, 10 flats for a cube. Keep trading until each student in the group has some of each type of block.

Counting Up and Down with Blocks Individually, start with each kind of block and count up by 1 and by 10. Write the resulting numbers. Then with each kind of block, count down by 1 and by 10. Write the resulting numbers.

*What strategies might students **invent** or construct?*

Since working with the manipulatives is the anchor for each activity, most students will begin by experimenting with each type of block and then try different ways to combine and arrange them. After several activities of building and representing different numbers with blocks, some students may want to skip the hands-on step and move directly to drawing numeral representations.

*What insights, connections, or applications might students **discover**?*

- Building numbers with base-10 blocks is easier than building them unit by unit with centimeter blocks.
- Sometimes it is simpler to work with groups of numbers than with individual units—for example, counting to 30 by 10s instead of one number at a time.
- The base-10 blocks show the structure of written numbers, with units for 1s, rods for 10s, flats for 100s, and cubes for 1,000s.

What extensions can you make?

Post additional questions for students to explore: How would you use base-10 blocks to show 10,000? 100,000? 1,000,000? What about the

Base-10 blocks come in units of one cube, rods of 10 cubes, flats of 100 cubes, and giant cubes of 1,000 unit cubes.

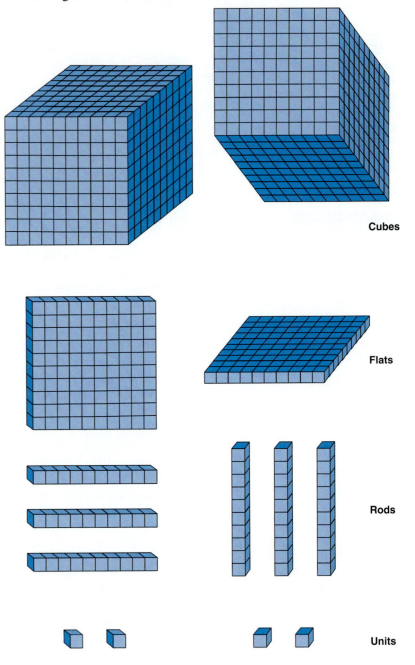

Cubes

Flats

Rods

Units

right side of a decimal point? Could you use coins to represent one and two places to the right of the decimal point? If you used blocks, what kind of blocks would you need? How large would 0.10 block have to be? A 0.01 block?

13 How Much Is That Pet?

Overview

The complexity of financial commitments, such as owning and caring for a pet, is neither immediately nor intuitively obvious to young people. Joanne Rocklin's story, *How Much Is That Guinea Pig in the Window?*, puts the financial implications of pet ownership in a context that students can relate to and provides a take-off point for the class pet-store experience. Shopping in the class pet store makes the activity hands-on and allows for experimentation and individual involvement.

Grade Levels 2–5

NCTM Standards	
Content	*Process*
■ Number and Operations	■ Problem Solving
☐ Algebra	☐ Reasoning and Proof
☐ Geometry	■ Communication
☐ Measurement	■ Connections
☐ Data Analysis and Probability	☐ Representation

Activity

What ideas or concepts will students explore?

- Money, value of items
- Making, adjusting, following through on a spending plan
- Adding, subtracting money
- Estimating costs

What materials will you need?

play money in denominations of $1, $5, $10, $20 • shopping lists and pencils • cutout store items • cartons, paper cups, sand, shredded paper • yarn, felt pieces • signs with prices of different items • cash box with dividers for denominations • Joanne Rocklin's story *How Much Is That Guinea Pig in the Window?* (New York: Scholastic, 1995)

What questions could you ask?

How many of you have pets? Did you buy your pet or adopt a pet at an animal shelter?

What do you think it costs to feed your pet?

Does your pet have toys, a special bed? How much do those cost?

How about vaccinations and visits to the vet?

Are there any pets you would like to have (for example, horses, elephants, and so forth) that might cost too much to take care of?

In the class pet store, are there any pets outside your price range?

Will you have to skip some items such as a fancy collar in order to buy your pet what it actually needs, such as food?

What is the most expensive pet you have seen in the class store or in other stores? The least expensive?

What will you do?

Set up a pet store with the cutouts, cartons, and other items. Read *How Much Is That Guinea Pig in the Window?* aloud and lead a discussion about the cost of pets. Ask the children if they have pets or would like to have pets. Have an aide or advanced student serve as cashier in the store so that you are free to answer questions and make suggestions.

What will students do?

You have $50 each to spend on a pet and everything the pet needs. As you shop, keep a record of your purchases and a running account of what you have left to spend. Write a report about your purchase. Explain why you chose the pet you did. Provide a detailed expense account of what you spent. Include a drawing of your pet in the report.

What strategies might students invent or construct?

They might shop for items one at a time, checking after each purchase to see how much they have left. Or they might window-shop first, make a list of what they can afford, and then buy all of the items at one time.

What insights, connections, or applications might students discover?

- How much you can buy depends upon how much money you have to spend rather than upon what you want or even need.
- Buying something means exchanging money for the item.
- As you spend, the amount of money you have left goes down.
- Keeping a pet can be expensive.

What extensions can you make?

Have students look at the business side of the store. Figure out how much money the pet shop took in during the class. Add additional questions: If we estimate the cost of the items, how much did the shop actually make? How about the clerk's wages? How much do you think a pet-shop clerk is paid? How much would the clerk's salary take away from the amount the shop took in?

Pose another budgeting problem: What if there's not enough money to buy a pet you want? Devise several ways to make money; you might include a bake sale or collecting cans and bottles, as the children do in the story. Find out how much people will pay for cakes, bottles, cans, or car washes; then figure out how long you will have to work to make enough money to buy and take care of your pet.

14 Filling Up or Filling Out: How Much Will Fit in Each Place on the Calculator Display?

Grade Levels 2–3, 4–5

NCTM Standards	
Content	*Process*
■ Number and Operations	■ Problem Solving
☐ Algebra	☐ Reasoning and Proof
☐ Geometry	☐ Communication
☐ Measurement	■ Connections
☐ Data Analysis and Probability	■ Representation

Overview

An important concept for understanding the base-10 system is the use of just 9 digits in different combinations to compose numbers. The idea is also an essential one for using a calculator. Having students work with a calculator to explore place and face value lets them discover for themselves how the system works.

Activity

What ideas or concepts will students explore?

- Patterns
- Place value
- Counting by 1s, 10s, 100s, 1,000s

What materials will you need?

calculators • recording sheets with a 10 × 10 grid of boxes, labeled from right to left: 1s, 10s, 100s, 1,000s, and so forth (see "Calculator Worksheet" in the Worksheets & Handouts section of the CD-ROM that accompanies this text)

What questions could you ask?

How many of you have used a calculator before?
What is a calculator used for?
What are the different keys on the pad used for?
What happens if you enter a very large number?
What happens if you want to add a whole column of numbers?
What if you want to add some numbers and subtract some?

What will students do?

In teams of two, explore how much will fit in each number place, starting with the 1s box. Take turns recording and calculating.

Counting by 1s Count to 10, one at a time. What happens when you get to 10? Record the highest number in the 1s box.

Counting by 10s Count to 100, 10 at a time. What happens when you get to 100? Record the highest numbers in the 10s box.

Counting by 100s Count to 1,000, 100 at a time. What happens when you get to 1,000? Record the highest number in the 100s box.

Counting by 1,000s Count to 10,000, 1,000 at a time. What happens when you get to 10,000? Record the highest number in the 1,000s box.

What is the highest number in each number place? What do you have to do to move to the next place? How many different ways can you find to move up to the next number place? Try out the combinations and write each one that works in a box on the grid under the name of the place value.

*What strategies might students **invent** or construct?*

Some might record their counting on the grid with tally marks and then count all. Others might write and cross out successive totals on the display until they answer the question.

*What insights, connections, or applications might students **discover**?*

- The highest number in any place-value box is 9: nine 1s, nine 10s, nine 100s, nine 1,000s.
- When the count reaches 10 (ten 1s, ten 10s, ten 100s, ten 1,000s) it causes a shift to the left.
- The pattern is consistent: count 9, stay in place; count 10, move to the left.
- The bigger the number, the more places it moves to the left.

15 Quipus

Grade Levels 3–6

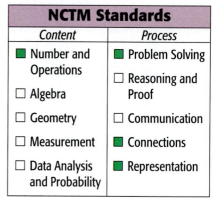

NCTM Standards	
Content	*Process*
■ Number and Operations	■ Problem Solving
☐ Algebra	☐ Reasoning and Proof
☐ Geometry	☐ Communication
☐ Measurement	■ Connections
☐ Data Analysis and Probability	■ Representation

Overview

The ancient Incas developed a complex trading system using oral rather than written records and a base-10 number system that could be represented with knotted cords. To show numbers or groups of numbers, they used a base cord with knotted cords attached. Where the knot was made on the cord determined the place value: 1s were knotted closest to the end, 10s next, then 100s, and so forth. A base cord could have several knotted cords attached and a separate cord to show the total of the others.

Activity

What ideas or concepts will students *explore*?

- Oral number traditions
- Base-10 number systems
- Representing place value with physical objects

What materials will you need?

2-foot lengths of heavy macramé cording • 18-inch lengths of lighter cording in a variety of colors • access to printed or Internet information about Incan civilization

What questions could you ask?

Who were the Incas? When did their civilization flourish?
Does the *quipu* system seem easier or harder than a written system to you?
What special demands does the *quipu* and the oral tradition place on the tallier?
What if we had no way to write out numbers? How could you keep track of important numbers, such as the number of students in your school or the amount of money it costs to buy a bagful of groceries?
What are some of the advantages of a written number system? Can you think of any advantages to an oral system?

What will students do?

Work with a length of heavy macramé cording and four lengths of lighter macramé cording in various colors. Three of the lighter cords are tied with loops to the main cord to create a narrow curtain of loose cords. The fourth cord, a sum-up cord, is tied in a loop to the top of the other three.

In *quipus,* numbers are represented by knots tied in cords. To keep the different parts of a tally separate, there may be separate cords with knots for each tally and then a summary cord that adds the other tallies together.

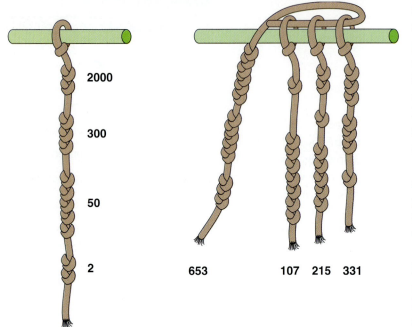

2000

300

50

2

653   107   215   331

Choose three items to tally—different items for different colors of cord. For a classroom activity the items might be chairs, desks, books in the resource center, floor or ceiling tiles, window panes, pencils, crayons, paper clips, and so forth. For a take-home activity, items might be dogs or cats observed in the neighborhood, cars on the streets or in the parking lots, street lamps, bicycles, skate boarders, and so forth. Use only the *quipus* to record your observations; don't write numbers and then transfer them to the cords.

Record each group of items selected on a different cord. If you are observing over a period of time, you may find that you have to unknot and reknot your cords several times.

When you have finished the three tallies, knot the sum of the three on the fourth cord—again, not writing out the addition but doing it mentally and recording the results with knots.

What strategies might students *invent* or construct?

Some might keep track of their tallies with mnemonic aids such as fingers or other body parts. Some might knot and reknot their *quipus* as they add to their tallies.

What insights, connections, or applications might students *discover*?

- Working with an oral numbers tradition requires users to develop their memory skills since they keep track of quantities as well as order and do many operations in their heads.
- Showing quantity with knots is more time-consuming than using written numbers.
- The system provides for simple classification and tallies but could make it difficult to develop and work with more sophisticated numerical concepts.

What extensions can you make?

Have older students do some research about other methods of hand-tallying (for example, the English tally sticks for tax records) and then share what they have found.

16 The Circle of Time

Overview

Grade Levels 5–8

NCTM Standards	
Content	*Process*
■ Number and Operations	■ Problem Solving
☐ Algebra	☐ Reasoning and Proof
☐ Geometry	☐ Communication
■ Measurement	■ Connections
☐ Data Analysis and Probability	■ Representation

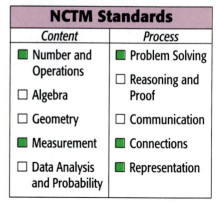

Math is everywhere, and we are doing math all the time. Telling time is one of the earliest math skills students master. The basic skill involves reading numbers and being able to count, but much more is involved in the mathematics of time. In this activity students discover the complexity of the concepts and measurements behind telling time. They discover that time is more than a measurement of minutes and hours; it is a measurement of the movement of the earth in space.

Activity

What ideas or concepts will students explore?
- Time standards
- Relationship between degrees of a circle and longitude and latitude
- Earth's rotation on its axis and orbit around the sun
- Moon's orbit around the earth

What materials will you need?
round clock • globe • model or map of the solar system • world map with time zones • Internet access or reference books • compass, ruler • pencils, colored pencils, markers • drawing paper, lined paper

What questions could you ask?
Why are there 24 hours in a day and 365 days in most years?
Why do we have leap years, and what are they?
Where do days begin, and where do they end?
Why are many clocks round?
What is a month?
What is the international dateline?

What will you do?
Talk about time and its effects on living things—day, night, seasons, entropy. Discuss the clock as a symbol developed to measure the passage of time. Discuss the appropriateness of a circular clock as a symbol of time—its relation to the rotation of the earth and the movement of the earth around the sun. Use the globe and maps as aids in the discussion.

What will students do?
Compose and write down questions about time, including or in addition to those posed by the teacher; the focus and details of the questions might

be revised as you learn more about the topic. Search for answers, beginning with classroom resources and extending searches as necessary to libraries, planetariums, and authorities. Findings should be represented in words and illustrations—for example, a drawing or diagram of the moon circling the earth or of the earth circling the sun.

*What strategies might students **invent** or construct?*

They might look first for an overall discussion of time in a reference work or on the Internet and then for the answers to their specific questions. They might study a map with time zones and do the math to discover relative times around the world. They might use the globe and maps of the solar system to understand night, day, months, and years.

*What insights, connections, or applications might students **discover**?*

- Time on earth is tied to the motion of heavenly bodies and of the earth itself.
- We use time standards to help us define our position in the universe and help us make sense of what is happening around us.
- Much depends upon people around the world accepting the same time standards.
- A better symbol for a day might be a round clock with 24 instead of 12 hours.

What extensions can you make?

Have students work with time-related numbers—circumference at earth's equator, distance across time zones, distance the moon travels in a month or the earth in a year. Discuss the time-lag phenomenon of jet travel—the apparent loss or gain of time as you travel east or west. What effect might this have on people traveling and on daily activities, such as watching television? Older students might explore the idea of time as a measure of distance (light years) and its implications for what we see in the night sky and for space travel.

17 What If You Had a Million Dollars?

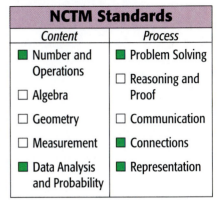
Grade Levels 5–8

NCTM Standards	
Content	*Process*
■ Number and Operations	■ Problem Solving
☐ Algebra	☐ Reasoning and Proof
☐ Geometry	☐ Communication
☐ Measurement	■ Connections
■ Data Analysis and Probability	■ Representation

Overview

It seems that everyone likes to daydream about becoming rich by winning the lottery or placing first in a game or reality show. These fantasies are used to engage students' interest in an activity that combines basic financial calculations with more complex tasks of computing taxes, making judgments based on value, and sticking to a budget.

Activity

What ideas or concepts will students ***explore****?*

- Cost, worth, value
- Taxes as part of item cost and amount available
- Estimation
- Working with large numbers
- Pricing, figuring costs
- Computing tax with percentages
- Computing costs

What materials will you need?

calculators ● catalogs, advertisements, websites for prices ● construction paper, markers, staples for expense-book cover ● ledger or lined paper for pages of expense book ● pencils

What questions could you ask?

Have you ever watched a television game or reality show where the winner becomes a millionaire?

Is a million dollars much money today?

If you had a million dollars, could you buy everything you want or just some of the things you want?

If you spent all of your money on things, how much would you need to live on?

How would you get money to run the car you bought or maintain the house?

Is there anything you might have bought that would be an investment— something that would increase in value and give you more money?

How about education? Did anyone think about school tuition as something to spend the money on? What do you think it costs to become a teacher (5 years of college), a doctor (8–12 years of college), an attorney (7 years of college)?

What will students do?	Make an expense book by folding and cutting ledger or lined paper. Make a cover for your book with construction paper and use markers to write your name and create a cover title and design. Staple the pages and cover together at the spine.

Spend $1,000,000. Write items and costs in your expense book. Spend all of the money down to the last dime. Be sure to include sales taxes in a separate column in your book.

Estimate the federal and state taxes on $1,000,000 using percentages given to you by your teacher. You might need to deduct items from your expense book until you have enough to pay those taxes.

*What strategies might students **invent** or construct?*

They might start with a wish list, estimate costs, and then look for exact costs. They might buy one item at a time, deduct the cost, and make their next choices based on how much they have left. Some might comparison-shop, buying the cheapest of some items to leave money for others. Some might try different combinations of items to get the greatest value for the money.

*What insights, connections, or applications might students **discover**?*

- A million dollars is a lot of money, but it is not unlimited.
- Costs of items depend upon a variety of factors—brand name, size, quality, and so forth.
- Taxes reduce the amount of money you have to spend and increase the cost of items you want to buy.

18 Discovering EightWorld

Grade Levels 6–8

NCTM Standards	
Content	*Process*
■ Number and Operations	■ Problem Solving
☐ Algebra	■ Reasoning and Proof
☐ Geometry	■ Communication
☐ Measurement	■ Connections
☐ Data Analysis and Probability	■ Representation

Overview

Discovering different number systems is an important part of working with numbers. Students work with different base systems when they learn to tell time and measure length or weight. Learning about the metric and standard systems prepares them to understand that there can be multiple standards for measurement. Exploring different base systems expands that understanding to include numbers in general. In this activity a fantasy world provides the context for exploring a base-8 number system.

Activity

What ideas or concepts will students *explore*?
- Base-8 number system
- Base-8 place value
- Base-8 biology

What materials will you need?
calculators ● drawing paper, lined paper ● pencils, colored pencils

What questions could you ask?
What do we mean when we say our number system uses a base of 10?
How do you think people might have arrived at a base of 10 for basic number operations such as counting?
Using the calculator, what can you tell us about place values in our system?
What if there were a world where the inhabitants had four fingers on each hand, like frogs? What kind of base-8 number system might they develop?

What will students do?
Write a story and draw a picture about EightWorld. Cover biology—organic structure of the inhabitants, including animals; social structure, with details such as language related to number of fingers; commerce and technology—for example, whether the inhabitants show the dexterity of opposable thumbs and build ornate, complex structures and tools or are restricted to simpler buildings and machines.

Develop a number system for EightWorld. Create new numerals or borrow familiar ones from earth, such as Arabic or even Chinese stick numerals. Work out the place values for base-8 numbers. Set up one or two counting problems with tally marks; then write the answer in base-8 and base-10. Use calculators to compute values.

*What strategies might students **invent** or construct?*

To understand the base-8 system, some of the students might use drawings to represent place values. They could use stick numerals that translate easily from base-10 to base-8.

*What insights, connections, or applications might students **discover**?*

- The base system does not affect the answers to mathematics problems, just the way they are arrived at.
- When we get past the counting stage, the number of fingers or even fingers and toes has little effect on our "doing" mathematics.
- Base-10 is easy for us to use because we are accustomed to it, but other systems will work also.

What extensions can you make?

Have the students research another number system, such as the Babylonian, Chinese, or Mayan system. Try as a class to do some basic operations such as adding or subtracting with different types of numerals. Helpful websites include http://it.stlawu.edu/dmelvill/mesomath/sumerian.html, http://www.groups.dcs.st.andrews.ac.uk/history/HistTopics/Babylonian_numerals.html, http://www.groups.dcs.st-and.ac.uk/history/HistTopics/Mayan_mathematics.html.

Have the students research the binary or base-2 number system. The simplest of all the positional number systems, the binary system is basic to computer technology. Discuss how base-2 differs from base-10. A helpful site is http://www.cut-the-knot.com/do_you_know/BinaryHistory.html.

19 The 250-Mile Race

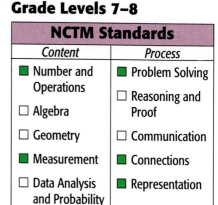

NCTM Standards	
Content	*Process*
■ Number and Operations	■ Problem Solving
☐ Algebra	☐ Reasoning and Proof
☐ Geometry	☐ Communication
■ Measurement	■ Connections
☐ Data Analysis and Probability	■ Representation

Overview

Usually a race matches like against like: horses against horses, cars against cars, and so forth. However, this race matches different types of transportation and even allows racers to plot different courses. In the process they must analyze the effect of different characteristics on their ability to run the race—on speed, terrain, fueling stops, and so forth. The result is a race that asks students to see relationships and understand and manipulate a variety of numbers in a variety of ways.

Activity

What ideas or concepts will students *explore*?

- Time, distance, speed
- Reading maps
- Measurement

What materials will you need?

copies of a state map including highways, towns, and rest stops and large enough to plot a 250-mile race • cards for five teams of racers: hot-air balloon, dog sled (on wheels or runners), bicycle, donkey cart, electric golf cart (see "Race Cards for 250-Mile Race" in the Worksheets & Handouts section of the CD-ROM that accompanies this text, or make your own) • measuring tapes or sticks • race logs, pencils • calculators

What questions could you ask?

What is the most important factor in a race, the race vehicle or the person driving it?

Is it possible for something slow like a hot-air balloon to beat something faster like a a golf cart?

What are some of the factors that might affect the outcome of a race?

In planning your race strategy, how much math would you need to know and use?

What will students do?

Divide into five different racing teams. Select one of the five racing vehicles. Working with a map marked with a beginning and ending point 250 miles apart, plot a route, choosing terrain or roads that will work best for your vehicle—for example, west to east with the wind pattern for the balloon, populated with many towns for the electric cart which will need to be recharged frequently. Pay special attention to any special requirements described on the vehicle card—number of stops needed, top speed, and so forth.

Keep a written log of the racer's progress and also plot the courses on the race maps, marking stops and hazards. Each team should identify and log 5 obstacles or hazards on their course and make a plan (including time spent) to overcome them.

The team that correctly logs the least time to finish wins the race.

*What strategies might students **invent** or construct?*

They could figure race time by dividing distance by speed and then add time for hazards and stops. They could plot the course, step by step, adding time for stops and obstacles as they occur. In the first case, the race log will emphasize numbers; in the second, events.

*What insights, connections, or applications might students **discover**?*

- Race time involves more than distance and speed.
- Average speed over a race course may be much lower than best speed.
- Most U.S. maps list distances in miles; to measure the kilometers traveled in the race, students will have to convert English miles to metric kilometers.
- Running the race calls for a knowledge of science and geography as well as mathematics.

Working with Whole Numbers: Addition and Subtraction

20 Animals, Numbered and On the Town: A Bilingual Lesson in Spanish and English*

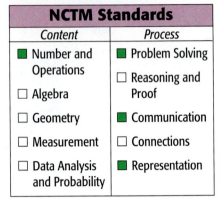

Overview

The simple vocabulary and the easy-to-interpret visuals in Susan Middleton Elya's story, *Eight Animals on the Town*, make this book the ideal anchor for a bilingual math and reading lesson. Students who know Spanish will learn English words for numbers, animals, and simple things like milk. Students who know English will learn the Spanish words for the same things. The story provides a context—the animals' shopping trip—and a story line within which the number sequence can be visualized and ordinal number words understood.

Grade Levels K–2

NCTM Standards	
Content	*Process*
■ Number and Operations	■ Problem Solving
□ Algebra	□ Reasoning and Proof
□ Geometry	■ Communication
□ Measurement	□ Connections
□ Data Analysis and Probability	■ Representation

Activity

*What ideas or concepts will students **explore**?*

- Ordinal numbers
- Cardinal numbers
- English/Spanish number words
- Number sequence and order

What materials will you need?

Susan Middleton Elya's *Eight Animals on the Town* (New York: Putnam, 2000) ● 11 sheets of paper for each student, half lined for text, half blank for illustrations ● construction paper for book covers and animal hats ● crayons, colored pencils, markers ● stapler or binder with plastic rings for binding ● overhead projector ● transparencies for book pages

What questions could you ask?

What do you think would happen if a group of animals decided to take a ride and go shopping?

Which animals would be noticed first? Which animals might not be noticed?

What would happen if the animals all went to the market at the same time?

Which animal in the story is the biggest? The smallest? The longest? The shortest? The most colorful?

How many taxis would you need to take all of the animals in the story for a ride? How many buses?

---

*Adapted from a lesson taught by Thelma Aragon

What will students do?

Watch and follow along as the teacher reads *Eight Animals on the Town* aloud and projects the story a page at a time on the overhead projector. Then reread the story silently a page at a time on the overhead projector; then read aloud as a group. Discuss any words that seem difficult to understand or pronounce.

Rewrite the story a page at a time. Use your own words or repeat the author's. Illustrate each page (see one student's drawing on page 46 as an example). Be sure to include Spanish words for numbers, English ordinal number words, and numerals. Draw a cover for the book that shows the eight animals and gives the author's name and your name as illustrator.

Extend and act out the story, adding new animals and new numbers for each additional student in class. Use construction paper and markers to create animal hats. Write the name, number, and order (12th, 16th, and so forth) for each animal on a sign or tag.

What strategies might students *invent* or construct?

They might illustrate the story with drawings of the animals and the items and numbers mentioned in the text, or they might show the animals in action—going to the market, eating, or dancing.

The animal hats could be paper ears for cats and dogs, horns for the cow, or strips of paper for a mane and forelock for the horse. Or students could use colored cones to match the creatures—green for the frog, pink for the pig, and so on.

What insights, connections, or applications might students *discover*?

- Ordinal number words refer to places in a number line.
- Being first means being at the start of the line; being last (in this case, eighth) means being at the end of the line.
- To tell how many animals there are, we need to change the order number of the last animal into a quantity word like *eight* or *sixteen*.
- Ordinal numbers can be used with time and space words like *then, next, after, behind.*

"Numero cuatro is a large bird."

1. Número cuatro is a large bird.

2. Fourth in line after first, second,

3. third Bird flies along to

4. purchase some seed. "Semillas,"

5. chirps Pájaro. "That's what I need."

21 Change for More/Change for Less

Overview

Grade Levels K–2

NCTM Standards	
Content	*Process*
■ Number and Operations	■ Problem Solving
☐ Algebra	■ Reasoning and Proof
☐ Geometry	☐ Communication
☐ Measurement	☐ Connections
☐ Data Analysis and Probability	■ Representation

Before developing algorithms for addition and subtraction, students need to discover the processes of changing quantities to make more or less. This activity uses counters for the discovery stage and stickers for representing changes in quantity.

Activity

What ideas or concepts will students explore?

- Changing quantities
- Changing to make more
- Changing to make less
- Counting for totals

What materials will you need?

plastic counters in cups—circles, cats, dinosaurs, bugs, bears, other shapes • peelable stickers or "Pattern: Counters" (in the Make Manipulatives section of the CD-ROM that accompanies this text) • crayons or colored pencils • paper

What questions could you ask?

If I pour out some but not all of the counting objects from a plastic cup, how many counters are there?
If I pour out the remaining counters, how many counters are there?
If I add the remaining counters to the first group, how many **more** counters have we added?
What is the total number of counters?

What will students do?

In small groups, count the objects in a pile of counters poured from a plastic cup. Show the quantity with drawings or marks and write the total in numerals. Then do the same for the remaining counters and for the combined pile.

What strategies might students invent or construct?

Some will adopt a counting-in-sequence strategy for each stage of the problem, counting the first and second piles and then starting over to count the combined pile. Others will count in sequence for the first and second pile but begin with the total for the first pile and continue counting in sequence for the remaining counters.

Some will draw circles, cats, or actual objects to represent quantities; some will abbreviate the process with tally marks or invented symbols.

What questions could you ask?

If I pour all of the counters in the plastic cup into one pile, how many counters are there?

If I take away a handful of counters, how many did I take away?

How many counters are left?

What will students do?

Again in small groups, count all of the counters in a plastic cup. Draw the quantity and show the total in numerals. Then take away a handful. Draw and write the number in that handful. Then determine the number of counters left in the ongoing pile. Draw and write that quantity as well.

*What strategies might students **invent** or construct?*

They might count each object in each pile and draw the actual objects, or they might shorten the process by using tally marks and counting by 2s or 3s. A few might reverse the count to find the total, although reverse processes are very difficult conceptually for many children.

*What insights, connections, or applications might students **discover**?*

- Quantities can be increased or decreased by specific amounts.
- When quantities change for more, the total will be a larger number than the one you started with.
- When quantities change for less, the total will be a smaller number than the one you started with.
- Counting can be used to find more or less.

What extensions can you make?

Have the children work individually and use peelable stickers or the cut-outs from the CD-ROM that accompanies this text to show quantities. Have them show a starting quantity with stickers and write the number. Then change the quantity to make it more or less and write the result of each change in numerals. You may want to introduce plus (+) and minus (−) symbols to indicate changing for more and changing for less.

22 One-Handed Fingermath
Part I: Counting All and On to Add Single-Digit Numbers

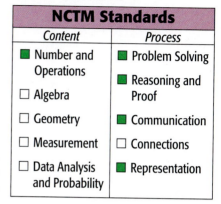

Grade Levels K–1

NCTM Standards	
Content	*Process*
■ Number and Operations	■ Problem Solving
☐ Algebra	■ Reasoning and Proof
☐ Geometry	■ Communication
☐ Measurement	☐ Connections
☐ Data Analysis and Probability	■ Representation

Overview

Because of the emphasis on memorizing math facts, teachers once considered using the fingers to count and do basic calculations a major infraction. Many adults have horror stories about early math instruction, such as having their hands slapped or hit with a ruler, being sent to the board to write a problem as punishment, or feeling guilty for counting on their fingers even if they got away with it. Although the use of manipulatives has helped make fingers more respectable as counting tools, some of the stigma remains. Nonetheless, research in early math learning by Fuson and others has shown that counting on fingers is an important intuitive strategy for working with numbers and that learning a one-handed version of fingermath helps children understand addition and subtraction.*

Activity

*What ideas or concepts will students **explore**?*
- Counting to determine quantity
- Adding single-digit numbers
- Using fingers as a calculator
- Counting all and on to add

What materials will you need?
chart with finger patterns (printed at the end of this activity)
• counting objects or pictures • rolls of paper • colored pencils or crayons • pencils • paper

What questions could you ask?
Do you ever use your fingers to help you do math?
How do you or could you use your fingers to keep track of numbers when you are counting?
How could you use your fingers to add or combine numbers?

---

*See Fuson, Karen C. *Children's Counting and Concepts of Number.* New York: Springer-Verlag, 1988.

What will students do?

Observe the teacher count on her or his fingers using the method shown on the finger pattern chart. Practice making the finger patterns in sequence, then at random. To reinforce learning, draw the patterns in sequence on sheets of rolled paper by forming the pattern for each number and tracing around your fingers with markers or colored pencils.

What will you do?

Introduce the idea of addition as a change-for-more strategy. Use counting objects or pictures to model the process. Ask the children how they can use finger patterns to change quantities (3, 5, 7) by adding more (2, 4, 3).

What will students do?

Model addition situations with objects or pictures; then use finger patterns to find answers. Each situation and solution should also be written in numerals on paper. Also draw the finger pattern for the solution.

What strategies might students invent or construct?

Some students will count all (sum procedure), using their fingers to count out the numbers of the first addend and then continue on in sequence for the number in the second addend. Some may start with counting all but then devise a counting-on (min procedure) strategy. They will start by showing the pattern for the larger addend; then count on for the number of the smaller addend.

What insights, connections, or applications might students discover?

- Adding numbers is as simple as counting out the numbers.
- Counting on takes less time than counting all.
- You can count on from either addend and get the same number, but it is easiest to start with the larger addend.

What extensions can you make?

Some children may prefer to use all 10 fingers in their calculations. Ask them to think about and explain their methods; then add a variety of numbers both by counting all and by counting on.

Ask the children how they could use their fingers to count larger numbers, including the teens and the decades above 20. You might also introduce the 10-fingered method from Edwin M. Lieberthal's *The Complete Book of Fingermath* (New York: McGraw-Hill, 1979), see p. 73 in Activity 30.

Finger patterns for one-handed fingermath

Source: Adapted from Lieberthal, Edwin M. *The Complete Book of Fingermath* (New York: McGraw-Hill, 1979.)

Right-hand numbers:

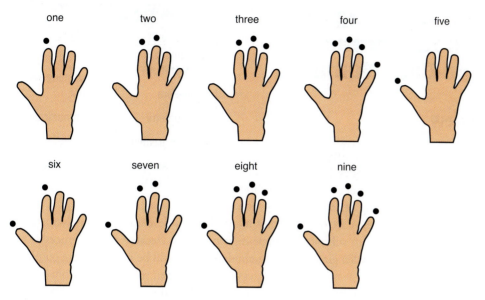

23 One-Handed Fingermath
Part II: Counting Up and Down to Subtract Single-Digit Numbers

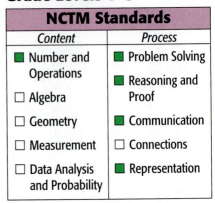

Math Manipulatives

Grade Levels 1–3

NCTM Standards	
Content	*Process*
☑ Number and Operations	☑ Problem Solving
☐ Algebra	☑ Reasoning and Proof
☐ Geometry	☑ Communication
☐ Measurement	☐ Connections
☐ Data Analysis and Probability	☑ Representation

Overview

Just as counting-all and counting-on strategies build on children's intuitive algorithms for addition, counting up and counting down to subtract are methods that many children develop for themselves as they work with subtracting single-digit numbers. Because reverse processes are more challenging for young children, most will be initially more comfortable with a counting-up strategy—that is, when subtracting 3 from 6, they will count up from the 3 to the 6 to find the difference instead of counting down from 6 to 3.

Activity

*What ideas or concepts will students **explore**?*
- Counting to determine quantity
- Subtracting single-digit numbers
- Using fingers as a calculator
- Counting up and down to subtract

What materials will you need?
chart with finger patterns (see p. 51 in Activity 22) • counting objects or pictures • rolls of paper • colored pencils or crayons • pencils • paper

What questions could you ask?
Why might it be helpful to count with your fingers when you do math? If you are asked to do math in your head, do you use your fingers to keep track of the numbers?
How could you use your fingers to subtract or take away numbers?

What will you do?
Review the one-handed finger patterns for numbers as well as any two-handed patterns the children have developed. Introduce subtraction as a change-for-less procedure. Model the ideas with counting objects or pictures: the larger to start, the lesser quantity to take away, the quantity left as the problem solution. Model the counting-up process to subtract: starting with the quantity to be taken away, counting up with finger numbers to the larger quantity, reading the final finger patterns for the answer.

What will students do?   Practice one- or two-handed finger patterns from 1 to 20 (see p. 73 in Activity 30 for a two-handed chart). Set up problems with counters and fingers and then work out solutions by counting up. Draw the problem on paper with circles or other objects to represent the numbers. Write out problems and answers in numerals.

What questions could you ask?
- In each subtraction problem, how many do you have to start?
- How many are you taking away?
- How many do you have left?

What will you do?   Demonstrate the concept of reverse counting. Model counting down with objects by taking away a counter with each number you count down. Ask if the children know of any situations where people use counting down to time events—for example, the countdown to the start of a race or a shuttle launch. Model counting down with finger numbers.

What will students do?   Count backwards from 4 to 1, 10 to 1, then 20 to 1 with objects, words, fingers, and numerals. Act out counting down by standing up, sitting down, walking around, standing still, and so forth.

What will you do?   Review subtraction as a change-for-less procedure. Model counting down with objects and fingers to subtract: starting with the larger number, counting down by the smaller number, reading the final finger pattern or counting the objects left for the answer.

What questions could you ask?   How many do you have to start?
How many are you counting down?
At what number do you stop counting down?

What will students do?   Set up problems with counters and fingers; then work out problems by counting down. Write out problems and answers in numerals.

*What strategies might students **invent** or construct?*   They might work through the subtraction situations three times: first with objects, then with fingers, and finally on paper with numerals. Or they might work step by step with objects, finger patterns, and numerals. Some may want to reaffirm their answers by counting up with fingers or by doing a take-away activity with objects and counting all that are left.

What insights, connections, or applications might students discover?

- The number line remains stable whether you are counting up or counting down.
- Subtracting is like going backwards from addition. The answers will be the same whether you count up, count down, or take away and count all that are left.
- Counting down is quicker and takes one less step than counting up to subtract.

What extensions can you make?

Have older children develop strategies for using counting-up and counting-down finger patterns with multi-digit subtraction. Talk about the role memory must play in keeping track of the numbers.

24 Exploring Multi-Unit Concepts with Base-10 Blocks

Grade Levels 1–5

NCTM Standards	
Content	*Process*
■ Number and Operations	■ Problem Solving
□ Algebra	■ Reasoning and Proof
□ Geometry	■ Communication
□ Measurement	□ Connections
□ Data Analysis and Probability	■ Representation

Overview

Moving from single-unit concepts to multi-unit concepts can be challenging for students. Thinking in terms of multi-units calls for a greater level of abstraction, and modeling multi-unit mathematical situations is more difficult with single-unit manipulatives such as counters. Base-10 blocks help students bridge the gap because multi-units are integral to their structure, with 10s represented by rods, 100s by flats, and 1,000s by cubes. When students model multi-digit numbers with multi-unit blocks, they begin to create the mental structures needed to work with large numbers and to understand the base-10 number system.

Activity

What ideas or concepts will students *explore*?
- Base-10 number structure
- Place and face value
- Quantity-by number relationships

What materials will you need?
sets of base-10 blocks or "Pattern: Base-10 Blocks" in the Make Manipulatives section of the CD-ROM that accompanies this text ● cubes of 1,000, flats of 100, rods of 10, units of 1 ● pencils ● "Base-10 Blocks Worksheet" in the Worksheets & Handouts section of the CD-ROM

What questions could you ask?
Is it easier to work with single-digit or multi-digit numbers? Why?
Would there be any differences in the way you show 9 and 99? Why or why not?
How is the way we represent numbers affected by our base-10 number system?
How many ways can you show 10 with blocks? 25? 50? 100? 1,000?
What are the advantages of using rods, flats, and cubes instead of representing all numbers with units? Are there any disadvantages?

What will students do?
In small groups explore different combinations of blocks, including two combinations of rods and units; two of flats, rods, and units; and two of cubes, flats, rods, and units. For each combination draw the combination, interpret and write the quantity in words, and write the number in the appropriate boxes of the worksheet.

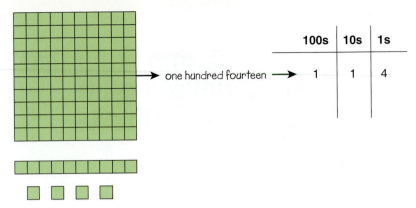

	100s	10s	1s
one hundred fourteen →	1	1	4

In small groups explore the relationship of units to rods, rods to flats, flats to cubes. Start with a random collection of units and organize them into rods and units. Draw and write the results in numbers and words individually. Do the same for rods and flats and flats and cubes.

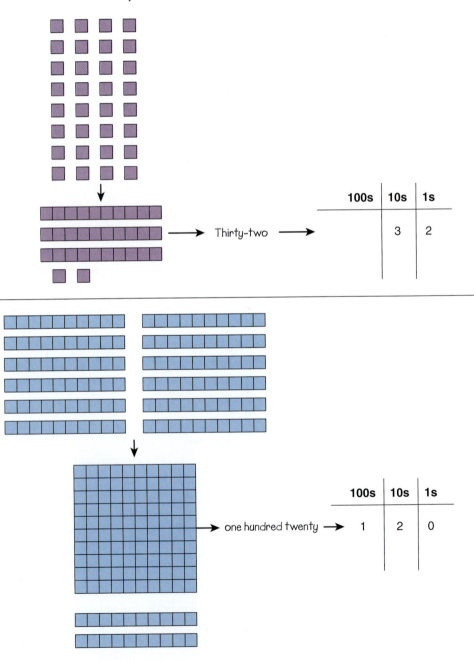

	100s	10s	1s
Thirty-two →		3	2

	100s	10s	1s
one hundred twenty →	1	2	0

Develop a 10-for-1 trading scheme by trading back and forth units for rods, rods for units, rods for flats, flats for rods, flats for cubes, and cubes for flats. Model the trades first with blocks; then represent each trade in a sketch, words, and numerals.

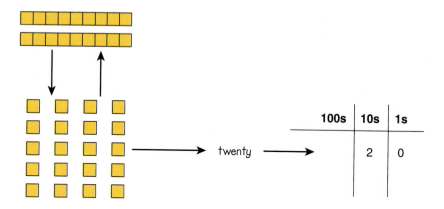

*What strategies might students **invent** or construct?*

The students might count and circle units to organize them by 10s, or they might organize units in rows to speed counting. Some may count by 2s, 5s, 10s, and so forth to group and find totals.

*What insights, connections, or applications might students **discover?***

- The blocks have a 10-for-1 relationship—10 units for a rod and so forth.
- Number places have the same relationship—ten 1s for one 10, ten 10s for one 100, ten 100s for one 1,000.
- Blocks and numbers are flexible—units and 1s can be traded for rods and 10s, and rods and 10s can be traded for units and 1s.
- Grouping blocks and numbers into multi-units makes them easier to work with: it is easier to count 10, 20, 30, 40 than to start at 1 and count to 40.

25 Adding Multi-Digit Numbers with Base-10 Blocks

Math Manipulatives

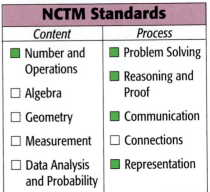

Overview

Grade Levels 2–4

NCTM Standards	
Content	*Process*
☑ Number and Operations	☑ Problem Solving
☐ Algebra	☑ Reasoning and Proof
☐ Geometry	☑ Communication
☐ Measurement	☐ Connections
☐ Data Analysis and Probability	☑ Representation

Early experiences with addition often begin with students counting and combining groups of individual counters. Base-10 blocks let students continue to model the combining process concretely but at the same time allow for multi-unit and base-10 factors. The activity goes beyond modeling with the blocks to ask students to represent numbers with drawings, words, and numerals—a process that provides different avenues to express and reinforce understanding.

Activity

What ideas or concepts will students *explore*?

- Base-10 number structure applied to addition
- 10-for-1 trading scheme
- Trading up or carrying with multi-digit addends
- Representing procedures and solutions concretely, visually, verbally, and symbolically

What materials will you need?

sets of base-10 blocks or "Pattern: Base-10 Blocks" in the Make Manipulatives section of the CD-ROM that accompanies this text, cubes of 1,000, flats of 100, rods of 10, units of 1 • pencils • "Base-10 Blocks Worksheet" in the Worksheets & Handouts section of the CD-ROM

What questions could you ask?

How many units, rods, flats, or cubes are there in each addend?
If you combine the blocks representing the addends, how many trades can you make—how many rods can be made from the units, how many flats from the rods, and so forth?
Does it matter which number comes first?

What will students do?

Model multi-digit addition with base-10 blocks; then represent the process with drawings, words, and numerals. Use 10-for-1 trading scheme to demonstrate the meaning of carrying, and think aloud, verbalizing numbers and processes.

What strategies might students *invent* or construct?

For smaller combinations some students might still use a unit-by-unit counting strategy to find totals, but addends of three or more digits should encourage them to think and work with multi-units. Some students may approach the problems first by estimating, rounding off to 10s and counting on or down for answers.

*What insights, connections, or applications might students **discover**?*

- Carrying from 1s to 10s and 10s to 100s is like trading units for rods and rods for flats.
- The total will be the same whether you work out the addition with blocks, drawings, or numerals.
- It is important to align numbers by place value when you work with numerals; putting a number in the wrong column will result in a wrong answer.

Representing multi-digit addition and trading with drawings of base-10 blocks

Source: Adapted from Fuson, Karen C. *Children's Counting and Concepts of Number.* New York: Springer-Verlag, 1988.

26 Subtracting Multi-Digit Numbers with Base-10 Blocks

Math Manipulatives

Overview

Grade Levels 2–5

NCTM Standards	
Content	*Process*
☑ Number and Operations	☑ Problem Solving
☐ Algebra	☑ Reasoning and Proof
☐ Geometry	☑ Communication
☐ Measurement	☐ Connections
☐ Data Analysis and Probability	☑ Representation

As with addition, students usually begin exploring subtraction with single-unit counters. Although the counters help them visualize taking away one quantity from another, they do not work well to show trading or working with multi-digit numbers. Base-10 blocks show the 10-for-1 relationships and provide a concrete referent for 10-for-1 trading—that is, trading a rod for 10 individual units or a flat for 10 rods.

Activity

What ideas or concepts will students *explore*?

- Base-10 structure applied to subtraction
- 10-for-1 trading scheme
- Trading down or borrowing with multi-digit numbers
- Representing procedures and solutions concretely, visually, verbally, and symbolically

What materials will you need?

sets of base-10 blocks or "Pattern: Base-10 Blocks" in the Make Manipulatives section of the CD-ROM that accompanies this text • cubes of 1,000, flats of 100, rods of 10, units of 1 • pencils • "Base-10 Blocks Worksheet" in the Worksheets & Handouts section of the CD-ROM

What questions could you ask?

How many units, rods, flats, or cubes are there in each number of the problem?
Does it matter which number comes first?
How can you tell the take-away number?
How many trades can you make in the number you are subtracting from—how many units can be made from the rods, how many rods from the flats, how many flats from the cubes?

What will students do?

Model multi-digit subtraction with base-10 blocks; then represent the process with drawings, words, and numerals. Use 10-for-1 trading scheme to demonstrate the meaning of borrowing, and think aloud, verbalizing numbers and processes.

*What strategies might students **invent** or construct?*

For smaller combinations some students might still use a unit-by-unit take-away strategy, but numbers of three or more digits should encourage them to think and work with multi-units. Some students may approach the problems first by estimating, rounding off to 10s and counting up or down for answers.

*What insights, connections, or applications might students **discover**?*

- Trading down or borrowing from 10s to 1s, 100s to 10s, and 1,000s to 100s is like trading rods for units, flats for rods, and cubes for flats.
- The answer should be the same whether you subtract with blocks, drawings, or numerals.
- It is important to align numerals carefully; putting numbers in the wrong columns will change the answer.

Representing multi-digit subtraction and trading with drawings of base-10 blocks

Source: adapted from Fuson, Karen C. *Children's Counting and Concept of Number.* New York: Springer-Verlag, 1988.

Drawings — Numbers

27 $100 Shopping Spree

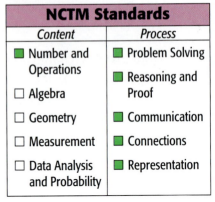

Overview

Shopping is both an important survival skill and an effective motivational tool. In this activity, students are able to apply what they have learned about the base-10 system and adding and subtracting multi-digit numbers to a real-life situation—shopping on a strict budget.

Grade Levels 3–6

NCTM Standards	
Content	*Process*
■ Number and Operations	■ Problem Solving
☐ Algebra	■ Reasoning and Proof
☐ Geometry	■ Communication
☐ Measurement	■ Connections
☐ Data Analysis and Probability	■ Representation

Activity

What ideas or concepts will students *explore*?

- Multi-digit addition/subtraction with money
- Budgeting
- Balancing amount spent, amount available
- Adding/subtracting multi-digit numbers with the calculator

What materials will you need?

calculators • shopping lists • posters with store names and lists of items with prices rounded to the nearest dollar • cash boxes for each store • play money • shopping scenarios

What questions could you ask?

Do you like to shop? Why or why not?
When you shop, how important is the cost?
Would you rather buy the exact item you want, whatever the price, or would you be willing to buy a similar but cheaper item?
What if you are shopping for a list of items? How would you make sure you don't select more items than you can pay for?
What does it mean to look for the best buy?

What will you do?

Turn your classroom into a mini-mall with posters for each store. Set up one area with a sign and ads to sell groceries, another to sell toys, another for costumes, another for party items, and so forth. Create shopping scenarios for four or five groups—birthday party, costume party, picnic, camping trip, special dinner.

What will students do?

Working in small groups, select a shopping scenario and collect $100 in play money. You may window-shop to check prices at the store sites and then make a shopping list with items, amounts, and prices. Shopping will consist of putting money into the cash boxes and making change, using your calculators to figure exact amounts.

Each group must spend exactly $100, with every dollar accounted for on the shopping list. After the activity, each group will report on the list and purchases and talk about how well it fulfilled the shopping scenario—for example, whether it bought enough toys or cake for the party or enough supplies for the camping trip.

What strategies might students *invent* or construct?

During window shopping the students might keep a running tally in their heads or on their calculators to estimate how much they are spending. The first shopping list will probably not be the final list. Some may need to return items and select others to keep their purchases within the $100 budget.

What insights, connections, or applications might students *discover*?

- Shopping with a budget is more complicated than simply buying what you want.
- You may need to buy less-expensive brands or items to stretch your money.
- The $100 budget was plenty for some scenarios—like the birthday party and dinner—but not enough for others—like the camping trip and costume party.

What extensions can you make?

Do some cross-over work with economics. Have the groups total the cash boxes for the different classroom stores, subtract the amount that was in the cash box to start with, and find out how much that store took in. Compare the amounts taken in by the different stores. Which store took in the most? The least? Talk about why.

With older students who are more familiar with decimal points and dollars-and-cents notation, use newspaper advertisements and printed circulars for store items and costs. Add play-money coins to the budgeted amount, and work with exact dollars and cents instead of rounding off.

28 Adding and Subtracting with Chinese Stick Math

Grade Levels 4–8

NCTM Standards	
Content	*Process*
■ Number and Operations	■ Problem Solving
☐ Algebra	■ Reasoning and Proof
☐ Geometry	☐ Communication
☐ Measurement	■ Connections
☐ Data Analysis and Probability	■ Representation

Overview

Chinese stick numbers are fun to learn. They also provide a new perspective on addition and subtraction concepts—concepts that students in the fourth grade and beyond may consider repetitive and boring even if they have not fully mastered applications. Working with the stick numbers on a counting board also reinforces base-10 and 10-for-1 trading concepts. Students consider the multicultural dimensions of this activity exotic and enjoy learning about Chinese contributions to mathematics.

Activity

What ideas or concepts will students explore?

- History of numbers
- Decimal system, place and face value
- Zero
- 10-for-1 trading schemes

What materials will you need?

red and black chenille wires • roll of colored paper for large sheets to serve as counting boards • markers • rulers, scissors • paper, pencils • "Chinese Stick Numbers" in the Worksheets & Handouts section of the CD-ROM that accompanies this text

What will you do?

Provide a historical context for the activity. Talk about *suan zi*, or calculation with rods; its use 2,000 years or more before the development of western number systems; its emphasis upon mental calculation, with the sticks as reminders; its decimal base and representation of zero with an empty space on the counting board.*

What questions could you ask?

Why might it be easier in the long run to write the numerals instead of using exact numbers of sticks in each box?
Is this system easier or harder than ours for you? For a beginner?

---

*Two excellent sources of information and examples are McLeish, John, *The Story of Numbers: How Mathematics Has Shaped Civilization* (New York: Fawcett Columbine, 1991), 55–68; and Ifrah, George, *The Universal History of Numbers: From PreHistory to the Invention of the Computer* (New York: Wiley, 2000), 278–88.

In this system *red* means positive and *black* means negative. How about our system, especially money?

Could you add more than two numbers with this system? How?

Could you add and subtract, like you can on a calculator?

What will students do?

Create your own individual counting boards with sheets of roll paper, rulers, and markers. Cut chenille wires into lengths small enough to make stick numbers on the counting board squares (about 2″ for 4″ squares). You will need about twice as many red sticks for positive numbers as black sticks for negative numbers.

Once the boards and sticks are ready, you can practice making multi-digit numbers on the board, including two-, three-, four-, and even five-digit numbers. To help keep the numbers straight as they worked quickly on the board, the Chinese alternated the direction of the numbers—up and down or sideways for numerals 1 through 5 and right-side up or up-side down for numerals 6 through 9.

Once you are comfortable with laying out the numbers, you can set up an addition problem with the addends lined up in two rows. Then add the sticks from the second row to the first, practicing 10-for-1 trades, from right to left when the number in a box exceeds 9.

Subtraction problems are set up with the first row in red sticks for positive numbers and the second in black for negative numbers. The process of subtraction involves matching red stick numbers to black stick numbers in each column and taking that number away. When the black numeral is larger than the red, you can borrow by making 10-for-1 trades from left to right.

What strategies might students *invent* or construct?

Some students may prefer to use the exact number of sticks to represent numbers instead of forming the stick numerals. Some devise a three-row system, akin to traditional western mathematics, with the third row for the answers.

Although the Chinese worked from left to right, many students will perform the calculations in the western right-to-left order.

What insights, connections, or applications might students *discover*?

- Numerals are easier to work with when you understand the procedures, but it is harder to make mistakes with sticks.
- With numerals you borrow and carry in your head; with sticks you do it with your hands.
- There are 10 major numbers; the others are made by putting those 10 numbers in different order.
- You have to read the face value and the place value of numbers.

What extensions can you make?

Experiment with color coding for different place values—for example, red sticks for 1s, blue for 10s, green for 100s, and so forth.

Compare the sticks-and-counting-board process to its offshoots—the abacus and even Cuisenaire rods.

Working with Whole Numbers: Multiplication and Division

29 *A Remainder of One* *

Overview

Elinor J. Pinczes's story *A Remainder of One* engages students by presenting a mathematical dilemma with personal applications. Everyone has been left out of an activity or has observed someone who has been left out

Grade Levels 2–5

NCTM Standards	
Content	*Process*
☑ Number and Operations	☑ Problem Solving
☐ Algebra	☑ Reasoning and Proof
☐ Geometry	☑ Communication
☐ Measurement	☑ Connections
☐ Data Analysis and Probability	☑ Representation

after team members have been chosen or partners assigned. Dealing with the situation in a mathematical way encourages a rational response to an emotional situation. It calls for thinking mathematically in creative ways and proposing and testing multiple solutions.

Activity

What ideas or concepts will students explore?

- Multiplication
- Division
- Factors
- Prime numbers

What materials will you need?

Elinor J. Pinczes's, *A Remainder of One* (New York: Scholastic, 1995)
• writing paper, construction paper • yarn • crayons or colored markers
• counters or peel-and-apply stickers or see "Pattern: Counters"
in the Make Manipulatives section of the CD-ROM that accompanies
this text • lyrics to "The Ants Go Marching" (reprinted in this activity)
• celery, creamy peanut butter, raisins • knives, plates

What questions could you ask?

What does it mean to have "a remainder of one"?
Why do you think the ant in the story wants so badly to march in the parade?
What suggestions can you make to help the ant solve his problem?
What do you think of the ant's solution? Do you have a better one?
How could you model the ant's problem with counters?
How could you show the ant's problem on paper with drawings or numbers?
Could you write a word problem that explains the ant's situation?

What will you do?

Activity A Read the story aloud. Stop after each marching order and ask, "Will this marching order let Joe march with the others?"

---

*Adapted from activities taught by Beth Krawczyk

What will students do?	Use manipulatives, stickers, or drawings to model the different marching orders.
*What strategies might students **invent** or construct?*	The students might use grouping or matching strategies to try out different number combinations.
*What insights, connections, or applications might students **discover**?*	■ They can put together uneven numbers and come up with even rows. ■ Several combinations will result in equal rows but leave remainders of one or more than one. ■ Only one combination will work to give even rows and no remainder.

What will you do?

Activity B Teach the class "The Ants Go Marching" song (sung to the tune of "When Johnny Comes Marching Home").

The ants go marching one by one, hurrah, hurrah.
[Repeat]
The ants go marching one by one,
The last one stops to have some fun,
And they all go marching
Down to the ground to get out of the rain,
Boom, boom, boom, boom, boom, boom.

Repeat verse, changing end to rhyme with number: two by two, tie its shoe; three by three, climb a tree; four by four, shut the door; five by five, say good-bye; six by six, to pick up sticks; seven by seven, to count to eleven; eight by eight, shut the gate; nine by nine, to tell the time; ten by ten, to say "the END!"

After each regrouping, show the pattern in numbers on the board, pointing out any remainders from the combination. You might also mix up the verses to increase the challenge.

What will students do?

Model the song as you sing, grouping yourselves to march one by one, two by two, and so forth.

*What insights, connections, or applications might students **discover**?*

■ The marching song shows marching orders with and without remainders.
■ If the number of students in the class is even, only one and an even number will arrange the marching order without a remainder.
■ If the number of students is odd, there may not be a combination that will turn out to be even.

What will students do?

Activity C Working in pairs, put a handful of raisins, celery in various lengths, and creamy peanut butter on the plates to make "Ants Marching on a Log." Fill the celery with peanut butter and arrange the raisin ants in various combinations so that there are no remainders. Create and record as many combinations as possible before you eat the project.

*What insights, connections, or applications might students **discover**?*

- Some numbers cannot be divided equally.
- The width of the celery stalk may vary; the width of the raisin ant line cannot exceed the narrowest width of the celery stalk.

What will students do?

Activity D Use construction paper and crayons or colored markers to make bug counters. Use yarn to make rows for the bug counters. Look for all number combinations that will make even rows of bugs; then work with the number 25 to re-create the remainder of one situation from the story.

What will you do?

Explain factors, factor pairs, and prime numbers shown by the students' manipulations of the bug counters. Record prime numbers and factor pairs for various numbers on the board for class reference and discussion.

*What strategies might students **invent** or construct?*

They might use calculators to work out number combinations or follow a model-and-count procedure. As they investigate number combinations, some students may skip pairings, recognizing they reflect the commutative law (for example, with the number 12, both 4 bugs in 3 lines and 3 bugs in 4 lines work).

*What insights, connections, or applications might students **discover**?*

- When factors of a number are multiplied, the result is the number; when a number is divided by one of its factors, the result will be another factor.
- Many numbers have many factors, but a prime number has just two—itself and 1.

What extensions can you make?

Students who work out the number combinations with calculators will discover that, for division problems with remainders, the calculator gives numbers to the right of the decimal point. You might take the opportunity to introduce the decimal point and the ideas of rational and irrational numbers and tie them to what students already know about place-value and base-10 structure.

30 Two-Handed Fingermath

Grade Levels 2–8

NCTM Standards	
Content	*Process*
■ Number and Operations	■ Problem Solving
☐ Algebra	☐ Reasoning and Proof
☐ Geometry	☐ Communication
☐ Measurement	☐ Connections
☐ Data Analysis and Probability	■ Representation

Overview

The number patterns of two-handed fingermath (like one-handed fingermath) are adaptations of strategies many students have already developed for themselves. Counting and calculating on the fingers is a favorite intuitive strategy; therefore, most students will be able to relate directly to the method. In two-handed fingermath, single digits are patterned with the right hand and 10s on the left hand. Using both hands allows students to work with multi-digit numbers, adding, subtracting, multiplying, and dividing. For the most part multiplication will be handled as repeated addition and division as repeated subtraction.

Activity

What ideas or concepts will students *explore*?

- Representing numbers with fingers
- Manipulating numbers with fingers
- Recognizing number patterns visually
- Recognizing number patterns tactilely

What materials will you need?

fingermath charts—large chart for class reference, individual charts for students • Edwin M. Lieberthal, *The Complete Book of Fingermath* (New York: McGraw-Hill, 1979)

What questions could you ask?

Do you ever use your fingers to count or keep track of calculations?
How might you use your fingers to count to 10? To 20? To 46?
What if you wanted to add 15 and 9? Could you use your fingers? How?
Are you comfortable using your fingers to do math? Why or why not?

What will you do?

Demonstrate the starting position for fingermath—fingers fanned, none touching the table. Then walk students through the number positions from 1 to 99. For each number the finger or fingers marked with dots touch the table; the others are lifted.

What will students do?

Counting Count aloud from 1 to 99, forming the finger positions for each number. Practice forming the positions in forward and reverse order. Then, working with a partner, practice calling and forming numbers at random.

Adding Use a counting-on strategy to add. Take the finger position for the first addend; then count on for each additional addend. Read the final position of fingers for the answer.

Subtracting Use a counting-down strategy to subtract. Take the finger position for the number to be subtracted from (the minuend) and count down the number to be subtracted (the subtrahend). Read the final position of fingers for the answer.

Multiplying Use a repeated-addition strategy to multiply. Take the finger position for the number to be multiplied. Count on by the same number, continuing until it has been repeated the number of times indicated by the multiplier. Read the final position of the fingers for the answer.

Dividing Use a repeated subtraction strategy to divide. Fingershape the number to be divided, then subtract the divider repeatedly by counting in reverse. Keep track of the number of times you subtract; the total will be your answer. If any number is left on your fingers, read it to find the remainder.

What strategies might students ***invent*** *or construct?*

Some students might use counting-all strategies for each procedure; others will use shortcuts: start with the largest number; factor 10s and 5s or other numbers; skip-count. Some will keep track of repeated addition or subtraction in their heads; others will use tally marks or even keep track by counting on toes.

What insights, connections, or applications might students ***discover***?

- Numbers can be "felt" as well as seen or read.
- Numbers can be added, subtracted, multiplied, and divided by moving up or down the number sequence.
- Doing fingermath is something like playing scales on a keyboard.
- Some of fingermath is mental math—keeping track of operations in your head.

What extensions can you make?

Investigate and introduce Lieberthal's fingermath methods for working with triple-digit and larger numbers. Test Lieberthal's claim that fingermath is faster than calculator math. Is he correct for some numbers but not others? For some procedures but not others? For the experiment you might divide the class into teams of four with two members to pose problems, time the calculations, and record results; one to do the problems with fingermath; and one to do the problems with a calculator.

Fingermath for two hands

Source: Adapted from Lieberthal, Edwin M., *The Complete Book of Fingermath* (New York: McGraw-Hill, 1979).

Right-Hand numbers:

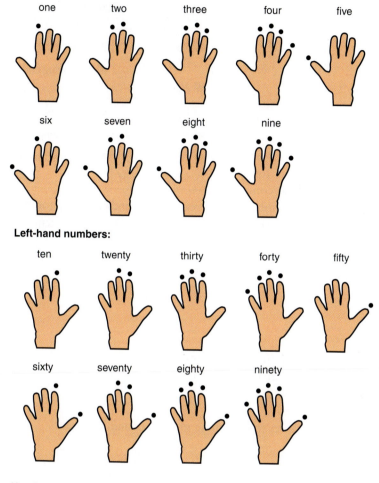

one two three four five

six seven eight nine

Left-hand numbers:

ten twenty thirty forty fifty

sixty seventy eighty ninety

Numbers with both hands:

twenty-two   seventy-four

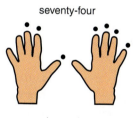
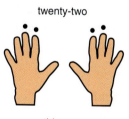
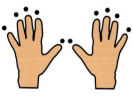

thirteen   ninety-nine

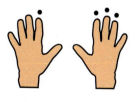

31 Jumping Critters: Kids, Frogs, and Bugs

Grade Levels 3–6

NCTM Standards	
Content	*Process*
■ Number and Operations	■ Problem Solving
■ Algebra	■ Reasoning and Proof
□ Geometry	■ Communication
■ Measurement	■ Connections
■ Data Analysis and Probability	■ Representation

Overview

This series of investigations involves both multiple content standards and multiple process standards. Students measure, multiply, divide, look for patterns, collect data, and compute averages. The investigations can be spread over a number of days for unit-connected activities and conclude with a review that calls for students not only to perform calculations but also to make judgments about farthest jumps and so forth. (See examples of student work later in this activity.)

Activity

*What ideas or concepts will students **explore**?*
- Measurement, both metric and standard
- Multiplication and division
- Number patterns with multiples
- Modeling multiples
- Comparing distances to determine more-than and less-than relationships
- Averaging
- Estimating

What materials will you need?
tape measures with metric and standard scales • newsprint • stapler • construction paper • pencils, colored markers, or crayons • calculators

What questions could you ask?
How many ways can you measure a jump?
What distances are important in measuring jumps?
What makes a good jumper?
For their size, who do you think jumps the farthest—people, frogs, or bugs? Why?

What will students do?
Make investigators' log books by cutting 8½″ × 11″ sheets of newsprint in half. Make a cover with construction paper, fold newsprint in half, and staple cover around it to make a small, easy-to-carry notebook to record data.

Investigation A How high and how far can kids jump? First, estimate and record how high and how far you think you can jump. Use both metric and English measures throughout. Second, working in teams, measure and record your height and weight. Third, take turns making two jumps for distance, marking and recording the length of each jump. Make two more jumps for height, then compare and discuss the results.

What strategies might students *invent* or construct?

The length of jumps may exceed the length of the measuring tapes. To compensate, some students might measure the distance in stages and add the results; others might use a secondary medium such as yarn or string to measure, fold it in half, measure, and double the results. To measure the height of jumps, students might use cross sticks and mark a paper scale. Some students might measure with one standard and then convert the numbers to the other standard rather than measure twice.

What insights, connections, or applications might students *discover*?

- Measurements for distance will generally be more accurate than measurements for height.
- Taller students may have the advantage in jumping; heavier students, a disadvantage.
- It takes 2.54 centimeters to make an inch but approximately 3.28 feet to make a meter.
- The base-10 system makes measuring and comparing distances with the metric system efficient and the values of the units easy to remember.

What extensions can you make?

Have the students find the average length of jumps for each team and then for the class as a whole. Use the opportunity to discuss the concept of an average.

What will students do?

Investigation B How far can a frog leap? Begin with a word problem about a jumping frog. Record the problem in your logs and then work out the solution with drawings and numbers:

> **Word problem:** A Goliath frog can jump 9 feet in one leap. If the frog makes 5 leaps, about what distance will it have covered?

What strategies might students *invent* or construct?

Strategies for representing the multiplication situation might include drawing the leaps, blocking the area to represent each leap, grouping tally marks to represent the leaps, and creating a 9×5 multiplication grid. Strategies for performing the calculations could include counting tally marks, repeated addition, doubling, and adding.

What insights, connections, or applications might students *discover*?

- They could generalize from the concrete representation to the multiplication fact: $5 \times 9 = 45$.
- If they compare the frog's "average" leap with their own, they could conclude that frogs jump farther for their size than people.

What extensions can you make?

Turn the multiplication problem around and create a division problem:

> **Word problem:** A Goliath frog is sitting in the middle of a pond. The shore is 45 feet (or about 13.7 meters) away. If the frog leaps 5 times, how far will it have to leap each time to reach the shore?

What will students do?

Investigation C Who can jump farther—a little frog, a flea, or a grasshopper? Working individually in your logs, record three facts and then respond to four questions:

Facts
A little frog jumps 36 inches.
A flea jumps 15 inches.
A grasshopper jumps 42 inches.

Questions
Which can jump the farthest?
How much farther can the frog jump than the flea?
How much farther can the grasshopper jump than the frog?
If the flea jumped 5 times, how far could it go?

What strategies might students ***invent*** *or construct?*

To make the comparisons, they might draw a frog, a flea, and a grasshopper lined up for a race and then make tally marks on the lines for inches and count and color the distance for each. They might use repeated addition or doubling plus addition to find out how far the flea jumped; or they could use their knowledge of multiplication facts, decompose the problem into $5 \times 10 = 50$ and $5 \times 5 = 25$, and add the results for 75.

What insights, connections, or applications might students ***discover***?

- A measuring rod or tape will *show* how much longer or shorter the leaps are concretely.
- Subtracting a smaller jump from a larger tells us the difference in numbers of inches or other units of measure.

What extensions can you make?

Have the students use both metric and English measures in their calculations. Look for data in the encyclopedia or on the Web about how far other "critters" such as kangaroos, rabbits, cheetahs, or even Olympic athletes can jump. Compare that data to what the students collected about their own jumps.

Student math reviews of jumping bugs and frogs

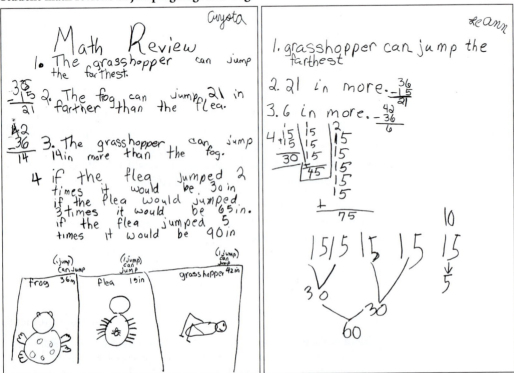

32 Multiplication and Division: Maps of Facts

Overview

Discovering patterns is an important mathematical thinking skill. When students can see relationships between numbers and sets of numbers, they can go beyond the facts to the reasons for the facts. Creating maps of numbers facts encourages students to organize the facts in meaningful ways. Rather than memorizing the facts, students construct patterns that show what the facts mean and how they fit into the bigger picture of mathematical concepts.

Grade Levels 4–6

NCTM Standards	
Content	*Process*
■ Number and Operations	■ Problem Solving
■ Algebra	■ Reasoning and Proof
■ Geometry	■ Communication
☐ Measurement	☐ Connections
☐ Data Analysis and Probability	■ Representation

Activity

*What ideas or concepts will students **explore**?*

- Mathematical operations for multiplication and division facts
- Multiplication and division as inverse operations
- Patterns, relationships

What materials will you need?

unlined paper for facts maps • "Multiplication/Division Facts Worksheet" in the Worksheets & Handouts section of the CD-ROM that accompanies this text • rulers • pencils, crayons, or colored markers • graph paper

What questions could you ask?

What is the relationship of multiplication and division?
What patterns can you find for multiples of 5? For squares? For 10s?
What patterns can you find horizontally? Diagonally? What about geometric patterns?
How might you use the 10 × 10 grid to add and subtract numbers?

What will students do?

Part A Use the calculator to explore multiples. Record the results and then map the numbers in some meaningful way. For example, cluster groups of multiples (the results of multiplying by 2, 3, 4, and so forth) or stack them in columns. Look for and discuss patterns or any areas of duplication and overlap.

Part B Working in teams, build and explore a 100 numbers table. Use the "Multiplication/Division Facts Worksheet" or develop your own 10 × 10 matrix on graph paper. Start with 1 at the left and use multiplication and division to fill in the blanks. Identify and mark patterns with colored markers. Describe observations in writing and discuss them as a group. Here is an example of a 100 numbers table:

Identifying patterns in a 100 numbers table

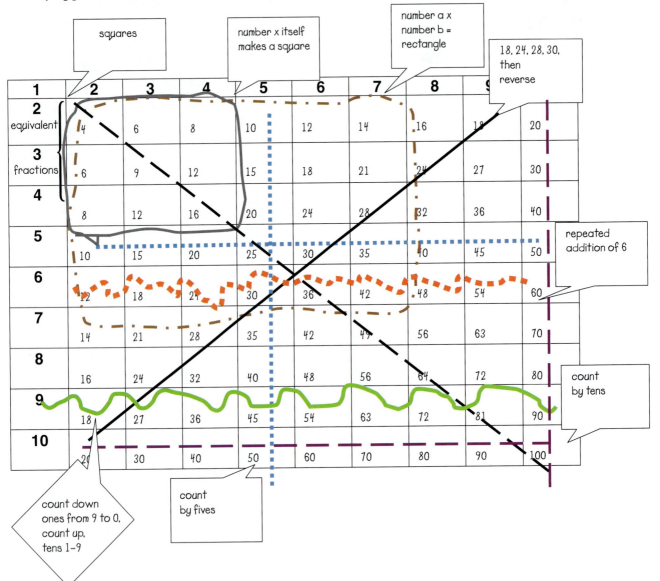

*What strategies might students **invent** or construct?*

Some will notice the duplication of across and up-and-down numbers and perform the calculations once. Others will use the commutative principle to avoid duplicating calculations. Students might make several copies of their tables to enable them to color in various patterns they discover. If they mark patterns for each combination or set of combinations, they might use 9 tables.

*What insights, connections, or applications might students **discover**?*

- Multiplying numbers by themselves creates a square on the table; multiplying one number by a smaller or larger number creates a rectangle.
- Reading across or down from 2 results in skip-counting by 2, 4, and so forth.

- To multiply, find the number across, the number down, and plot the intersecting point.
- To divide, find the number divided inside the table and the divider on either the horizontal or the vertical axis; the answer will be on the other axis.

What extensions can you make?   Extend the 10×10 table to 12×12, 15×15, 20×20. Discuss any changes or similarities among the different tables.

Tie the table to base-10 concepts by modeling calculations and patterns with blocks or by exploring the abacus. Discuss the similarities and differences between an electronic calculator and manual, hands-on calculators such as the abacus or numbers tables.

33 Writing Mathematics: Telling Tales by the Numbers

Overview

Grade Levels 6–8

NCTM Standards	
Content	*Process*
■ Number and Operations	■ Problem Solving
□ Algebra	■ Reasoning and Proof
□ Geometry	■ Communication
□ Measurement	■ Connections
□ Data Analysis and Probability	■ Representation

Writing mathematics gives students a different perspective on concepts. Writing stories engages students creatively but also puts them in the unique position of seeing ideas from the teacher's viewpoint—as something to be demonstrated clearly, set in problem-solving contexts, and taught to someone else. Students can develop their own story plots and characters or use a well-known tale, such as "Little Red Riding Hood" or "The Three Little Pigs."

Activity

*What ideas or concepts will students **explore**?*
- Connecting mathematics and language arts
- Communicating mathematical ideas in natural language
- Interpreting mathematical ideas in the context of story plot and characters
- Creating imaginative contexts for mathematics

What materials will you need?
- construction paper, plain paper for illustrations, lined paper for story • crayons, colored pencils, or markers • stapler • scissors • "Little Red Riding Hood Turns the Times Tables on the Wolf" (reprinted later in this activity)

What questions could you ask?
What is your favorite fairy tale? Is there any math in that story? How could you add math to the story?
In "Little Red Riding Hood Turns the Times Tables on the Wolf," how does Red use math to trick the wolf? What kinds of mistakes does the wolf make?
What do we mean when we say someone is telling a tall tale?
What role does math play in tall tales? Can you think of any examples?
Have you ever told a tall tale in which you used imaginary measurements ("I jumped 20 feet in the broad jump!" or "I caught a fish that was a yard long?) or made-up numbers ("I ate 6 whole pizzas!" or "My dog chased 1,000 cats and 100 mail deliverers!")?

What will students do?   Read and talk about the math in "Little Red Riding Hood Turns the Times Tables on the Wolf." Then write and illustrate a story in which mathematics plays a key role. The story might be an original creation or a revision of a story you already know. Some possibilities include

- Adding math to a well-known fairy tale, such as "The Three Little Pigs" or "Cinderella"
- Telling a tall tale with large numbers to support your "lies"—for example, a Paul Bunyan–style story in which the main character eats 12 dozen eggs and 20 helpings of 20 flapjacks for breakfast
- Daydreaming on paper with rags-to-riches stories that involve manipulating large amounts of money
- Posing and solving a complex problem or a problem involving large numbers and then writing a story to fit the problem

What strategies might students *invent* or construct?   Some might develop a storybook using construction paper for a cover and lined and blank pages for text and drawings. Others might write the story and illustrate with one large drawing or a collage of images. The composing process itself could begin with mathematics (a problem or a concept) and then overlay narrative. Or it could begin with narrative and integrate operations such as multiplication or division into the story.

What insights, connections, or applications might students *discover*?
- Mathematical ideas can be expressed with words and ordered sentences as well as with numbers and symbols.
- Using mathematics in a story—for example, adding costs to the pigs' building projects in "The Three Little Pigs"—adds a new layer of meaning to the story.
- Stories can make mathematics more interesting and provide the impetus needed to work out complex, step-by-step problems.

Little Red Riding Hood Turns the Times Tables on the Wolf

Not so long ago a small girl lived in Montana near a forest. The weather was often cold—10°F at night and 30°F during the day—so the girl usually wore a red parka with a pointed hood. People called her Little Red Riding Hood after the girl in the fairy tale, or Little Red for short.

One snowy day, when school had been canceled, Little Red's mother baked 4 dozen chocolate chip cookies.

"The snow plows have cleared the roads," she said, "If you watch carefully for traffic, you can take these cookies and a 48-ounce jug of apple cider and visit your grandmother.

Little Red's grandmother lived in an A-frame cabin 2 miles away on the side of the mountain. Little Red enjoyed visiting her grandmother and going skiing on the mountain. Besides, she had already finished her math homework and had nothing else to do.

The girl loaded her backpack with cookies and cider, put on her red parka, and started out in the snow. It was slow going. The plows had cleared the center of the road, leaving the snow in a ridge 3 feet deep. As Little Red walked on the shoulder of the road, her boots sometimes sank a foot into the snow.

To pass the time, Little Red began repeating the multiplication tables: "$2 \times 2 = 4$, $2 \times 3 = 6$, $2 \times 4 = 8$, $2 \times 5 = 10$, $2 \times 6 = 12$ . . ." She had gotten as far as $6 \times 8 = 48$ when she met a wolf.

He was sitting at the side of the road looking bored and out of sorts, like someone waiting for trouble. "Where are you going, little girl in the red parka?" he asked.

"None of your business," said Little Red, who never talked to strangers, and kept walking. But the wolf, who had nothing else to do, followed along behind.

(continues)

Soon Little Red saw some friends from school shoveling snow from their driveway.

"Where are you off to?" they called.

"I'm going to my grandma's for a ski party," she called back, pointing up the mountain to her grandmother's cabin. "Want to come?"

"Sure, but we have to finish the driveway first."

"I'll help you," said Little Red; "then we can all go together, and you can help me carry all of these goodies." After a mile of walking, the 4 dozen cookies and 48-ounce jug of cider in her backpack felt like a load of bricks.

So Little Red joined her friends shoveling snow. Meanwhile, the wolf had been eavesdropping. He had seen the girl point to her grandmother's cabin. He had heard her mention goodies, and he wanted some. Racing along the road on all fours, he arrived at the cabin in less than 10 minutes. He knocked on the door—tap, tap.

"Is that you, Little Red?" called the grandmother, who was expecting her granddaughter because the mother had phoned ahead.

"Yes," croaked the wolf, sounding more like a frog than a little girl.

Thinking her granddaughter had caught a cold in the snow, the grandmother ran to the door and flung it open. The wolf leaped in, pushed the woman into the coat closet, and closed and locked the closet door.

The wolf had a plan. Not having looked at himself in a mirror recently, he thought he could dress up as the grandmother and trick the little girl into giving him all the goodies. He wrapped himself in the grandmother's size 10 housecoat, tied a chef's apron over that, and stuck the grandmother's ski cap over his ears and 2 oven mitts on his paws.

When the little girl and her friends knocked at the door, he called, "Come in," in a high voice that did not sound at all like the grandmother's.

Of course, Little Red knew immediately what had happened. She could see the wolf's head under the ski cap and his tail sticking out the back of the housecoat, and she could hear her grandmother's pounding on the door of the closet. But she decided to play along to find out what the wolf wanted.

"What big ears you have, Grandma," she said while her friends snickered behind their mittens.

"The better to hear you with, my dear," said the wolf in his fake voice.

"What big eyes you have, Grandma," said Little Red and reached outside the door for a snow shovel.

"The better to see you with, my dear," said the wolf, thinking his disguise was working.

"What big teeth you have, Grandma," said Little Red.

"The better to eat up all your goodies," said the wolf and pounced just as Little Red hit him with the snow shovel.

The girl and her friends chased the wolf outside, let Grandmother out of the coat closet, and unpacked the goodies. Then Little Red had an idea. She had noticed that her grandmother's driveway and walks needed shoveling. She guessed the wolf was the kind of animal that always ditched school and had never learned his multiplication tables.

She went to the door with a plate of cookies and called to the wolf, who was sitting on the porch and rubbing his head where the snow shovel had hit him. "Wolfie, I'll make you a deal. If you will shovel the walks and the driveway, you can have all of the cookies and cider left from our party."

The wolf was suspicious. "How do I know you will leave any," he growled.

"Figure it out for yourself," said Little Red. "We have 48 cookies and 48 ounces of cider. There are just 4 of us and we each want 2 helpings of 6 cookies and two 6-ounce mugs of cider."

The wolf, adding the numbers instead of multiplying them, thought, "$4 + 2 + 6 = 12$ cookies; that leaves 36 cookies for me. And $4 + 2 + 8$ equals 14 ounces of cider; that leaves 34 ounces all for me."

And so while the wolf shoveled the snow, Little Red, her two friends, and her grandmother ate their two helpings of 6 cookies and drank their two mugs of hot cider.

How many cookies and how much cider were left for the wolf?

Source: Joseph G. R. and Nancy C. Martinez, *Math without Fear*, 122–24. Published by Allyn & Bacon, Boston, MA, Copyright © 1966 by Pearson Education. Used by permission of the publisher.

34 Modeling Multiplication

Grade Levels 3–5

NCTM Standards	
Content	*Process*
▣ Number and Operations	▣ Problem Solving
☐ Algebra	☐ Reasoning and Proof
☐ Geometry	☐ Communication
☐ Measurement	▣ Connections
☐ Data Analysis and Probability	▣ Representation

Overview

Showing both the process and the product of multiplication is an essential step in understanding the operation of multiplication and moving from additive to multiplicative thinking. It is important that students not only use manipulatives to explore multiplication but also represent their explorations in a variety of ways, including with words and numerals.

Activity

*What ideas or concepts will students **explore**?*

- Representing mathematics with manipulatives, drawings, words, and symbols
- Applying base-10 concepts to multiplication
- Using 10-for-1 trading schemes

What materials will you need?

Base-10 blocks or "Pattern: Base-10 Blocks" in the Make Manipulatives section of the CD-ROM that accompanies this text ● centimeter paper (see the Make Manipulatives section of the CD-ROM), plain paper ● pencils or markers

What questions could you ask?

What does it mean to multiply numbers?
How does multiplication differ from addition? How is it like addition?
How many different ways can you think of to multiply 4 times 5? 5 times 5? 10 times 10? 10 times 100?
How useful is multiplication? How many different real-life situations can you think of where you need to multiply?

What will students do?

Explore multiplication word problems involving one- and two-digit numbers. For example—

> George is going door to door in his neighborhood collecting canned goods for needy families. If each neighbor gives him 4 cans and he visits 32 neighbors, how many cans will he collect?
>
> You are running for school president. You and your friends are making campaign buttons to hand out to all of the students in your school. If there are 12 classes and 25 students in each class, how many buttons will you need to make?

For each problem—

1. Model and work out the problem with blocks and/or drawings.
2. Write the elements of the solution in words.
3. Write the problem and solution as a mathematical sentence.

As you work through and discuss the problems, your teacher can help by listing approaches and summarizing conclusions on the board. (An example of modeling with blocks and drawings and writing in words and numbers appears on page 85.)

*What strategies might students **invent** or construct?*

Students might model the multiplicand with blocks and then duplicate the number of sets according to the number in the multiplier. Then they may translate the results into words and a mathematical sentence.

Students might also use centimeter paper to model multiplication. They can begin by counting across for the number in the multiplicand and down for the number in the multiplier and then use markers to block off the rectangular array generated by the numbers. To determine the total number of centimeter squares in the rectangle, they might count a column and use repeated addition or mark off blocks of 100, 10, and single-unit squares and then add.

*What insights, connections, or applications might students **discover**?*

- There are many ways to multiply.
- Multiplication can be represented with objects and space and also with words and numbers.
- Adding 1 to the 10s column or the 100s column in written numbers is the same as trading 10 units for a rod or 10 rods for a flat in base-10 blocks.
- Doing a problem in more than one way serves as a kind of quality control to check and understand answers.

Multiplication in blocks, words, and numbers

Model: Make 4 sets of 3 rods and 2 units

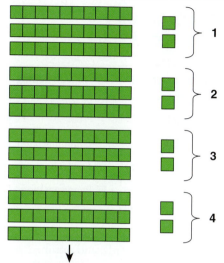

↓

Combine for 12 rods and 8 units

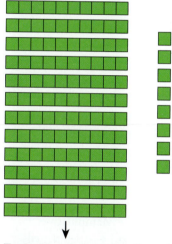

↓

Trade 10 rods for a solution of 1 flat, 2 rods, and 8 units

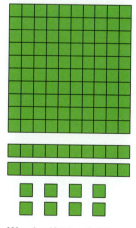

Words: If 32 neighbors give George 4 cans each, he will collect 128 cans.

Numbers: 32 × 4 = 128

35 Modeling Division

Grade Levels 4–6

NCTM Standards	
Content	*Process*
■ Number and Operations	■ Problem Solving
☐ Algebra	☐ Reasoning and Proof
☐ Geometry	☐ Communication
☐ Measurement	■ Connections
☐ Data Analysis and Probability	■ Representation

Overview

Understanding the difference between partitive and measurement division can be challenging, even for older students. Building the concepts with base-10 blocks helps student see and feel the operations; representing the operations in drawings, words, and numbers reinforces the hands-on experiences and helps create mental pictures and pathways for understanding division.

Activity

What ideas or concepts will students *explore*?

- Representing division with manipulatives, drawings, words, and numbers
- Applying base-10 concepts and 10-for-1 trading schemes to division
- Modeling partitive division
- Modeling measurement division
- Showing remainders

What materials will you need?

counting disks or "Pattern: Counters" (in the Make Manipulatives section of the CD-ROM that accompanies this text.) ● paper, pencils ● base-10 blocks or "Pattern: Base-10 Blocks" (in the Make Manipulatives section of the CD-ROM that accompanies this text.)

What questions could you ask?

What does it mean to divide?
How is division like subtraction? How is it different?
What is the relationship of multiplication and division?
Which is easier to do, multiply 22 × 144 or divide 3,168 by 144? Why?
How useful is division? Is it important to know how to divide? Why or why not?
How many examples can you find of division in the real world?

What will students do?

Explore division word problems involving measurement and partitive situations. For example—

Measurement division: Josepha has 54 balloons. She wants to give each of her friends 6 balloons. To how many friends does Josepha give balloons?
Partitive division: Abdul just won 49 packages of bubblegum. He wants to share his prize equally among himself and 6 friends. How many packages of bubblegum will each receive?

For each problem—

1. Use counting disks and base-10 blocks to model the division situations.
2. Explain the solutions and write them in words.
3. Write mathematical sentences showing the problems and the solutions.

As you model and discuss your solutions, your teacher may periodically ask questions, discuss answers, and translate words to numbers, numbers to words.

What strategies might students *invent* or construct?

They might count out disks equal to the number to be divided and then "deal out" the disks into the number of groups indicated by the divisor. They might use tally marks and trial-and-error grouping. Or they might represent the total with base-10 blocks, sort the blocks into equal groups, and count.

What will students do?

Explore a division word problem that will result in a remainder. For example—

> There are 81 fifth graders at Wilson Middle School. All have signed up for a field trip to the top of Sandia Crest on the tram. If each tram car holds 25 people, how many tram cars will the class fill? How many students will be left over? How many cars will be needed to take all of the students to the top of the crest?

For each problem—

1. Model the problem situations with base-10 blocks and pencil-and-paper drawings.
2. Explain the solutions and write them in words.
3. Write mathematical sentences showing the problems and the solutions.

What will you do?

After you have modeled the situation, discuss the idea of remainders and think of ways to deal with the remaining students in the problem. You and the students might also work the problem with calculators and talk about the calculator's representation of rational numbers. Discuss whether the calculator's answer or the model's answer is more helpful in this case.

What strategies might students *invent* or construct?

The students might use a tally-and-count strategy, making 81 tally marks and then counting off 25 tally marks at a time. They might estimate 4 tram cars, and then draw the cars and mark or draw in passengers until they fill three cars and have 6 passengers in the fourth. Some might create an array with 5 or 10 in each row and then skip-count to mark off three sets of 25 each and leave 6 left over.

What insights, connections, or applications might students *discover*?

- Not all division situations will turn out to be even.
- How remainders are handled can be influenced by the problem situation. For example, a rational-number solution will not work when we are dealing with whole people or whole tram cars.
- The number to be divided may be represented by concrete objects, but the divisor could represent a number of sets instead of individual objects.
- A mathematical sentence is an efficient way to represent a complex process.

36 Calculating with Chinese Stick Math

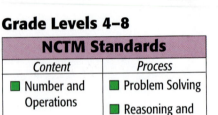

Grade Levels 4–8

NCTM Standards	
Content	*Process*
■ Number and Operations	■ Problem Solving
☐ Algebra	■ Reasoning and Proof
☐ Geometry	☐ Communication
☐ Measurement	■ Connections
☐ Data Analysis and Probability	■ Representation

Overview

Developing flexibility in mathematical thinking begins with understanding that there may be multiple pathways to mathematical solutions and in some cases even multiple solutions. Using a counting board and Chinese stick numbers to multiply and divide not only shows students a different way to do these operations but also calls on them to break out of some traditional and potentially rigid procedures for visualizing and working through problems. For example, to multiply on the counting board, students will work from left to right instead of right to left; results will be laid out on the middle row between the multiplicand and the multiplier instead of in the familiar three-row pattern of multiplicand, multiplier, and product.

Activity

What ideas or concepts will students explore?
- Using an alternative number system
- Using a left-to-right procedure to multiply and divide
- Translating stick number operations into Arabic numeral operations
- Representing base-10 and 10-for-1 trading schemes with sticks

What materials will you need?
red and black chenille wires • roll of colored paper for large sheets to serve as counting boards • markers • rulers or yardsticks • scissors • paper, pencils • "Chinese Stick Numbers II" in the Worksheets & Handouts section of the CD-ROM that accompanies this text.

What questions could you ask?
How important is it to follow exact procedures when you multiply and divide? Can you get the same answer if you vary the procedures?
How many different ways can you think of to multiply 22 × 22? To divide 100 by 5? Are some methods better than others?
What are some of the contributions the Chinese have made to mathematics?
When you use the counting board to make calculations, how many things do you have to keep track of in your mind?
Could you use this system to multiply a multi-digit number by a multi-digit number? What problems might you encounter?
What advantages or disadvantages do you find in this system?

What will you do?

Part A: Multiplication (Grades 4–8) Show the students a sample counting board with several rows of counting blocks. Talk about the stick numbers on the worksheet and demonstrate how single- and multi-digit numbers are laid out on the board. Call attention to the right-to-left decimal pattern, with the place values matching those in Arabic notation.

What will students do?

Use the colored paper, yardsticks or rulers, and markers to make individual counting boards. Cut chenille wires into lengths that will allow the formation of any of the stick numerals within the blocks. Practice laying out and reading multi-digit numbers on the board.

To multiply a multi-digit number by a single-digit number, use three horizontal rows. Lay out the multiplicand on the top row and the multiplier on the third row. Use the middle row to record results.

Working from left to right, multiply the first number in the multiplicand by the multiplier and record the result in the same column of the second row. Move the multiplier to the right. Multiply the second number in the multiplicand by the multiplier and record the number in the second row. Continue until all of the numbers have been multiplied. Read the result in the second row.

*What strategies might students **invent** or construct?*

Some students might work out the problem first using a more familiar system and then translate the results into stick numerals. Following the left-to-right procedure, some might use extended notation to separate Arabic numbers into place-value units and then deal with 100s, 10s, 1s, and so forth separately and add the results.

*What insights, connections, or applications might students **discover**?*

- There is more than one way to multiply.
- Stick math relies heavily on performing mental calculations and remembering multiplication facts.
- Because calculation begins at the left, you may have to change some numbers if multiplying a numeral to the right results in a total greater than 9.

What will you do?

Part B: Division (Grades 5–8) Talk about division as reversing the process of multiplication. Where multiplication joins groups together, division separates them into groups again. Show how dividing with Chinese stick math starts at the end point of multiplication—the middle of three horizontal rows. Discuss the place value of the different columns and how both the multiplier and the divisor work outside those relationships by moving from digit to digit.

What will students do?

To divide a multi-digit number by a single-digit number, use three horizontal rows (as in multiplying). Lay out the number to be divided in the middle row. Move the divisor from left to right in the third row and record the digit-by-digit results of the procedure in the top row.

*What strategies might students **invent** or construct?*

Although the Chinese actually removed sticks as they manipulated the numbers, many students leave numerals intact as they work through a problem. Again, some students may work out the problem first using Arabic numerals and the traditional algorithm and then translate into stick numbers. Some students, following Chinese practice, might do the calculations in their heads and use the counting board as a way to keep track as they work their way through a problem.

*What insights, connections, or applications might students **discover**?*

- The procedure works for single-digit divisors but could become awkward with multi-digit divisors.
- Representing remainders seems awkward with the system.
- The left-to-right pattern in Chinese stick division seems more like our traditional division algorithm than Chinese stick multiplication is like our traditional multiplication algorithm.

Discovering Geometry and Developing Geometric Thinking

37 Friendship Quilt*

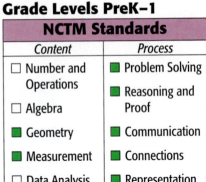

Overview

Creating a friendship quilt is a cooperative activity. Each student makes a section of the quilt, using construction paper, markers, and watercolors to create designs. The pieces are joined together with yarn threaded through holes punched around the edges. The activity combines elements of geometry and measurement as well as art and design.

Grade Levels PreK–1

NCTM Standards	
Content	*Process*
☐ Number and Operations	■ Problem Solving
☐ Algebra	■ Reasoning and Proof
■ Geometry	■ Communication
■ Measurement	■ Connections
☐ Data Analysis and Probability	■ Representation

Activity

What ideas or concepts will students explore?

- Geometric shapes and relationships between quadrilaterals
- Spatial reasoning
- Measurement
- Cooperative learning skills

What materials will you need?

colored and white construction paper • rulers • pencils • watercolors and markers • hole punch • glue • scissors • yarn

What questions could you ask?

What do you know about quadrilaterals?
Can you show me a square? A rectangle?
How is a square like a rectangle? A rectangle like a square?
Have you ever seen a hand-pieced quilt? What was it like? Do you know how it was made?
If we all draw rectangles and squares, how can we make sure all of them are the same size?

What will you do?

Show the students one or more examples of actual quilts. Let them touch and handle the material. Talk about the different shapes that go into the design. Point out the stitches that show where the pieces were put together. Then look at pictures of some famous friendship quilts, such as quilts made for cancer or AIDS victims with names and other tributes written in each square.

---

*Adapted from a lesson taught by Aida J. Homs-Rivera

What will students do?

Select a large piece of rectangular colored construction paper and a smaller piece of white construction paper. Use a ruler to construct a square of the white paper. Divide the square into 4 or more boxes. Talk about the difference between the rectangular and square shapes.

Glue the square directly into the center of the colored construction paper. Talk about how to find the center and whether you think the square looks best there and why. Then with a black marker outline the square and the boxes in it; write the names of friends and draw pictures in the boxes. Use watercolors and markers to decorate the entire sheet.

Punch holes around the colored paper and thread them with yarn. As a class, lay out the different quilt pieces on the floor until the pieces form one large rectangle. Experiment with arranging the pieces so that there are no holes in the quilt. Discuss which arrangement works best. Then use additional pieces of yarn to tie the entire quilt together.

What strategies might students *invent* or construct?

To draw the square and boxes, some may experiment with eye-balling and free-handing the shape, using the ruler primarily as a straight edge. Others could measure with the ruler but use trial-and-error to make the four sides and boxes come together exactly. Still others may use the right-angle edge of a sheet of paper as a guide. For the yarn borders and ties, some students will punch holes first in the corners, then halfway in between, and so forth.

What insights, connections, or applications might students *discover*?

- A quadrilateral has four sides.
- Both a rectangle and a square are quadrilaterals.
- To make a quilt, the parts need to fit together to make a giant quadrilateral.
- You can form a quadrilateral with four sides that is not a square.
- Dividing a square into 4 equal parts in terms of area makes 4 smaller squares.

38 7 "Magic" Pieces: Tangrams

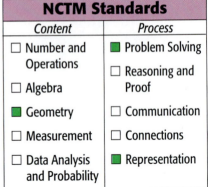

Overview

Tangrams continue to be a favorite manipulative, among both teachers and students. Making sets of tangrams from construction paper, rather than working with prepared or manufactured pieces, lets students experience the shapes from a new perspective. The pieces provide a good introduction to several geometric shapes and can be manipulated creatively to make a variety of other shapes and designs.

Grade Levels K–2

NCTM Standards	
Content	*Process*
☐ Number and Operations	☑ Problem Solving
☐ Algebra	☐ Reasoning and Proof
☑ Geometry	☐ Communication
☐ Measurement	☐ Connections
☐ Data Analysis and Probability	☑ Representation

Activity

What ideas or concepts will students explore?
- Visualization
- Spatial reasoning
- Triangle, square, rectangle, parallelogram

What materials will you need?
Tangram pattern in a square or "Pattern: Tangrams" on the Make Manipulatives section of the CD-ROM that accompanies this text • construction paper • scissors • glue • lined paper • pencils • tangram puzzles and solutions on the Make Manipulatives section of the CD-ROM

What questions could you ask?
How would you describe each of the different tangram pieces?
Are any alike? Are any different? Are any shaped the same but different in size? How many?
How do you know the tangram pieces will form a square?
What would happen if we took away one piece?
How do the tangram creatures you made differ from the ones in the printed puzzles?
How many sides and corners does each tangram piece have? How do the corners and sides help us identify the pieces?

What will you do?
Show students examples of each shape—triangle, square, rectangle, parallelogram. Talk about the corners and number of sides. Then show them how a square can be broken down into 7 tangram pieces and reformed from the same pieces.

What will students do?

Cut out the tangram pieces from the pattern square. Identify each piece and explore sides and angles tactilely and visually. Select construction paper in various colors, trace around the pattern pieces, and cut out two complete sets of 7 pieces.

Use one set of tangrams to make a tangram creature—real or imaginary. Add faces or other features with a pencil. Glue your creature to a sheet of paper and write a sentence about it. (Examples appear at the bottom of this page.)

With the other set of tangrams, practice assembling and disassembling a tangram square. Follow a tangram puzzle pattern to make the shapes of various animals, human figures, and other objects.

What strategies might students _invent_ or construct?

Students might use a cover-the-pattern strategy to make squares and other shapes, fitting the tangram pieces carefully over a pattern or printed image. Some may be careful to create symmetrical patterns, balancing a triangle with a triangle; others might create asymmetrical patterns with a triangle on one side and a parallelogram on the other.

What insights, connections, or applications might students _discover_?

- Triangles can be joined to make squares, another triangle, or a parallelogram.
- Hundreds of shapes can be made from the tangram pieces—hence the designation 7 "magic" pieces.
- Taking a tangram square apart is easy; putting it back together from memory is hard.

What extensions can you make?

Have pairs of students play Tangoes—a game in which they use tangram pieces to form the puzzle shapes on the cards.

Access one of the many websites devoted to tangrams for additional activities. If your classroom has interactive geometry software available, you can use tangrams to introduce transformations as students slide, flip, and rotate pieces to form geometric shapes.

Students manipulate tangram pieces, exploring the shapes and being creative. They can follow the traditional tangram puzzles or make their own patterns for animals and objects.

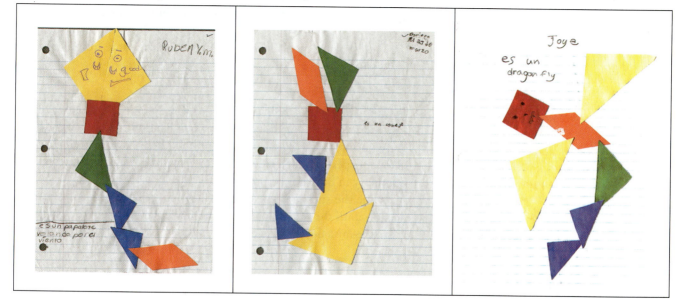

39 "Buggy" Geometry

Grade Levels K–3

NCTM Standards	
Content	*Process*
☐ Number and Operations	☐ Problem Solving
☐ Algebra	☐ Reasoning and Proof ■
■ Geometry	☐ Communication
☐ Measurement	■ Connections
☐ Data Analysis and Probability	■ Representation

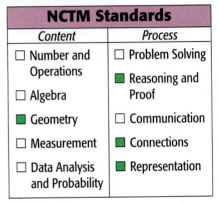

Overview

This activity deals with the big idea of symmetry, but it can also connect math with biology. The use of bugs as a subject engages students' interest and helps them focus on the task, but it also offers them the opportunity to spend time studying the insect world and introduces various science projects, such as observing and identifying real insects.

Activity

What ideas or concepts will students explore?
- Line symmetry
- Rotational symmetry
- Spatial reasoning
- Visualization

What materials will you need?
colored paper with outlines of bugs or "Bug Worksheet" in the Worksheets & Handout section of the CD-ROM that accompanies this text • pencils • straight edge • mira • bug stickers or pictures • cutout shapes for making monster bugs

What questions could you ask?
What parts of the bugs are alike? What parts are different?
Can you fold the bug so that the sides match? So that they don't match?
Can you make a monster bug that can be folded to match two different ways?
Can you make a monster bug that will look the same from 3 or more directions?

What will students do?
Working individually or in pairs, explore line symmetry by folding, drawing, and reflecting bug shapes in your bug handout. Start by cutting out shapes printed on colored paper. Find the lines of symmetry by folding cutout shapes to match sides. Then use the mira device to find lines of symmetry in bug stickers or pictures.

Glue the stickers or pictures on a piece of paper and adjust the reflection until the sides match exactly. Draw a line through the center, remove the mira device and compare the sides. Draw a symmetrical bug of your own.

Explore rotational symmetry by creating monster bugs. Use cutout shapes to create bugs with two or more heads, antennae, and sets of feet. Rotate the monster bugs and use a straight edge to help you find the different axes of symmetry. Draw a line through each axis with a straight edge.

What strategies might students *invent* or construct?

To make their own symmetrical bugs, students might start with folded paper, draw half the bug, cut along the drawn lines, and unfold. Or they might work with a mira device, drawing one side and tracing the reflection. To make a monster bug with rotational symmetry, students might begin again with folded paper but increase the number of folds, or they could work with multiple cutouts.

What insights, connections, or applications might students *discover*?

- The left and right sides of bugs are symmetrical.
- The left and right sides of most living things are symmetrical.
- A monster bug with rotational symmetry probably could not move since every head would be going in a different direction.

What extensions can you make?

Look for line and rotational symmetry in other living things—animals, people, trees, leaves, flowers, and so forth. Draw, fold, and cut paper representations. Redesign one or more symmetrical objects to be asymmetrical. What is the effect?

40 Exploring the Many Faces of Geometry

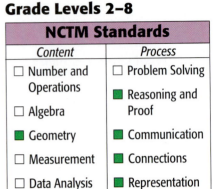

Overview

Grade Levels 2–8

NCTM Standards	
Content	*Process*
☐ Number and Operations	☐ Problem Solving
☐ Algebra	■ Reasoning and Proof
■ Geometry	■ Communication
☐ Measurement	■ Connections
☐ Data Analysis and Probability	■ Representation

To many students and adults who remember high school geometry classes, geometry is a formal subject filled with formulas and information to be memorized. Placing the geometry of classrooms and textbooks in context makes geometry less intimidating and more interesting. Discovering informal geometry in crafts such as quilting and formal geometry in art and architecture emphasizes the importance of the subject and also demonstrates that geometry is a subject to be enjoyed rather than simply endured.

Activity

What ideas or concepts will students *explore*?
- Formal and informal geometry
- Applications of geometric concepts and thinking
- Connections with everyday objects and behaviors
- Visualization, description, representation

What materials will you need? printed map or grid paper for making a map • construction paper • yarn • lined paper • ruler • compass • protractor • pencils

What questions could you ask? What is geometry?
How many geometric shapes do you know?
How many shapes can you show me in this room?
Is geometry really everywhere?
How have you used geometry?
Where can you find geometry in everyday life?

What will you do? Use overhead pictures of architecture and art objects and examples of common applications such as quilts and puzzles to show students the many faces of geometry. Ask students to recall other examples from their own experiences.

What will students do? In pairs or groups plan an expedition to find examples of formal and informal geometry in the real world. You may want to search at a mall, an amusement park, or a downtown area such as a town square. Use a printed map of the area to mark your discoveries or draw a map on grid paper.

As you explore, keep a log of your discoveries. Use lined paper for log sheets and construction paper for a cover. Tie the book together with yarn and decorate with pictures or drawings of geometric shapes. For each example you find of geometry in the real world, make an entry in your log with location, names of shapes, descriptions, and either pictures or drawings. Try to find examples of *recreational geometry* as in rug or quilt patterns; *everyday geometry* in shapes of packaging or food like an ice-cream cone; *technical geometry* as in buildings or bridges; and *academic geometry* as in textbook explanations. Categories may overlap—for example, academic and recreational geometry in an educational pyramid puzzle.

*What strategies might students **invent** or construct?*

Students might use a one-use camera to take pictures of their discoveries and post the results in their logs. They might focus on the big picture with an emphasis on skyscraper shapes, bridges, and street patterns. Others might take a narrower perspective, looking for items in store windows or on store shelves. Some might interpret their findings in terms of two-dimensional shapes and others a combination of two- and three-dimensional shapes.

*What insights, connections, or applications might students **discover**?*

- Geometry is everywhere.
- Most objects in the real world can be described in terms of geometric shapes.
- We use geometry every day when we select bags to fill with items purchased, decide how large a rug or bedspread to buy, or estimate the number of cans of soup that will fit on a shelf.
- Everyone is a geometrician, including hair stylists who work with shapes and symmetry; quilters who design and piece together complex patterns; and carpenters who use angles, straight lines, and shapes such as triangles.

What extensions can you make?

Have students select a favorite face of geometry (for example, recreational geometry in a 3-D puzzle or a game such as chess). Have them explain in writing how geometry is involved and then demonstrate and discuss with the class their examples.

41 Tangrams and *Grandfather Tang's Story**

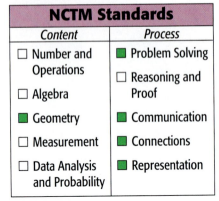

Overview

Ann Tompert's classic work, *Grandfather Tang's Story*, presents an imaginative context for the geometry of tangrams. The illustrations in the story include puzzles that students can model as the narrative progresses. They can make their own tangrams from construction paper and even create their own illustrations for the different episodes in the story.

Grade Levels 1–5

NCTM Standards	
Content	*Process*
☐ Number and Operations	■ Problem Solving
☐ Algebra	☐ Reasoning and Proof
■ Geometry	■ Communication
☐ Measurement	■ Connections
☐ Data Analysis and Probability	■ Representation

Activity

*What ideas or concepts will students **explore**?*
- Spatial relationships
- Properties of geometric shapes
- Names of shapes
- Connections between shapes

What materials will you need?
- Ann Tompert's, *Grandfather Tang's Story*. (New York: Crown, 1990)
- sets of tangram pieces printed on different colors of construction paper or "Pattern: Tangrams" in the Make Manipulatives section of the CD-ROM that accompanies this text • scissors • glue • sheets of blank 8½″ × 11″ paper • three-prong folders • pencils • crayons or colored pencils

What questions could you ask?
How many pieces are in each puzzle?
Can you make a square (or other shape) with all of the pieces?
With some of the pieces?
What makes tangram puzzles so interesting?
How do you feel about the foxes' choice of shapes? Would you have chosen differently?
When you formed the shapes, what pieces did you use to make each part?

What will students do?
Cut out tangrams in several different colors. Manipulate the pieces into groups of 2, 4, or 7 to form geometric shapes, such as squares, triangles, pentagons, and hexagons.

---

*Adapted from units taught by Thelma Aragon

Listen to the reading of *Grandfather Tang's Story*. Ask questions about any words or ideas you don't understand.

Rewrite the story in your own words on the bottom half of your blank page. On the top half, follow your teacher's model on the overhead projector to form each of the foxes' shape changes with tangram pieces.

What strategies might students *invent* or construct?

Solving a tangram puzzle takes trial-and-error efforts. It is possible to form one part of a puzzle correctly but miss the rest; a true solution requires all of the pieces to fit exactly. Some students will try several combinations of tans, then consult the solutions. Others will use the tans to form their own shapes instead of trying to duplicate the puzzle pattern. Some will embellish the puzzle illustrations by drawing faces on the tans and drawing backgrounds.

What insights, connections, or applications might students *discover*?

- Geometric shapes can be put together to create other geometric shapes.
- Geometric shapes can be put together to make animals, people, buildings, and other objects.
- The 7 tangram pieces can be combined in hundreds of ways.
- Geometry can be fun.

What extensions can you make?

Introduce another tangram story, Grace Maccarone's *Three Pigs, One Wolf, and Seven Magic Shapes* (New York: Scholastic, 1997). Have students continue making shapes from the story with tangrams—duck, cat, candle, swan, house, boat, and so forth. But, instead of rewriting and illustrating this story, have them compose and illustrate their own magic-shapes story with tangrams.

42 Building Polygons and Polyhedrons with Gumdrops and Toothpicks

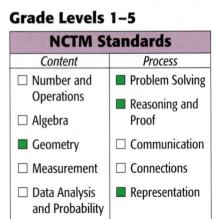

Overview

Building polygons and polyhedrons with physical objects gives students hands-on experience with the shapes and a functional perspective on the shapes and

Grade Levels 1–5

NCTM Standards	
Content	*Process*
☐ Number and Operations	■ Problem Solving
☐ Algebra	■ Reasoning and Proof
■ Geometry	☐ Communication
☐ Measurement	☐ Connections
☐ Data Analysis and Probability	■ Representation

their properties. The gumdrops work as a motivational device; when the students have finished working with them as manipulatives, they can be given fresh gumdrops to eat. Other eatables such as miniature marshmallows can also be used, although they do not hold the toothpicks as firmly.

Activity

What ideas or concepts will students *explore*?

- Angles and lines
- Polygons
- Polyhedrons
- Spatial relationships in two and three dimensions

What materials will you need?

• gumdrops • toothpicks • models (overhead and hands-on) of polygons and polyhedrons or "Pattern: Polygon Cutouts" in the Make Manipulative section of the CD-ROM that accompanies this text • "Building Shapes Worksheet: Polygons" and "Building Shapes Worksheet: Three Dimensions" in the Worksheets & Handout section of the CD-ROM.

What questions could you ask?

What shapes can you make with gumdrops and toothpicks?
Are there any shapes you cannot make?
What are the easiest shapes to make? The hardest?
How does making a two-dimensional shape differ from making a three-dimensional shape?
What is the difference between two-dimensional shapes and three-dimensional shapes?

What will students do?

Use the gumdrops and toothpicks to build polygons with three and more sides. On the worksheet write the name of the polygon and a brief description with the number of sides and angles and draw the shape. Talk about what you learned. Then create a "crazy" polygon shape with irregular angles and sides. Name your polygon for yourself (a jamiegon or a mishagon) or for something it reminds you of (a monstergon or a buggygon).

Build three-dimensional shapes, beginning with a pyramid. Record on your worksheet the names of the polyhedrons and a brief description, including the number of sides and angles.

What strategies might students *invent* or construct?

Some students build shapes individually and then count angles and sides; others use an add-on approach, adding a side and an angle to a pentagon to make a hexagon and so forth. When the number of sides and angles becomes awkward for the building materials, students might continue with their worksheets by working deductively.

What insights, connections, or applications might students *discover*?

- To make new polygons, add lines and angles.
- To make a new polyhedron, add new plane surfaces with multiple angles and lines.
- Polyhedrons are more complex structures than polygons.
- The faces and base of polyhedrons are polygons.

What extensions can you make?

For your younger students read Marilyn Burns's *The Greedy Triangle* (New York: Scholastic, 1994). Talk about advantages and disadvantages of adding sides to the Triangle. Have students choose their favorite *Greedy Triangle* shape, draw a picture of it, and write a sentence about the shape.

For older students introduce a commercial product such as Zometools to extend the study of polyhedrons. Have students in small groups build a small model of a three-dimensional shape such as an octahedron (the faces are 8 equilateral triangles) or a dodecahedron (the faces are 12 pentagons). Have them analyze and describe shapes and spatial relationships. Dipping the structures in bubble solution will help with visualization.

43 Symmetry and Geometric Transformations: Creating a Frieze Pattern*

Overview

Grade Levels: 3–6

NCTM Standards	
Content	*Process*
☐ Number and Operations	■ Problem Solving
☐ Algebra	☐ Reasoning and Proof
■ Geometry	■ Communication
■ Measurement	■ Connections
☐ Data Analysis and Probability	■ Representation

Learning about geometry in art can be interesting, but having the students apply what they see in others' work to their own art provides a dimension of ownership of the artistic and mathematical ideas involved. The focus of this activity is how artists use symmetry and transformations of shapes to create frieze patterns. The students look for the patterns in artwork and the world around them and then create their own friezes on long strips of rolled paper. The students' friezes can be used to decorate doors or to make a border along bulletin boards or the ceiling of the classroom.

Activity

What ideas or concepts will students explore?

- Symmetry
- Transformations (reflection, rotation, slide)
- Frieze patterns in art
- Everyday applications in geometry

What materials will you need?

pictures of frieze patterns (from community buildings, art books, rugs, tiling patterns, and so on • "Frieze Patterns" in the Worksheets & Handout section of the CD-ROM that accompanies this text • pencils • rulers • transparent mirrors • triangular grid paper (small sheets, large roll) in the Make Manipulatives section of the CD-ROM, and large rolled grid paper • tracing paper • pattern blocks • colored pencils, crayons, paints

What questions could you ask?

How are the objects in transformations alike?
How are the objects different?
What are frieze patterns? Who uses them? Why?
What kind of frieze pattern can be made by sliding, reflecting, and rotating designs?
What kinds of shapes can be used to create frieze patterns?

What will students do?

Identify and discuss frieze patterns in art and in the world around you. You might find the patterns on a building or in wallpaper borders, in rugs or in a dress design. Talk about the symmetrical shapes in the patterns and how the designer or artist uses transformations (slips, slides, rotations, flips, and so forth) in the pattern.

*Adapted from an activity developed by Becca Rainey

Trace frieze patterns from models you find in books or on worksheets; then use a straight edge and a transparent mirror to help identify the various transformations in the friezes.

Use pattern blocks to design your own frieze pattern; then transfer the pattern to sheets of grid paper. Highlight the design with color.

On a small sheet of grid paper, design a frieze pattern for a classroom area such as a door frame, the top of a chalkboard, or another space. Use geometric shapes, tangram puzzles, stick figures, animals, flowers, or other objects in your design. Then determine the scale of your sheet design and increase the size for the large rolled grid paper. Transfer the design and highlight with color. Display the frieze in your classroom.

What strategies might students *invent* or construct?

Students might use transparent mirrors to help them create a reflecting or sliding frieze pattern or cut out traced objects and draw around them for rotating and combination designs. They might use the objects themselves or a ruler to space the design. Working from scale, some students could use a measure-multiply-measure-again strategy; others may use magnification with an overhead projector; others may choose a small-square-to-large-square approach, cutting out the large-square design and drawing around it.

What insights, connections, or applications might students *discover*?

- To be balanced, a frieze needs a beginning point, a center point, and an ending point.
- The right side of a frieze can repeat or reflect the left side.
- The most successful designs, especially for a large space, are often simple; smaller pieces (like book covers) can use more intricate patterns.
- Three simple transformations lead to dozens of different designs.

What extensions can you make?

Emphasize the multicultural dimensions of transformations by studying rug, tile, and other designs from a variety of cultures. After students have analyzed transformations in several designs, they can create their own designs to be joined together in strips for a paper rug or an afghan.

Have students work on the computer to create patterns. If they are using a common software program such as Microsoft Word, they can use the autoshapes feature and manipulate it with the flip and rotate buttons to create the various transformations.

44 Spinning Polygons*

Math
Manipulatives

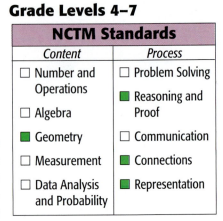

Grade Levels 4–7

NCTM Standards	
Content	*Process*
☐ Number and Operations	☐ Problem Solving
☐ Algebra	▣ Reasoning and Proof
▣ Geometry	☐ Communication
☐ Measurement	▣ Connections
☐ Data Analysis and Probability	▣ Representation

Overview

Experimenting with polygons to create various artistic designs lets students not only use geometric shapes to make art but also explore the properties of those shapes. Rotating the shapes reveals properties related to number of sides and degrees of angles. Students can also investigate the world around them to find rotating polygons in business logos, trademarks, and other everyday designs.

Activity

What ideas or concepts will students explore?

- Visualization
- Spatial relationships
- Polygons
- Rotation transformation
- Vertices
- Lines of symmetry

What materials will you need?

card stock • ruler, protractor • scissors • plain paper, colored paper • colored markers or paints • overhead transparencies and cutouts of polygons of various shapes, including combinations of triangles, squares, and so forth (See "Pattern: Polygon Cutouts" in the Make Manipulatives section of the CD-ROM that accompanies this text.)

What questions could you ask?

What happens when you rotate a polygon? Does it change? Does your view of it change?

How many different ways can you rotate a triangle, a rhombus; a trapezoid, or other polygons? Which positions look alike? Different?

What happens if you combine polygons—a triangle with a parallelogram, a square with two triangles, and so forth?

What figure do you make if you rotate a polygon all the way around a central point?

What will you do?

Use the transparencies of various polygons to show what happens when they are rotated a quarter, half, three-quarters, or full turn. Talk about vertices and lines of symmetry. Show a design made by forming a geometric design from polygons and then repeating the pattern eight or more times, rotating around a central point.

---

*Adapted from an activity developed by Rebecca Kennedy

What will students do?

Explore the rotating transformation by turning different polygon cutouts a quarter, a half, three-quarters, and a full turn. Look for and comment on differences or likenesses in how the rotating polygons look.

Combine two or more polygon cutouts to make one segment of a flower petal or windmill design. Trace your design on card stock. Then on plain paper make a dot for the center point of your design. Rotate your card-stock pattern around the dot, tracing the design eight or more times to make a complete circle. Use markers or paints to add color to different parts of the design.

*What strategies might students **invent** or construct?*

Students might record their polygon explorations in a log with names, descriptions, and sketches. Students might experiment with single polygon designs until they find the base they prefer and then add the second polygon. Some students will estimate the position visually for tracing the design. Others will start with quarter turns and then fill in the gaps. Color might follow the pattern (green triangles, blue parallelograms) or vary (green and blue triangles alternating with blue, green, and yellow parallelograms). Some students may want to work on clear plastic instead of paper to make suncatchers.

*What insights, connections, or applications might students **discover**?*

- Designs made from simple polygons can be pleasingly artistic.
- Polygons with fewer sides, such as triangles, work better in rotating designs than do polygons with more sides, such as hexagons.
- The names of polygons use Latin prefixes for the number of sides.

What extensions can you make?

Move from stationary to moving patterns by making polygon spinners. Start with a rotating polygon design on colored paper. Cut out the design. Experiment with folding segments of the outer edge to catch the wind. Stick a pin through the center point and attach to a straw. Then blow to make the design spin. As a group, discuss which designs, size of spinner, and edge folds result in the best spin.

45 Dimensions:
Exploring *Flatland*

Overview

Grade Levels 6–8

NCTM Standards	
Content	*Process*
☐ Number and Operations	■ Problem Solving
☐ Algebra	■ Reasoning and Proof
■ Geometry	■ Communication
☐ Measurement	■ Connections
☐ Data Analysis and Probability	■ Representation

Edwin A. Abbott's story *Flatland: A Romance of Many Dimensions* captures students' imaginations with its unusual premise (that there might be a world with just two dimensions) and engages their problem-solving and reasoning skills as they explore the implications of two-dimensional creatures in a two-dimensional environment.

Activity

What ideas or concepts will students *explore*?

- Properties of two- and three-dimensional objects
- Two- and three-dimensional perspectives (physical and philosophical)
- Spatial relationships
- Connections with social issues and ideas

What materials will you need?

Edwin A. Abbott's *Flatland: A Romance of Many Dimensions* (1884; reprint, New York: Barnes & Noble, 1983) • drawing or drafting paper • construction paper • protractor, ruler, compass • pencils • patterns of two- and three-dimensional shapes to be cut or folded

What questions could you ask?

What would a two-dimensional world—a Flatland—be like?
How would inhabitants of a two-dimensional world view objects and beings in a three-dimensional world?
If everything in Flatland looks like a point or a line to Flatlanders, how can Flatlanders tell the difference between things and people or between different things and different people?
How have geometric shapes impacted social structure in Flatland? Can you see any problems with that social system?

What will students do?

Read the first six or seven sections of Abbott's *Flatland*. Discuss Flatland's physical and social structures.

In groups, use construction-paper cutouts to create a model of Flatland. Work on a flat surface such as a table. Try to duplicate a Flatlander's perspective by looking at the model from table-top eye level and discuss what you see. Experiment with moving figures around in your model and discuss the problems with movement and with recognizing people and structures in a two-dimensional world.

Imagine what Spaceland, the home of the Sphere who visits Flatland, might look like. Construct shapes and structures by folding and cutting paper and then build a model of Spaceland. Experiment with different shapes for people, houses, and so forth. Discuss how Spaceland might look to a Flatlander and how Flatland might look to a Spacelander.

Design a house for a Flatland family. You may need to make some assumptions about Flatlanders' sizes and the amount of space they need to live in comfortably. Set up a scale and use a ruler and a protractor to draw the house and its furnishings. Discuss as a group the way your designs respond to the physical and social realities of Flatland living.

Write your own story about a Spacelander visiting Flatland or a Flatlander visiting Spaceland. Imagine, for example, what would happen if a visitor from one world got lost in the other or if an explorer from Flatland visited Spaceland and then went back home to tell Flatlanders about his or her discoveries.

What strategies might students *invent* or construct?

Students might act out the movements of various Flatland inhabitants, trying to imagine what it would be like to be a straight line, a triangle, or another polygon. They could use cutouts of various shapes and experiment with different arrangements before they begin drawing a Flatland house. They might keep a log of Flatland shapes and their characteristics as they read and then compare those characteristics with the geometric properties of the shapes.

What insights, connections, or applications might students *discover*?

- In Flatland both physical and social structures are rigid and unmoving.
- In designing a Flatland house, you must consider both the content and the shapes of the inhabitants, including pathways for them to move through the rooms and around each other.
- Flatlanders' limited visual perspectives seem to be mirrored by limited intellectual perspectives.
- In a two-dimensional world all objects are seen as lines and points; they only look two-dimensional from a viewpoint in three dimensions.

What extensions can you make?

Have students read Ian Stewart's *Flatterland: Like Flatland, Only More So* (Cambridge, MA: Perseus, 2001). Discuss the changes in and continuation of themes introduced in *Flatland*. Try representing three- as well as two-dimensional objects on flat paper by drawing a picture of an inhabitant of Spaceland visiting Flatland and an inhabitant of Flatland visiting Spaceland.

46 Origami Zoo

Grade Levels 4–8

NCTM Standards	
Content	*Process*
☐ Number and Operations	■ Problem Solving
☐ Algebra	■ Reasoning and Proof
■ Geometry	■ Communication
☐ Measurement	■ Connections
☐ Data Analysis and Probability	■ Representation

Overview

This activity connects math with art and science. Students explore three-dimensional objects by creating origami shapes. At the same time they study animals and animal habitats. The zoo animals and environments they create can also serve as an art project. The work can be done in small groups or individually.

Activity

What ideas or concepts will students explore?

- Three-dimensional shapes
- Spatial relationships in three-dimensional space
- Symmetry in three dimensions
- Habitat needs of zoo animals

What materials will you need?

origami paper in various sizes and colors • pencils or markers • ruler • grid paper • origami patterns of animals (various levels of difficulty) • resources such as Internet access so that students can research animals and their habitats

What questions could you ask?

How can we turn a two-dimensional piece of paper into a three-dimensional animal?

What role does symmetry play in folding?

What geometric shapes are involved in origami?

What does origami mean? Where does origami come from?

Is origami art or geometry?

Have you ever visited a zoo?

What do you know about zoo animals and their habitats?

What is your favorite animal at the zoo?

What will students do?

Select a zoo animal to study. Choose an origami pattern and a sheet of paper. Fold the animal, paying special attention to geometric shapes and symmetry of individual and repeated folds.

Do some research on the Internet or in the library about your animal's habitat. Then use grid paper and rulers to design a habitat, including shelter, exercise areas, feeding stations, visitor viewing areas, and so forth. Color the habitat and, if you wish, add features to your origami animal with colored pencils or markers.

What strategies might students *invent* or construct?

Some students prefer to fold a practice animal from newsprint and then use origami paper; others start with origami paper, unfolding and refolding as necessary. Similarly, some will make a rough sketch of their habitat plans and then transfer the plan to grid paper; others will start with grid paper and erase and redraw until they are satisfied with their plans.

Students might use the size of their origami animals to set a scale for the habitat—making it 10 or 20 times the animal's length and so forth; or they might work from researched material and build a scale from those numbers. Some will stop with a two-dimensional habitat design; others will take the next step and construct a three-dimensional habitat from their designs.

What insights, connections, or applications might students *discover*?

- Three-dimensional figures can be constructed from two-dimensional sheets of paper, one fold at a time.
- Because animals have symmetrical shapes, the right and left sides mirroring each other, the paper folds also follow a symmetrical design.
- Habitat size depends not only on an animal's size but also on special needs such as horizontal space for running or vertical space for climbing and flying.

What extensions can you make?

Have students write a story about animals and math. They can use origami to illustrate several scenes from the story.

Have students work in small groups to prepare and present a report on a category of zoo animals (for example, the big cats, monkeys, and so forth).

Take a field trip to a zoo. Have students keep logs of what they see. Include a math dimension in the log so that students record not only facts and observations but also the math they find at the zoo (shapes, numbers, sizes, and so forth).

Understanding and Using Measurement Concepts

47 How Much Time Does It Take to _____?

Grade Levels K–2

NCTM Standards	
Content	*Process*
☐ Number and Operations	■ Problem Solving
☐ Algebra	■ Reasoning and Proof
☐ Geometry	■ Communication
■ Measurement	■ Connections
■ Data Analysis and Probability	■ Representation

Overview

Discovering the relativity of time can begin simply by discovering relationships between time and actions or events. Students work as teams to investigate how long it takes to do a variety of things. They keep records in a log and use the information to draw conclusions about lengths of time.

Activity

*What ideas or concepts will students **explore**?*

- Standard measures of time, such as minutes and seconds
- Connections between actions or events and time
- Equal intervals of time
- Numerical scales in time
- Time tools and uses

What materials will you need?

"Timing Log Sheet" in the Worksheets & Handouts section of the CD-ROM that accompanies this text • pencils • stopwatches or clocks with second hands • cookies • cartons of milk • drawing materials • balloons

What questions could you ask?

Have you ever heard people say, "Just a second," or "In a minute"? What do you think they mean? Have you ever used those words? What do you mean?
Have you ever felt like there's too much time in a day? Or not enough time?
What things seem to take too long?
What things seem to go by too fast?
How can you tell how much time something really takes?

What will students do?

Working in teams of three or four, conduct time experiments. Choose one member of the group to keep the log. Choose another to use the clock to time events. The other member (or members) of the team will act out events for timing. Experiments might include how long it takes to eat a cookie, inflate a balloon, drink a small carton of milk, run around the room, hop across the room on one foot, sing a song, recite a poem, count to 100.

*What strategies might students **invent** or construct?*

Students might first estimate and then time events. Some will emphasize speed (least-time measurements); others, thoroughness. There may be some competition for best time at actions, like running around the room.

*What insights, connections, or applications might students **discover**?*

- Differences in things, such as size of the balloon or length of a song, will affect the time.
- Differences in people, such as being a fast or a slow runner or chewer, will also affect the time.
- A minute spent doing something difficult, such as blowing up a balloon, may seem longer than a minute spent doing something easy or absorbing, such as drawing a picture.

48 Exploring Perimeter and Area with Froot Loops™

 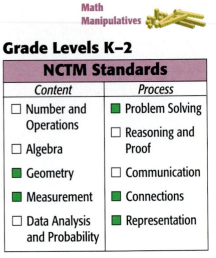
Overview

Grade Levels K–2

NCTM Standards	
Content	*Process*
☐ Number and Operations	■ Problem Solving
☐ Algebra	☐ Reasoning and Proof
■ Geometry	☐ Communication
■ Measurement	■ Connections
☐ Data Analysis and Probability	■ Representation

Working with edible manipulatives is a favorite with most students. Using Froot Loops as a measurement tool engages students in the process of measuring perimeter and area and at the same time prepares them for using more standard units of measurement such as centimeters and inches.

Activity

What ideas or concepts will students explore?
- Nonstandard and standard units of measurement
- Perimeter
- Area
- Numbers and measurement
- Two-dimensional space

What materials will you need?
drawing paper and pencils • bags of Froot Loops or other cereal • nonstretchy string • measuring sticks • centimeter blocks

What questions could you ask?
Who in this class has the biggest hand? The smallest?
How much larger is the biggest hand than the smallest? How can you tell?
When might it be important to know about the size of your hand?
What is the difference between the area inside a hand and the distance around it, or the perimeter? Will the biggest hand have the largest area and the longest perimeter? Why or why not?

What will you do?
Explain the concepts of perimeter and area. Use students' bodies to measure the perimeter of parts of the classroom. Have them make a measuring chain with held hands and then lead the chain around the sections to be measured, adding or subtracting students as needed. Have the students count and decide how many students make up each perimeter. Use the student measure again to find the area of different flat objects such as a rug. Have students lie down in rows, then count the number of students it takes to cover the rug.

What will students do?
Activity A Spread fingers wide on a piece of paper; then draw around the entire hand. Use Froot Loops to outline the hand and count the total to find the perimeter in Froot Loops. Then fill in the handprint with Froot Loops and count the number to find the area in Froot Loops. Compare and talk about the results.

Activity B Outline handprints with string to make a string the same length as the handprint perimeter. Then measure the string with a measuring tape or stick to find the perimeter in centimeters and inches. Cover the handprint with centimeter blocks to get an approximate area. Talk about the difficulties of covering an irregular area like the handprint completely with squares such as centimeter blocks.

What strategies might students ***invent*** *or construct?*

Students might count Froot Loops individually, starting over when they lose count, or group Froot Loops by 5s or 10s. Since filling the handprint completely with Froot Loops or centimeter blocks will be difficult, some will estimate the number for unfilled spaces, some will overfill, and some will fill what they can and ignore the rest.

What insights, connections, or applications might students ***discover***?

- Perimeter is the distance around something, even if there are many twists and turns, as with the fingers of a handprint
- Area means all the space inside the perimeter and none of the space outside it.
- Measuring with a tape or a stick can be easier than measuring with individual objects because you do not have to worry about overlap or gaps, and you do not have to count each unit.

What extensions can you make?

Have students experiment with the perimeter string they made to measure their handprints. Try putting the string into various geometric shapes like rectangles, triangles, or circles. They could use tape to hold the string in place. Then use Froot Loops to find the perimeters and areas of the different shapes. Compare with the results for their handprints and talk about what they find.

49 LOGO's Turtle Math

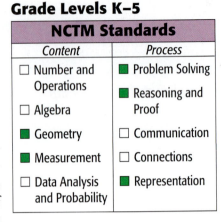

Grade Levels K–5

NCTM Standards	
Content	*Process*
☐ Number and Operations	■ Problem Solving
☐ Algebra	■ Reasoning and Proof
■ Geometry	☐ Communication
■ Measurement	☐ Connections
☐ Data Analysis and Probability	■ Representation

Overview

Creating geometric shapes by using LOGO and a turtle cursor introduces students to computer logic and at the same time allows them to explore properties of polygons. Working with turns lets students explore angles, and programming turtle steps helps them discover relationships such as the equal sides in a square or an equilateral triangle.

Activity

*What ideas or concepts will students **explore**?*

- Links between numerical scales and measurement scales
- Step-by-step logic of computer programming
- Importance of measurement in geometry
- Commands as a way to turn mental images into computer-screen images

What materials will you need?

computer terminals for each student or cooperative group • program using LOGO, such as Douglas H. Clements and J. S. Meredith, *Turtle Math*. [computer program] (Montreal: LOGO Computer Systems, 1994)

What questions could you ask?

Do you enjoy working on the computer?
What do you like best about working on the computer? Least?
What does it mean to give a command on the computer?
When you type a command on the keyboard, what are you trying to do?
What would happen if you left out a step in your commands?
What do you have to know to write commands for the turtle to draw a rectangle? Other polygons?

What will you do?

Introduce students to LOGO computer language. Demonstrate the operation of the turtle cursor and its response to basic commands. For easy reference, provide a large chart with the basic commands and their abbreviations: FORWARD FD, BACKWARD BK, RIGHT RT, LEFT LT, HOME HOME. Show how numbers following the commands tell the cursor how many turtle steps to take and how the PENUP (PU) and PENDOWN (PD) commands turn off and on the drawing feature.

What will students do?

Younger Students Become proficient at writing LOGO programs as you move the cursor around the screen, explore ways to move from one point to the other, and play games such as "Coming Home" on *Turtle Math*.

Older Students Write programs to draw a variety of regular and irregular polygons (including "crazy" polygons). Compare programs and discuss reasons for each command, bringing together your knowledge about geometric shapes, angles, numbers, and words and deepening your understanding of their relationships.

What strategies might students *invent* or construct?

Some students will act out commands to check for missed steps. Some will make drawings on paper as an intermediate step between mental image and computer image. Most will use trial-and-error to test and refine their control over the turtle cursor's movements.

What insights, connections, or applications might students *discover*?

- Precise results call for precise instructions to the cursor.
- Numbers and directions are equally important in writing a successful program.
- Mistakes can be corrected by composing reverse commands or by using the CLEARSCREEN (CS) command.
- You can avoid the necessity of rewriting a series of steps by using the repeat (REPEAT #) command.

What extensions can you make?

Have students experiment with changing the numbers of turtle steps and the angles of turns as they create geometric figures to explore congruence and proportion.

Explore internal angles of various polygons by keeping turtle steps constant but using different angles for turns. They might, for example, use the repeat command, a line length, and a turn angle to generate various regular-sided shapes such as a hexagon (REPEAT 6 [RT 60 FD 70]).

Use the turtle to explore various tessellation patterns, such as tessellations of individual or combinations of polygons.

Explore recursive procedures by constructing various rotating polygons in which the turtle begins at the same point but rotates its orientation to overwrite and create a circular, spinning figure.

50 Making Measurement Tools with Nonstandard and Standard Units

Overview

Two key ideas here are the use of standard units to measure objects and the use of tools to apply standard units in measurement situations. In addition to developing measurement strategies, students will apply division principles as they experiment with ways to divide bags of popcorn.

Grade Levels K–5

NCTM Standards	
Content	*Process*
■ Number and Operations	■ Problem Solving
☐ Algebra	☐ Reasoning and Proof
☐ Geometry	■ Communication
■ Measurement	☐ Connections
☐ Data Analysis and Probability	☐ Representation

Activity

What ideas or concepts will students *explore*?

- Linear space
- Volume or capacity
- Units of measurement
- Numerical scales in measurement

What materials will you need?

colored paper clips • rolls of adding-machine or cash-register tape • colored markers • rulers • bags of popcorn • one large container and two small containers for each group • clear Styrofoam cups • plastic baggies • measuring cups with common and metric measurements

What questions could you ask?

What does it mean if something is big, small, tall, or short?
Do I seem tall to you? Do you think I would seem tall to the tallest basketball player in the NBA? Why or why not?
What if that tall basketball player wanted to come to visit our class? How could we make sure he could get through our door without bumping his head or sit at a table and have enough room for his legs?
Can someone tell me what volume is? Perimeter?
How many children could we fit around this table? How many grown-ups?
How many children would fit sitting cross-legged on this table? How many grown-ups?
How is measuring perimeter different from measuring volume?
When might it be important to measure perimeter? To measure volume?

What will students do?

Activity A Use paper clips to create a measuring chain. Use the chain to measure people or things in your classroom. Then compare results and discuss the value or problems you encountered using paper clips as a measuring tool.

Activity B Create a measuring tape with narrow rolls of paper and markers. Select units of measurement and develop a way to mark the tape at regular intervals. Number the intervals. Then use the tape to measure objects, including those measured with paper clips. Compare the results.

Activity C On the reverse side of the paper tape, use markers to create metric and/or common measurement scales. Remeasure objects measured in activities B and C and compare results. Discuss which tape worked best.

Activity D Working in small groups, make Styrofoam cups into measuring cups by creating a scale and marking it on the outside of the cup. Experiment to see how much each cup will hold and how the intervals should be marked to show equal parts of that whole.

Activity E Use the marked Styrofoam cups and the large and small containers to find out how much popcorn is in a bag. Then remeasure with manufactured cups and compare the results.

Activity F Make a plan to share a bag of popcorn among the students in your group. Each member of the group should get a plastic baggie with an equal portion of popcorn. No popcorn should be left in the bag. Measure the portions with both your Styrofoam cup and your standard tools. Compare and discuss the results with those of other groups.

What strategies might students *invent* or construct?

To simplify counting paper clips, some students group the clips in their chains by color—five red, five blue, and so forth. Others count clips one by one for each measurement. To create regular intervals for dividing the paper tape measure, students might "walk" a paper clip or other unit down the tape, marking the intervals with short lines. Others could fold the paper repeatedly in half and use the fold lines as intervals.

Younger children often measure the popcorn one cup at a time; older children sometimes use the two smaller containers, filling the first one a cup at a time, then the second container all at once, and doubling the total.

The division of the popcorn could be done in a sharing fashion, one cup at a time, or by dividing the total cups in the bag by the number of students in the group, with any remainders shared in round-robin fashion.

What insights, connections, or applications might students *discover*?

- Linking measurement scales to numbers by writing the numbers directly on the tape makes the measuring process easier and more accurate.
- Nonstandard measurements can give the measurer valuable information, but standard measurements are easier to discuss and compare.
- When measuring volume, the shape of the cup along with height must be considered when you mark intervals such as $\frac{1}{2}$, $\frac{1}{4}$, or $\frac{1}{3}$.

51 Cooking on the Oregon Trail with Nonstandard and Standard Measurements

Grade Levels 3–5

NCTM Standards	
Content	*Process*
☐ Number and Operations	☑ Problem Solving
☐ Algebra	☐ Reasoning and Proof
☐ Geometry	☑ Communication
☑ Measurement	☑ Connections
☐ Data Analysis and Probability	☑ Representation

Overview

The way people cook outdoors has changed dramatically since the pioneers made their meals over open fires. To most students, campfire cooking is limited to roasting marshmallows and hotdogs on a stick; the real camp-out cooking is done on a grill fueled by bottles of butane. In addition, for many students cooking means microwaving prepared dishes or following simple directions on a box or a can. Looking at old-fashioned ways to measure ingredients and cook from scratch will itself seem novel; comparing that method to the even more old-fashioned pinch-of-this, handful-of-that method will seem exotic. The activity provides a good link between using personal, nonstandard units of measure and using standard units.

Activity

*What ideas or concepts will students **explore**?*
- Nonstandard and standard measures in cooking
- Volume, temperature, time, space
- Connections with history

What materials will you need?
access to a stove with an oven • ingredients for potato cake (white and brown sugar; butter; mashed potatoes; cocoa; milk or cream; walnuts; salt; ground cloves, cinnamon, and nutmeg; eggs; flour; baking powder) • heavy iron skillet • measuring cups and spoons • stove clock • cake knife • paper napkins • shortening for greasing skillet • toothpick • "Cooking on the Oregon Trail" recipes (reprinted on page 123)

What questions could you ask?
How important are exact measurements in cooking?
What kinds of things do we measure when we cook?
What kinds of foods did the pioneers probably eat on the trail?
What kinds of things did they probably not eat?
How long do you think it took the pioneers to travel west in their wagons? How long would it take us today?

What will you do?
Talk about the immigration west along the Oregon Trail. Describe the living conditions—sleeping in or under the wagons, cooking over an open fire or in a sheepherder's fold-up stove. Explain how trail cooks often worked by memory and feel rather than with a recipe when they cooked.

What will students do? **Activity A** Explore the nonstandard measurements of the pioneer recipes. Compare "double handfuls" and "pinches" to the cup and teaspoon measurements of the modern verion of the pioneer recipe. Discuss the differences in different students' measurements and the possible effect on the cake.

COOKING ON THE OREGON TRAIL

Pioneer Recipe for Potato Cake

Double handful of sugar	Pinches of salt, spices to taste
Large hunk of butter	Nuts
Heaping helping of mashed potatoes	Double handful of flour
Squares of chocolate (grated)	Several pinches of baking powder
Enough milk or cream to make a thick batter	Eggs
Bake slowly for about 1 hour	

Modern Version

2 cups sugar (about ½ brown)	2 cups flour (sifted)
1 cup butter or margarine	2 teaspoons baking powder
½ cup grated chocolate or cocoa	½ cup milk or cream
1 teaspoon each of ground cloves, cinnamon, nutmeg	4 eggs
1 heaping cup mashed potatoes	1 cup nuts

Activity B Preheat oven to 350°. Measure and combine the cake ingredients in the order given in the recipe. Bake in a well-greased iron skillet for 1 hour or until a toothpick inserted in the middle comes out clean. Cut the cake so that each student will have a small slice. The cake's texture will be somewhat bread-like and can be served on napkins as finger food.

*What strategies might students **invent** or construct?* Some students will focus first on the pioneer recipe, experimenting with how much flour they can hold in two hands and how much of the spices they can pinch. Others will start with the standard recipe and work backwards, seeing how many of their double handfuls equal 1 or 2 cups and how many pinches of spices equals a teaspoon.

*What insights, connections, or applications might students **discover**?*
- The nonstandard measurements change from person to person and depend upon differences such as hand and finger size.
- The results of the nonstandard recipe probably change a bit each time it's cooked.

- Standard cooking measurements often used in the United States are common rather than metric.
- Newer cooking tools usually have both metric and common systems, but older tools have just common measurements. When a recipe says a "cup" or a "teaspoon," it isn't referring to tableware but to specific measuring versions of them.

What extensions can you make?   Have students research the diet of western pioneers and then prepare and sample other dishes.

52 Estimating Length, Volume, and Weight

Overview

Grade Levels 3–5

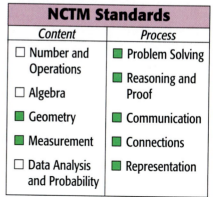

NCTM Standards	
Content	*Process*
☐ Number and Operations	■ Problem Solving
☐ Algebra	■ Reasoning and Proof
■ Geometry	■ Communication
■ Measurement	■ Connections
☐ Data Analysis and Probability	■ Representation

Developing the mind tools needed to estimate properties of size begins with experimentation. Students explore length, weight, and volume through a series of investigations that allow them to experience those properties directly—for example, to discover the volume of a box by seeing how many children can fit inside. They begin with nonstandard units such as footprints to measure length and then move on to using standard measuring units and tools.

Activity

*What ideas or concepts will students **explore**?*

- Measurement with nonstandard and standard units
- Mental measurement tools
- Direct and indirect measurement strategies
- Properties of physical objects

What materials will you need?

tape measures, meter sticks • scales • centimeter-block manipulatives • log sheets • collection of large and small objects to be measured, such as a box large enough for several children to fit into, a long strip of rug that can be measured with footsteps or body lengths, cereal or other boxes, one- or two-pound barbells, and so forth; include objects that cannot be measured directly, such as a long frieze design too high on the wall to reach or a container observed through a glass door

What questions could you ask?

How important is it for us to know how big or small things are? Can you think of a time when having something too big could be a problem? How about something too small?

What if you were shopping and wanted to get a rug to fit your room? How would you know what size to buy?

Or how about buying snacks for a party? How would you tell how much to buy?

What will students do?

Activity A Use nonstandard units (such as footprints or body lengths) and standard units (such as feet and decimeters) to estimate the length of various objects. Record estimates; then check answers by measuring with nonstandard units and a tape measure or meter stick. Reflect on, compare, and discuss answers.

Activity B Explore volume or capacity of objects by standing in them, emptying and feeling contents, or filling them with other objects, such as centimeter blocks. Estimate capacity with both nonstandard and standard units; then test with objects directly or measure to show capacity. Reflect on, compare, and discuss results.

Activity C Estimate the weight of various objects; then measure with scales. Reflect on, compare, and discuss answers. Also compare the measured weight of commercial packaging, such as cereal boxes, with the weight printed on the box.

What strategies might students *invent* or construct?

Most will use visual clues to estimate length but will touch and lift objects to estimate volume and weight. For objects such as frieze designs that cannot be measured directly, students might measure another object instead, such as a chalkboard, that appears to be the same length. For a box they can see but not touch, they might look for a comparable substitute that can be measured directly or attempt to take measurements with a ruler through the glass or other barrier. Many will use comparisons to estimate weight, holding an object in one hand and weighing it against objects in the other hand.

What insights, connections, or applications might students *discover*?

- Visual clues about size can be deceiving, with objects appearing smaller than they are in a large space and larger than they are in a small space.
- Estimates may improve with practice but often will be better for length and sometimes weight than they will for volume.
- Most products, such as cereal seem to fill only part of their packages' volume.
- A small object made of metal or wood will weigh more than a large object made of cardboard and filled with light material such as cereal.

What extensions can you make?

In teams, draw a plan for the perfect bedroom or playroom. Include room dimensions and locations and sizes of doors and windows. Then use a catalog to select furnishings, being sure to include dimensions of items. Develop strategies to determine whether your furnishings will fit into your room. Discuss and compare the results.

53 Boiling a Potato for Inca Time*

Grade Levels 5–8

NCTM Standards	
Content	*Process*
☐ Number and Operations	■ Problem Solving
☐ Algebra	■ Reasoning and Proof
☐ Geometry	■ Communication
■ Measurement	■ Connections
■ Data Analysis and Probability	■ Representation

Overview

Linking time to the earth's rotation on its axis and revolution around the sun is so universally accepted that the idea of other standards may seem unnatural to students. However, we all have some nonstandard ways of looking at time. We might use events such as meal times or favorite television shows to pace our days. Looking at the measurement of time in terms of how long it takes to boil a potato gives students a dramatically different perspective on time and also on a society's value system. Potatoes are a common diet staple for us, but to the Incas they were so important that they helped define the pace of life.

Activity

What ideas or concepts will students explore?
- Historical and multicultural roots of measurement systems
- Links between physical objects and events and measurement standards
- Time measurement
- Numerical scales

What materials will you need?
average-sized potatoes • saucepans • water • forks • stove • clock • posterboard • markers • paper, pencils

What questions could you ask?
How many ways do we have to cook potatoes?
How many different kinds of potatoes do you know about?
How many times a week do you eat potatoes?
Do you think potatoes are as important to us as they were to the Incas?
Why do you think the boiling time for a potato might be important enough to serve as a measurement of time?

What will you do?
Provide background about Incan civilization. Explain that the Incas grew more than 200 kinds of potatoes and developed freeze-drying methods of storage hundreds of years ago. Show how potatoes came to us from the Incas by way of the Spanish conquistadors, European cooking, and finally immigrants to North America. Discuss the importance of the potato in Incan diets and their use of the time it takes to boil a potato as a basic unit of measure.

---

*Adapted from a lesson idea in "One Potato, Two Potato, Inca style" http://www.pbs.org/opb/conquistadors/teachers/teachers.htm

What will students do?

Activity A Working in teams, boil a potato and time how long it takes to cook. Test for doneness with a fork. Compare results with other teams, and discuss any differences.

Activity B Using posterboard and markers, create a potato-time clock. Use the time it takes to cook the potato instead of the hour as the basic unit of time.

Activity C Working individually, write a personal daily schedule using potato time. Include getting-up time, breakfast time, class times, lunch time, school's-out time, dinner time, as well as special times such as soccer or band practice and the times of your favorite TV shows. Compare and discuss your potato-time schedules. Talk about any advantages and disadvantages you identify with potato time.

*What strategies might students **invent** or construct?*

To make a potato clock, some students will start with hours in pencil and then try to make adjustments from there. Others will work with the 360° of a circle and divide by the number of potato "hours" in a standard 12-hour period. Similarly, for the daily schedule, some will create side-by-side hour and potato lists to give themselves familiar reference points, while others will outline a potato day and then guess about equivalent times based on a sequence of events.

*What insights, connections, or applications might students **discover**?*

- We learn our current time system when we are young and learn it so thoroughly that another system feels unnatural.
- How hard the water boils can change the time it takes to boil a potato.
- Altitude can also affect boiling time since water boils at a lower temperature at higher altitudes (see Boiling Point of Water Calculator at http://www.biggreenegg.com/boilingPoint.htm)
- Everyone needs to use the same time, or daily life would be chaotic.
- We take our time system for granted, but it plays a key role in organizing our lives and communities.

54 Sir Cumference

Overview

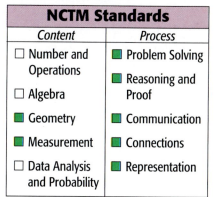

NCTM Standards	
Content	*Process*
☐ Number and Operations	■ Problem Solving
☐ Algebra	■ Reasoning and Proof
■ Geometry	■ Communication
■ Measurement	■ Connections
☐ Data Analysis and Probability	■ Representation

The series of math adventures by Cindy Neuschwander feature simple stories with some sophisticated play on words and math concepts that range from basic to complex. Students need to understand that the pseudo-history of the stories is purely fictional: that the circumference and diameter of a circle are not in fact named for a knight and lady of King Arthur's court, Sir Cumference and Lady Di of Meter, and that pi was not discovered when Sir Cumference's son Radius had to find the correct ratio of ingredients for a potion to change the Dragon of Pi back into Sir Cumference.

Activity

*What ideas or concepts will students **explore**?*

- Properties of circles and angles, including circumference, radius, diameter, degrees of angle
- Relationship of pi to circle measurements
- Measurement of circles and angles
- Use of compass, ruler, protractor

What materials will you need?

Sir Cumference books by Cindy Neuschwander: *Sir Cumference and the First Round Table* (Watertown, MA: Charlesbridge, 1997); *Sir Cumference and the Dragon of Pi* (Watertown, MA: Charlesbridge, 1999); *Sir Cumference and the Great Knight of Angleland* (Watertown, MA: Charlesbridge, 2001) ● drawing paper ● compasses, rulers, protractors ● pencils

What will you do?

Discuss stories and the concept of make-believe. Explain that the Sir Cumference math adventures are fiction, but they help us understand the ideas behind concepts such as the circumference of a circle and pi. Connect your discussion with language arts by talking about King Arthur, his knights, and legends of their quests.

What questions could you ask?

What shapes of tables have you seen? What did you think about those shapes?

Do you like pizza? Have you noticed how all of the pieces start at the center in a point and then get bigger at the edge?

How many of you ride bikes? What can happen if you make too sharp a turn?

What do you have to know to draw a polygon?

What makes a square different from a pentagon and a pentagon different from a hexagon or an octogon?

What will students do?

Activity A (Grades K–2) Listen to the story *Sir Cumference and the First Round Table*. Then join hands and try to make the various table shapes talked about in the story. Talk about the advantages and disadvantages of the various shapes. Discuss the final choice of a round table.

Activity B (Grades 3–5) Listen to or read the story *Sir Cumference and the Dragon of Pi*. Use a calculator to check Radius's figures, and help him out by drawing circles with compasses, measuring the circumferences and diameters of the circles, and dividing to find pi. Discuss the accuracy of the results and the significance of the final celebration: 3 days, 3 hours, and 24 minutes.

Activity C (Grades 6–7) Read *Sir Cumference and the Great Knight of Angleland*. Use the medallion in the book or individual protractors and rulers to draw and explore the angles and shapes that Radius encounters in the Angleland castle. Discuss Zig and Zag's warning and the significance of names in the story, such as the Mountains of Obtuse.

What strategies might students *invent* or construct?

Students might work directly from the story illustrations to make measurements, or they could draw and experiment with figures on scratch paper. Younger students might work with rounded numbers and estimates (like Radius's estimate of pi as slightly more than 3); older students may want to carry out calculations for pi to several decimal places.

What insights, connections, or applications might students *discover*?

- The vocabulary of geometry can be tied in a meaningful way to things we see and do.
- The world is filled with circles and other geometric shapes.
- Angles are an important part of our environment, and understanding them can help us interpret what we observe.
- Using tools such as compasses to draw circles and protractors to measure angles takes practice and precision.

What extensions can you make?

Each of the stories offers opportunities to make connections with history, writing, and art. Students can draw episodes or characters (such as the Dragon of Pi) or make maps (for example, of Radius's travels in Angleland). They might also write additional episodes of a story or a new math adventure for characters—for example, a quest to the Land of Polyhedra.

55 Measuring Pi

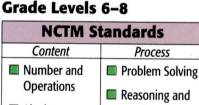

Grade Levels 6–8

NCTM Standards	
Content	*Process*
☑ Number and Operations	☑ Problem Solving
☐ Algebra	☑ Reasoning and Proof
☑ Geometry	☐ Communication
☑ Measurement	☑ Connections
☑ Data Analysis and Probability	☑ Representation

Overview

This activity places an investigation in an imaginative context. Students who know the value of pi must pretend they do not, and they must work within a fictional situation that requires them to discover pi in order to save a favorite teacher from aliens. Discovering pi encompasses not only geometry and measurement but also number systems and operations and data analysis. Students will be working with metric and standard measures and dividing the circumferences of various objects by the diameter to find pi, and they will be collecting and analyzing data about circles.

Activity

*What ideas or concepts will students **explore**?*

- Irrational numbers
- Standard and metric measurement systems
- Decimal numbers
- Rounding numbers
- Circumference, radius, and diameter of circles

What materials will you need?

measuring tapes, compasses, rulers • Worksheet "Measuring Circles to Find Pi" on the Worksheets & Handout section of the CD-ROM that accompanies this text • pencils, paper, and calculators for recording and manipulating data • assortment of round and spherical objects to measure (hula hoops, large and small balls, plates, cups, clocks, balloons, jars, cans, baskets, and so forth) • masking tape

What will you do?

Set up measurement stations around the classroom with baskets and shopping bags filled with round and spherical objects. Review the relationship between standard and metric measurement systems and tools and demonstrate a variety of ways to measure the radius, diameter, and circumference of a circle.

Then introduce pi. Talk about its history, its practical applications, and its applications in geometry, including the equation $C = \pi d$: circumference = pi × diameter and $\pi = C/d$ or pi = circumference ÷ diameter.

What questions could you ask?

Why is pi called a constant?
If you didn't know the value of pi, how could you find it?
Why is it important to know the value of pi?

If you have a circle with a radius of 10 centimeters, what will the circumference of the circle be?

If you have a circle with a radius of 5 inches, what will the circumference of the circle be? If you know the circumference and the radius of a circle but do not know pi, how could you estimate it?

What will students do?

Begin with an imaginary premise:

> Aliens from the planet Dragoon have abducted your favorite teacher. To get her back, your class must tell the aliens an important piece of information: the value of pi. Unfortunately, a mind sifter has drained that specific piece of information from everyone's brain. Your only hope is to discover pi for yourselves by dividing the circumferences of circles by their respective diameters. To be as accurate as possible, measure the circumferences and diameters of at least 10 circular objects using both standard and metric measurements. Use your calculator to divide circumference by diameter. Record all of the information on your worksheet. When you have 10 calculations, add and divide to find an average.

What strategies might students *invent* or construct?

Working in pairs, one student may do the measurements while the other records data. Measuring large circles such as hula hoops might be done in segments with tape to mark each section. For smaller circles, students often use a ruler to find the diameter. To find the diameter of a sphere, students might put the object on a piece of paper, hold straight edges to each side, mark the paper where the edges touch, and then measure the distance between the marks.

What insights, connections, or applications might students *discover*?

- Finding an accurate value of pi, even to two significant digits, can be difficult. The accuracy of the measurements and even the tools affect the outcome.
- The calculations can also be affected by variations in the roundness of the objects measured.
- If the measurements are equally accurate, pi should be the same for both standard and metric measurements.
- One or two errors in calculation can alter the average significantly.

What extensions can you make?

Make discovering pi part of a larger activity on discovering circles. Begin by looking for circles in the classroom and in the world outside the classroom. Discuss the uses of circles in design, construction, sports, packaging, and so forth. Compile a list of vocabulary words and expressions related to *circle* (*circular, circumference, inner circle*, and so forth). Discuss the relationship between the words and ideas or images suggested by the words.

56 Tessellating Polygons*

Grade Levels 6–8

NCTM Standards	
Content	*Process*
☐ Number and Operations	■ Problem Solving
☐ Algebra	■ Reasoning and Proof
■ Geometry	☐ Communication
■ Measurement	■ Connections
☐ Data Analysis and Probability	■ Representation

Overview

This activity is a hands-on exploration of the properties of polygons. As they discover which polygons will and will not tessellate, students also construct ways to measure angles and develop a firsthand understanding of the ways angles affect the ability of polygons to tessellate as well as of the spatial relationships among polygons. The activity can also be connected with art as students work creatively with different tessellations and patterns.

Activity

What ideas or concepts will students *explore*?

- Polygons
- Measuring angles and degrees
- Obtuse and acute angles
- Tessellation
- Spatial relationships

What materials will you need?

envelopes containing colored polygons made from a master worksheet: 10 each of triangles, squares, pentagons, and hexagons; 5 each of heptagons, octagons, nonagons, decagons, dodecagons (see "Pattern: Polygon Cutouts" in the Make Manipulatives section of the CD-ROM that accompanies this text ● "Tessellations Worksheet" and "Polygons and Angles Worksheet" in the Worksheets & Handouts section of the CD-ROM ● protractor

What will you do?

Introduce tessellating polygons as an arrangement of polygons that covers an entire space with no gaps. Describe the way tessellating hexagons helped Michigan State plan an indoor grass field for the Silverdome World Cup Soccer Championships in 1994 (see web.msu.edu/turf/). Discuss why the hexagon pattern was chosen instead of other shapes. Review the different polygon shapes represented in the envelopes; discuss other characteristics of the polygons, including obtuse and acute angles.

What questions could you ask?

What does it mean to tessellate?
Which polygons will tessellate and which ones will not? Why?
How many ways can you measure the degrees in an interior angle of a polygon?

---

*Adapted from ideas found in Blake E. Peterson "From Tessellations to Polyhedra: Big Polyhedra," *Mathematics Teaching in the Middle School* (February 2000): 348–57.

What is the sum of the interior angles of a triangle? A rectangle? A pentagon? How does the number of degrees in an interior angle affect the polygon's ability to tessellate?

What will students do?

Activity A Work with each of the polygon cutouts to try to create tessellating patterns. Record the results on the "Tessellations Worksheet." Explain in words why some polygons will not tessellate.

Activity B Explore each type of polygon to understand its characteristics. Count the number of sides. Measure the interior angles. Record the information on the "Polygons and Angles Worksheet." Discuss how the information obtained in this activity can be used to explain the results of Activity A.

*What strategies might students **invent** or construct?*

Students might work inductively, experimenting with each set of cutouts to try to find a tessellating pattern. Others might discover the need to fit the shapes around a single point early in the process and then proceed deductively to decide which shapes will or will not tessellate. Measuring of interior angles might be done individually with a protractor. Some students might use the triangle or square with known measurements of 60° and 90° to measure the other shapes. Or they could develop an intuitive method, segmenting the polygon around a central point into triangles and then working from the known interior angle sum of 180°.

*What insights, connections, or applications might students **discover**?*

- To tessellate, polygons must fit around a single point.
- Fitting around that point depends upon the size of the interior angles.
- The sum of the angles around the point of polygons that actually tessellate will always be 360°.
- Patterns developed with tessellating polygons are symmetrical and can be aesthetically pleasing.
- For the tessellations to work, the polygons should be regular, with all sides and interior angles equal.

What extensions can you make?

Have students work with combinations of two or more polygons to create semiregular tessellations. Keep a record of the combinations that tessellate and record the angles that fit around each point. Choose a pattern and create a full-page multicolor tessellation.

57 Tangram Conundrum*

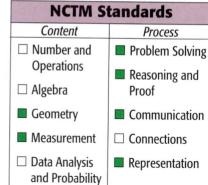

Overview

There are 9 ways to form a square from a set of 7 tangram pieces. The conundrum focuses not on one of the 9 ways but on something that does not work: Why can we not form a square with 6 tangram pieces? To solve the conundrum, students need to understand the properties of a square and also the properties of the tangram pieces they use to form squares. They need to discover the 9 ways to make a square with the pieces and then discover and find an explanation for the inability to form a square with 6 pieces.

Grade Levels 7–8

NCTM Standards	
Content	*Process*
☐ Number and Operations	■ Problem Solving
☐ Algebra	■ Reasoning and Proof
■ Geometry	■ Communication
■ Measurement	☐ Connections
☐ Data Analysis and Probability	■ Representation

Activity

What ideas or concepts will students explore?
- Area and perimeter
- Spatial relationships
- Squares and square roots

What materials will you need?
sets of tangrams duplicated on card stock in the shape of square (see "Pattern: Tangrams" in the Make Manipulatives section of the CD-ROM that accompanies this text) • pencils, paper • rulers • scissors

What will you do?
Talk about the tangram puzzle. Explain its origin in ancient China, its popularity as a pastime among prominent historical figures such as Napoleon, and the more than 1,600 shapes that can be made with the 7 pieces. Then focus on the square.

What questions could you ask?
What makes a square a square?
How might one square differ from another square—Square A with sides a centimeter long from Square B with sides a meter long?
How many squares can you make with the 7 tangram pieces?
How would you show that each of your arrangements of pieces is a true square?
The conundrum: Why can't you make a square with 6 pieces? What do we mean when we talk about the area and the perimeter of a square? How would you find them? How might the area and perimeter of a square differ from those of a rectangle?

---

*For more about the tangram conundrum, see Thatcher, Debra H., "The Tangram Conundrum," *Mathematics Teaching in the Middle School* (March 2001): 394–99.

What will students do?

Begin by cutting the printed tangram puzzle into its 7 pieces. Then re-form the square for a "freebie," the first of the 9 squares you will make. As you form each square, draw it with all the pieces on paper and explain briefly why each square is a square.

After you have formed all 9 squares, tackle the conundrum: why a square cannot be formed with 6 pieces. First, you will need to discover for yourselves that it cannot be by trying a variety of combinations. Then when you are convinced that the statement is true, you can look for an explanation.

What strategies might students invent or construct?

Students might proceed systematically, making squares with 1, 2, 3, and so forth pieces, or work at random, looking at the pieces and experimenting until they find the combination that forms a square. To answer the conundrum, they might explore area and perimeter of the squares. Some will use rule measurements; others might identify the smallest triangle as a unit and describe the other tans in terms of multiples of that unit. To prove that 6 tans cannot form a square, they might try a variety of combinations or work with area numbers.

What insights, connections, or applications might students discover?

- The area of a square can be expressed by squaring numbers; the perimeter, by multiplying sides by 4.
- If you work with the smallest triangle as a unit, all squares can be described in terms of powers of 2.

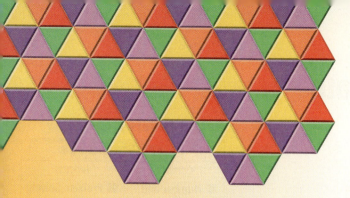

Algebraic Thinking

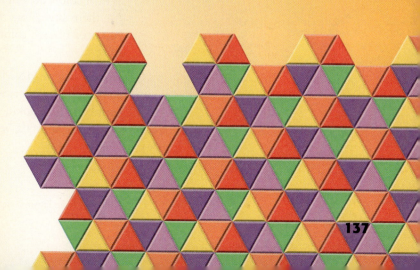

58 More M&M Math*

Grade Levels K–2

NCTM Standards	
Content	*Process*
☑ Number and Operations	☑ Problem Solving
	☐ Reasoning and Proof
☑ Algebra	
☐ Geometry	☑ Communication
☐ Measurement	☐ Connections
☐ Data Analysis and Probability	☑ Representation

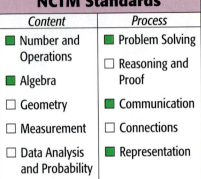

Overview

M&Ms are a favorite edible manipulative. Students are immediately engaged when they work with the candies, and the colors make them excellent subjects for sorting and graphing. This activity goes beyond counting and basic number operations. Students write equations and explore equivalencies.

Activity

What ideas or concepts will students explore?
- Sorting by color
- Counting
- Graphing
- Writing equations
- Exploring equivalencies

What materials will you need?
bags of M&Ms for each student • crayons • "M&Ms Worksheet 1" and "M&Ms Worksheet 2" in the Worksheets & Handouts section of the CD-ROM that accompanies this text • materials for making M&M equation booklets: colored paper, copies of circle equations for addition and subtraction, stapler (see illustration later in this activity)

What questions could you ask?
How many M&Ms are in your bag?
How many different colors do you find?
Which colors do you have more of? Which less?
Are there any colors that have equal numbers? How many more would you need of each color to make the numbers equal?

What will you do?
Open a bag of M&Ms. Hold up candies and have students identify the colors. Draw a chart with columns for each color. Put the candies from your bag on a napkin. Have students count the candies of each color. As they arrive at totals, write the number on the chart.

---

*Adapted from lessons taught by Louie Anaya

Make M&M equation booklets for each student. Begin by drawing circle equations for addition and subtraction:

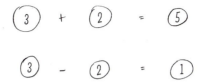

Copy one equation on colored paper to make a cover. Then make several copies of the addition and subtraction equations for booklet pages. Fasten with a stapler. Have students write their names on and decorate the booklet covers.

What will students do?

Activity A Hold and feel the bag of M&Ms and estimate the number of candies. Open the bag and sort candies by color. Then count the number of each color and write the numbers on "M&Ms Worksheet 1." Use crayons and the numbers from the worksheet to fill in the color graph on "M&Ms Worksheet 2." Compare numbers to see which color has the most, which the least. (The worksheets can be found on the CD-ROM that accompanies this text.)

Activity B Use "M&Ms Worksheet 1" as a guide to writing and solving your own M&M equations. Begin by adding the total number of orange M&Ms to the total number of blue M&Ms. For each equation use crayons to draw the problem in your equation book and then write it in numbers. Write three original equations. Work back and forth by turning around addition problems to make subtraction problems—for example, subtracting 5 blue M&Ms from the 12 total orange and blue M&Ms to get 7 orange M&Ms.

*What strategies might students **invent** or construct?*

Some students use crayons to underline the names of colors to help them make the correct match. Many use their M&Ms as place savers on the graph sheet, lining them up by color and then removing them one by one as they color in the circles. Most model their equations first with M&Ms and then draw, count, and write the equations in their M&Ms equations booklet.

*What insights, connections, or applications might students **discover**?*

- You can read more, less, or equal amounts from a bar graph without counting the number of M&Ms in each row.
- The answers for addition equations can be found by counting all of the M&Ms or by counting on from the first number.
- The answers for subtraction equations can be found by counting out the total in M&Ms and then taking away the number to be subtracted and counting what's left.
- With an equation you can work backwards or forwards to find totals from amounts added or amounts from totals.

What extensions can you make?   Have students work in pairs or groups, pooling their M&Ms for larger quantities. Students can take turns creating and solving M&M equations and explaining their thinking. Extend the worksheet questions to apply to the team or group, asking questions such as, "Who has the most orange M&Ms? Who has the least? Which color do most students have the most of?"

# Making and Guessing Patterns*

Overview

Grade Levels 1–3

NCTM Standards	
Content	*Process*
☑ Number and Operations	☑ Problem Solving
☑ Algebra	☑ Reasoning and Proof
☐ Geometry	☑ Communication
☐ Measurement	☐ Connections
☐ Data Analysis and Probability	☑ Representation

The auditory and movement dimensions of this activity (clapping, music notes, dance movements) make this a good activity for students whose learning styles emphasize sound and actions. Finding and representing patterns in a variety of ways encourages students to think flexibly and to look at patterns from a variety of perspectives. Representing the patterns with colors and shapes provides a crossover for art projects.

Activity

*What ideas or concepts will students **explore**?*

- Patterns: AB, ABC, AAB, AABB
- Functions
- Representing patterns with shapes, colors, sounds, movements, letters, and numbers

What materials will you need?

construction paper • scissors • colored tiles, pattern blocks, Cuisenaire rods, Unifix cubes, connecting disks, other manipulatives

What questions could you ask?

What is alike in the pattern? What is different?
What comes next in the pattern? Before?
How many patterns can you find in the classroom? How do you know they are patterns?
Can you hear, see, feel the patterns?

What will you do?

Demonstrate AB, ABC, AAB, AABB patterns by clapping, snapping, and stomping; by performing dance or exercise steps; by using colored tiles and other manipulatives; and by drawing shapes and writing letters on the white board. Form a variety of patterns with manipulatives, and ask students to identify and duplicate the patterns.

---

*Adapted from lessons taught by Amy Johnston

What will students do?

Activity A Identify and repeat patterns as you hear, see, and feel them; recognize that the same pattern can be represented with sounds (clapping), shapes, colors, and letters. Then create patterns using construction paper and die-cut shapes. Make one AB pattern, one AAB pattern, and one other. Share and explain the patterns.

Activity B In pairs, play "Guess My Pattern." Take turns making and guessing patterns with a variety of manipulatives. To encourage multiple perspectives, change the type of manipulative used every 5–10 minutes. Keep a record of the patterns made and those correctly guessed. Discuss why those missed may have presented difficulties.

What strategies might students ***invent*** *or construct?*

Some students will use the pattern labels (AB, AAB, and so forth) to keep patterns on track. Others will use colors to emphasize patterns in shape and designs. They might verify a manipulatives pattern by continuing it or by writing it out in letters.

What insights, connections, or applications might students ***discover***?

- Patterns are a way to organize and order items.
- The same pattern can be repeated in sounds, shapes, colors, letters, and objects. Once you have identified a pattern, you can continue it indefinitely.
- Patterns are all around us.

What extensions can you make?

Have students listen to and try to repeat patterns in popular and classical music. Identify and discuss the patterns in art, such as a Greek frieze or a Native American pottery design.

60 Pictographs*

Grade Levels 2–5

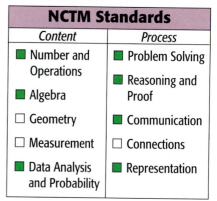

NCTM Standards	
Content	*Process*
■ Number and Operations	■ Problem Solving
■ Algebra	■ Reasoning and Proof
☐ Geometry	■ Communication
☐ Measurement	☐ Connections
■ Data Analysis and Probability	■ Representation

Overview

Representing quantities with pictures works at several levels. For very young students, it helps them connect number totals with things and groups of things. For older students, it fosters symbolizing and even multiplicative thinking. The activity can be done with pencil and paper or on a computer screen with clip art or other shapes and pictures.

Activity

*What ideas or concepts will students **explore**?*

- Tables
- Representing data with pictures
- Varying numerical value of pictures
- Collecting and analyzing data

What materials will you need?

pencil and paper to gather survey information and make tallies • for younger students: "Apple Pictograph Worksheet" in the Worksheets & Handouts section of the CD-ROM that accompanies this text • crayons • for older students: computer with clip art and graphics program and "McDonald's Farm Worksheet" in the Worksheets & Handouts section of the CD-ROM

What questions could you ask?

What does it mean when we say, "A picture is worth a thousand words"?
How is a pictograph like a picture? How is it different?
What does the graph key tell us?
How does a pictograph table help us make sense of information?

What will you do?

Do a whole-class pictograph activity. Ask students what their favorite breakfasts are: cereal, eggs and bacon, yogurt, pizza, and so forth. Then vote and do a tally chart on the favorites, using pictures or drawings as pictographs. Start with one-to-one relationships; then ask, "If one picture equals two people, then how many pictures would I put for six?"

---

*Adapted from lessons taught by Victoria Newcomm and Rand Barker

143

What will students do? **Activity A** (Younger Students) As a class, vote on and make a tally of students' favorite ways to eat apples: applesauce, juice, apple pie, caramel, or plain. Then individually make a pictograph table, using the "Apple Pictograph Worksheet," to show the result of the vote. Work with one-to-one relationships: one apple for one person's vote. (See the example below.)

Pictograph: Yummy apples

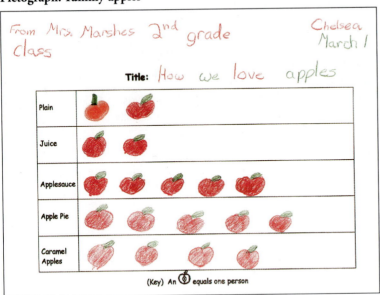

Activity B (Younger Students) Survey 20 people (classmates, teachers, aides, family members and so forth) to find out their favorite animal. Keep a tally sheet with the choices and votes. Once the survey is complete, use pictographs to show the results. Work with one-to-two relationships: one animal for two votes. Share and discuss the pictographs.

Activity C (Older Students) Work on the computer to construct a pictograph to show who lived on Old McDonald's Farm. Begin with the organizing table on the "McDonald's Farm Worksheet." Then use the computer to make the pictograph. Work with a one-to-four relationship: one picture for four animals. (See the example illustrated later in this activity.)

*What strategies might students **invent** or construct?* Students might use counters to help them organize the tables, using a counter as a placeholder for one or more pictures to be included in the graph. Working with the one-to-two relationship (Activity B), some start with enough counters for a one-to-one pictograph and then take away every other counter. Younger students typically ignore the remainders when results are uneven, but older students look for ways to show a half or a fourth—for example, making only part of a picture.

Pictograph: Old McDonald's Farm

COW		Key: each picture represents 4 animals or 4 people.
horses		
dogs		
cats		
cowboys		

*What insights, connections, or applications might students **discover**?*

- Without a key it is difficult to read a pictograph.
- Using multiples instead of one-to-one relationships can make the pictograph easier to read at a glance without the need to stop and count the pictures.
- A pictograph shows number totals and relationships effectively—which has most, least, about the same, and so forth. Changing from one relationship to another is simply a matter of multiplying or dividing.

61

Writing Story Problem Equations*

Overview

Asked what they liked least about math, a group of adults answered, "Word problems!" Demystifying word problems calls for a special approach. In this activity students model the quantities and relationships described in word problems directly with counters. Then they put the problems into their own words and write their own word problems. The result is an inside-out instead of an outside-in approach to the mathematical situations presented in word problems.

Grade Levels 1–3

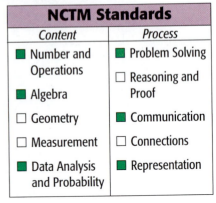

NCTM Standards	
Content	*Process*
■ Number and Operations	■ Problem Solving
■ Algebra	☐ Reasoning and Proof
☐ Geometry	■ Communication
☐ Measurement	☐ Connections
■ Data Analysis and Probability	■ Representation

Activity

*What ideas or concepts will students **explore**?*

- Writing equations
- Representing with pictures, words, and numbers
- Combining and separating

What materials will you need?

pencils • paper • counters • computers with clip-art software or other pictures

What questions could you ask?

How many ways can you show the number _____?
How can you use counters to set up the situation described in the story problem?
What in the story problem tells you to combine?
What in the story problem tells you to separate?

What will students do?

Listen as the teacher reads aloud the story problems:

> The other day I was watching some birds at the park. I saw 5 on one tree branch; then 2 more birds flew over and landed on the same branch.

> I was walking in the park, and I saw some squirrels playing together. There were 9 squirrels; then 4 got scared and ran away.

Activity A Retell the stories in your own words. Give the order of events. Model the events with counters; then show the problem and the solution with drawings and a number sentence or equation. Explain your problem-solving process in writing.

---

*Adapted from lessons taught by Amy Johnston

!!!!!! IMPORTANT — PLEASE READ !!!!!!

e quality of this book is not up to normal B&T Books standards,

_____ This is the best copy available

_____ This is an imported book and difficult to obtain.

erefore, we are supplying it in this condition for your inspection —
ase feel free to return it to us if it is unacceptable.

— ALERT —

Activity B Write story problems involving combining and separating. Model the problems with counters. Then show the problems in pictures, and write an equation to solve them. Share the problems and solutions. (See the example illustrated below.)

*What strategies might students **invent** or construct?*

Some students will work directly from the counters to numbers; others, from counters to drawings to numbers. Younger students frequently use a variation of the teacher's story problems ("I went to the park, and I saw. . . .") rather than create new situations. Older students often work backwards as well as forwards in the problem-creating and problem-solving process, starting with the answer and manipulating numbers to fit.

*What insights, connections, or applications might students **discover**?*

- You can write the same problem in different ways.
- An equation is a sentence written in numbers and symbols.
- A problem that involves combining results in more; a problem that involves separating results in less. Putting what you do into words can help you think the problem through and find errors.

"At the Beach" story problem

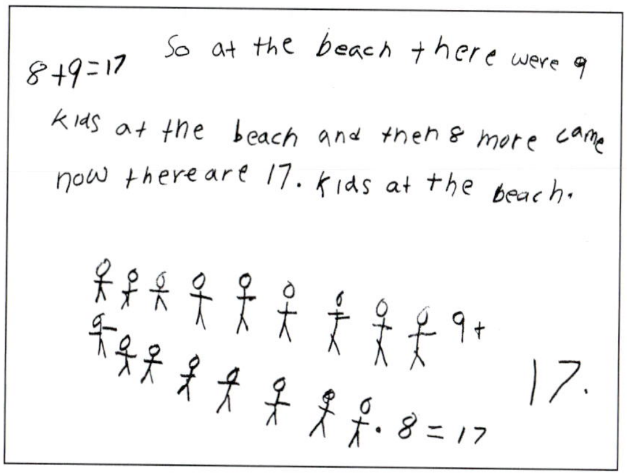

$8 + 9 = 17$ So at the beach there were 9 kids at the beach and then 8 more came now there are 17. kids at the beach.

$9 + 8 = 17$

$17.$

What extensions can you make?

Give students several equations, including equations with place savers or symbols. Have them write their own story problems to fit the equations; then model the problem-solving process with clip art or images on the computer.

62 The Pool Problem*

Grade Levels K–6

NCTM Standards	
Content	*Process*
■ Number and Operations	■ Problem Solving
■ Algebra	■ Reasoning and Proof
■ Geometry	■ Communication
■ Measurement	■ Connections
☐ Data Analysis and Probability	■ Representation

Overview

The pool activities work at a variety of levels. They combine geometry with measurement since students are working with area and squaring. They involve number operations and patterns. Students work hands-on to model the pool designs with blue and white tiles. They represent their models with drawings and also use tables to organize information and help them identify patterns. Versions of the investigations are adapted for students in various grade levels, with older students often starting with tasks designed for younger students and building on what they discover as a foundation for the more complex tasks.

Activity

What ideas or concepts will students *explore*?

- Patterns and functions
- Sorting by color
- Counting by 4s, 5s, and so forth
- Squares and squaring
- Fractions
- Tables and graphs

What materials will you need?

blue and white square tiles • pencils and paper • calculators • graph paper • "Pool Problem," illustrated later in this activity

What questions could you ask?

How many blue and white tiles are there in Pool 1, Pool 2, and Pool 3? What patterns do you see?

How many blue and white tiles would there be in Pools 4, 5, and 6?

How can you be sure the pools are squares?

For how many of the pools are there more white tiles than blue? More blue tiles than white?

As the size of the pools increases, how does the number of blue tiles increase? The number of white tiles?

---

*Adapted from Joan Ferrini-Mundy, Glenda Lappan, and Elizabeth Phillips, "Experiences with Patterning," in *Algebraic Thinking, Grades K–12,* edited by Barbara Moses (Reston, VA: NCTM, 1999), 112–19.

What will you do? Use an overhead to introduce the problem. Show how to use the blue and white tiles to create a model of a pool; then ask questions to encourage students to explore the problem from a variety of perspectives, including geometry, basic operations, and so forth.

What will students do? **Activity A** (Grades K–2) Sort the tiles by color: blue for the pool and white for the border. Count the number of blue and white tiles. Build the three pools shown in the problem. Count the number of blue and white tiles in each pool. Talk about the square shape of the pools and how the shape affects the number of blue and white tiles. Predict the number of tiles needed for Pool 4; then check the prediction by building the pool with tiles.

Activity B (Grades 3–4) Use tiles to make models of the first three pools. Record the data in a table. Look for patterns in the relationships of blue to white tiles and in the increases of blue and white tiles from Pool 1 to Pool 3. Represent the patterns in terms of fractions or proportions. Use the patterns identified to predict data about the next three pools. Explore the relationship between the pool squares and squaring numbers. Find the point when the increases in white tiles are exceeded by the increases in blue tiles.

Activity C (Grades 5–6) Construct a table to show the number of blue and white tiles for the first six square pools. Identify variables in the problem and describe their relationships. Make graphs to show the increases in blue and white pools. Predict the numbers of blue and white tiles in the 10th, 25th, and 100th pools.

What strategies might students _invent_ or construct? Most students will use the tiles to model only the smaller pools and then use the patterns they identify to predict the size and composition of larger pools. Some will emphasize addition and multiplication in their explanations; others will develop geometric explanations. Many students discover and demonstrate with tiles the relationship between squares and squaring numbers.

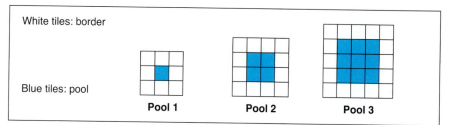

Pool Problem: Identify the pattern for building square swimming pools of blue tiles with a border of white tiles. Then use the pattern to find out how many blue and white tiles you will need to make larger pools.

Source: Adapted from Joan Ferrini-Mundy, Glenda Lappan, and Elizabeth Phillips, "Experiences with Patterning," in *Algebraic Thinking: (Grades K–12*, edited by Barbara Moses (Reston, VA: NCTM, 1999), 13.

*What insights, connections, or applications might students **discover**?*

- The increases in blue and white tiles follow regular but different patterns.
- Once you have identified the pattern in the three smallest pools, you can predict the number of blue and white tiles in larger pools.
- Starting with the fifth pool, there will be more blue tiles than white tiles.
- Squaring is a numerical way to describe geometric squares.
- Tables help organize data and make it easier to see the patterns.

What extensions can you make?

Have students create their own pool design; model the design with tiles or drawings and predict the increases in tiles or size for larger pools.

63 Patterns and Functions*

Grade Levels 2–3

NCTM Standards	
Content	*Process*
☐ Number and Operations	■ Problem Solving
■ Algebra	■ Reasoning and Proof
☐ Geometry	☐ Communication
☐ Measurement	☐ Connections
☐ Data Analysis and Probability	■ Representation

Overview

Students develop an understanding of patterns by identifying and making them. They look for relationships that can be expressed with numbers and for patterns expressed by numbers. The functionator box (described later in this activity) can be used as a game, with students keeping track of their answers and scores.

Activity

What ideas or concepts will students explore?
- Patterns, including dot patterns
- Functions
- T-charts
- Doubling and other multiples

What materials will you need?
overhead projector and transparency examples of dot patterns • "T-Chart Worksheet" in the Worksheets & Handouts section of the CD-ROM that accompanies this text • functionator box: box with two holes, one labeled "This goes in," the other labeled "This comes out" • number cards

What questions could you ask?
What is a pattern?
How can you tell when dots or numbers form a pattern?
Can you write rules to describe patterns?
What comes next? How do you know?

What will you do?
Using the overhead, show examples of dot patterns. Draw dot patterns and have students continue them. Draw a t-chart. Explain why it is called a t-chart and how it can help us find patterns and functions. Make and demonstrate the use of the functionator box. Show what happens when you put a number such as 2 in one side and then pull out a number such as 4.

---

*Adapted from lessons taught by Amy Johnston

What will students do? **Activity A** Complete dot patterns begun on the overhead; then make and continue an original dot pattern. Explain the patterns. Complete the chart begun on the overhead; then continue with the worksheet.

Activity B Take turns putting numbers into the functionator and pushing numbers out the other side. As a group guess the functions that explain the change of the first number to the second.

What strategies might students ***invent*** *or construct?*

Students may use counting and repeated addition and subtraction strategies to identify and continue patterns, or they might multiply and divide. To create t-charts, some will rely on calculators to find and check multiples. In the functionator activity, students might draw on basic operations for functions or emphasize counting by 2s, 4s, and so forth as well as doubling and tripling or halving and quartering.

What insights, connections, or applications might students ***discover***?

- Your eye can often see a pattern before you can explain or describe it.
- There may be more than one way to explain a relationship between numbers; for example, the relationship of 2 and 4 might be addition (2 + 2) or multiplication (2 × 2) and so forth.
- T-charts can help you "see" a relationship so that you can describe it.

64 Anno's Magic Seeds*

Overview

Grade Levels 3–5

NCTM Standards	
Content	*Process*
■ Number and Operations	■ Problem Solving
■ Algebra	■ Reasoning and Proof
☐ Geometry	■ Communication
☐ Measurement	■ Connections
☐ Data Analysis and Probability	■ Representation

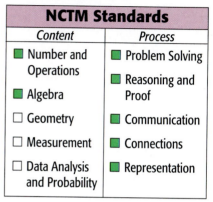

The magic in Mitsumasa Anno's story *Anno's Magic Seeds* is the magic of mathematics. The story presents an imaginative context for exploring variables and number patterns. Students can do the math as the story progresses and then continue working with and representing the mathematical situations in graphs and diagrams.

Activity

What ideas or concepts will students explore?

- Variables
- Representing with graphs and diagrams
- Doubling patterns
- Basic operations

What materials will you need?

Mitsumasa Anno's *Anno's Magic Seeds.* (New York: Philomel, 1995)
• beans • calculators • pencils • blank paper • graph paper

What questions could you ask?

What happened to the number of seeds when Jack ate one and planted one? What happened when he planted both seeds? When he planted three and ate one?

How many plants and seeds did Jack have at the beginning? How many at the end of the book?

What would have happened if Jack had never eaten any of the seeds but had planted them all?

What will you do?

Read the story aloud. Use beans to demonstrate and talk about the concept of doubling. Introduce the idea of the variable.

What will students do?

Listen and use pencil and paper or a calculator to keep track of the changes in the number of seeds as the story progresses. Compare results and check the book to settle any differences.

---

*Adapted from a lesson by Vicky McMath

Use beans to model doubling, and create a graph to show the concept. Then use beans to model the modified doubling plan in the story (2 beans, subtract 1, double 1; 3 beans, subtract 1, double 2, and so forth). Create a branching tree diagram, graph, or other representation to show the pattern of increase in the story.

*What strategies might students **invent** or construct?*

Students using calculators to keep track of the changing number of beans may also write the numbers on paper as a record of their calculations. Some use the beans as counters; others use a tally-mark method. Most students will describe the pattern in words; some, in mathematical sentences.

*What insights, connections, or applications might students **discover**?*

- When Jack eats half his crop, the number of seeds doesn't change from year to year; when he plants all of the seeds or more than he eats, the number increases.
- The rate of increase may stay the same, but the total amount doesn't.
- Doubling can be represented by adding the same number twice or by multiplying by 2.
- Graphs show how the increases jump when Jack plants more than he eats.

What extensions can you make?

Give students the classic problem of choosing a doubling penny or $1,000,000.

65 Playing Algebra with Equate

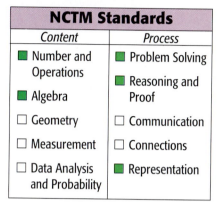

Overview

The game Equate is an equation-style version of Scrabble. Students work with tiles on a board. They form equations to win points, gaining double or triple scores if their equation tiles are placed on specific, marked squares on the board. The game has students apply what they already know about writing equations but also develop new skills as they work with tiles and the equations already on the board to gain a maximum number of points.

Grade Levels 5–8

NCTM Standards	
Content	*Process*
■ Number and Operations	■ Problem Solving
■ Algebra	■ Reasoning and Proof
☐ Geometry	☐ Communication
☐ Measurement	☐ Connections
☐ Data Analysis and Probability	■ Representation

Activity

What ideas or concepts will students explore?

- Equations
- Basic operations
- Fractions
- Variables

What materials will you need?

Classroom set of Equate: The Equation Thinking Game by Conceptual Math Media (www.PlayEquate.com) • overhead projector, with demonstration transparency and tiles • tally sheets and pencils for scoring

What questions could you ask?

What does "equals" mean?
What is an equation?
How many different equations can you make with the numbers 2, 2, and 4? With the numbers _____, _____, and _____?
Who knows how to play Scrabble? How are numbers involved in playing Scrabble?
Can you think of a way to turn Scrabble into a math game?

What will you do?

Use the board transparency to show how to set up horizontal and vertical equations and how to determine the score for each equation. Explain the difference between the 2S and 3S (two- and three-times symbol scores) and the 2E and 3E (two- and three-times equation scores). Explain how to use high-scoring tiles, such as fractions, to achieve larger scores.

What will students do?   Individually, practice making equations from the Equate tiles. Draw a game hand of 9 tiles and select equals tiles as needed. In groups, discuss the equations. Look for any way to use a player's hand to achieve a higher score. (Conceptual Math Media also produces tear-apart strips of paper tiles that can be used in a make-all-the-equations activity.)

In groups of four, play the Equate game. For younger students, the game can use basic-operations tiles; for older students, fractions, variables, and exponents. For a cooperative learning experience, students can play in teams.

What strategies might students *invent* or construct?   Some students will create simple number sentences; others will try for more complicated equations to achieve higher scores. Once they understand the value of the multiple S and E squares, students will develop strategies to position their highest-scoring tiles on those squares. Although the game can be competitive, many students encourage each other by helping create equations and looking for ways to use high-scoring tiles.

What insights, connections, or applications might students *discover*?
- An equation can be worked with from several directions—beginning, middle, end.
- Equations can involve several operations and combine whole numbers, fractions, and variables.
- The same set of tiles can result in a variety of equations.

66 Equivalence

Grade Levels K–8

NCTM Standards	
Content	*Process*
☐ Number and Operations	🟩 Problem Solving
🟩 Algebra	🟩 Reasoning and Proof
☐ Geometry	🟩 Communication
🟩 Measurement	🟩 Connections
☐ Data Analysis and Probability	🟩 Representation

Overview

NCTM's math investigations (part of the Illuminations e-resource) give students hands-on experience with the basic ideas of balance and equivalence. The website uses balance scales to weigh and compare objects and expressions. Different levels of investigation are provided for students in different grade strands.

Activity

*What ideas or concepts will students **explore**?*

- Equivalence and balance
- Numerical expressions
- Symbolic expressions

What materials will you need?

Equivalence i-Math investigation from NCTM's website (http://illuminations.nctm.org) • computer with Internet access • copies of worksheets from site • pan balances and objects for balancing for each small group

What questions could you ask?

What do you learn when things balance?
Can you tell by looking at something whether it will balance on the scales? Why or why not?
How is balance related to equivalence?
What happens if we look at equations as balances with the equal sign in the middle?
How many 2-inch squares would it take to balance a 4-inch square?
Can you balance variables? How?

What will you do?

Begin with a demonstration of balance and equivalence. Use a balance to show how to determine weight equivalence. Then introduce the idea of a virtual balance. As a class, try balancing objects using the virtual pan balance at the NCTM website. Answer some of the worksheet questions together.

What will students do?   **Activity A** Work in small groups with a set of pan balances for each group. Explore balancing like and unlike objects. Keep a record of findings to share with the class.

Activity B Individually or in teams, explore equivalence with the NCTM website virtual balances. Begin with the Balancing Act and compare weights of different collections of objects. Continue with Stability in Numbers to investigate the equivalence of numeric expressions. Older and advanced students may also do Extending to Symbols, which extends the investigation to symbolic expressions, and Exploring Equations Further, which investigates equivalence and systems of equations. For each section of the i-Math investigation, complete the accompanying worksheet and answer the questions.

What strategies might students ***invent*** *or construct?*   Most students will use guess-and-test. They will model the problems with the virtual balance and record their findings on the worksheets. As the investigation progresses, some will find that, after one or two tests, they can supply answers without actually testing expressions on the balance. Some students will need to work through all the problems; others will understand the concept well enough after a few experiments to make generalizations and draw conclusions.

What insights, connections, or applications might students ***discover***?
- Balance can apply to shape, weight, numbers, or symbols.
- You may need to work with both sides of an equation to achieve equivalence.
- Balance might be achieved with one object, number, or symbol or with a combination of different objects, numbers, and symbols.
- There may be a variety of answers for each problem.

67 Golden Rectangle

Grade Levels 6–8

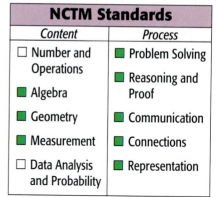

NCTM Standards	
Content	*Process*
☐ Number and Operations	■ Problem Solving
■ Algebra	■ Reasoning and Proof
■ Geometry	■ Communication
■ Measurement	■ Connections
☐ Data Analysis and Probability	■ Representation

Overview

Tying ratio and proportion to what students can see and measure helps make the abstract concepts concrete and real. Tying the golden rectangle to young people's values—such as the desire to be personally attractive or judgments about attractiveness in others—provides a context that many will find meaningful. The activity uses literature, art, history, and hands-on measurements to explore the relationship of proportion and aesthetic factors such as symmetry.

Activity

What ideas or concepts will students *explore*?

- Ratio and proportion, decimal and fraction numbers
- Geometry of rectangles and squares
- Variables
- Measurement

What materials will you need?

measuring tape • calculators • 46″ length of cardboard or paper • butcher paper and markers • Theoni Pappas's story "Penrose and the Golden Rectangle," from *Fractals, Googols and Other Mathematical Tales* (San Carlos, CA: Wide World Publishing/Tetra, 1993)

What questions could you ask?

Why would the Greeks call a rectangle "golden"?
How common are rectangles in the world around you?
How can we measure rectangles to find out if they are golden?
If we have a small golden rectangle, how can we make a large one?
What is the difference between a golden rectangle and an everyday rectangle?
Could any other polygons show the golden ratio?

What will students do?

Study examples from art of the golden rectangle—for example, pictures of the Parthenon or of the work of Phidias, da Vinci, Bellows, and others who used golden rectangles to create dynamic symmetry.

Activity A Working in small groups, find rectangles in the everyday world. Measure the rectangles, either directly or indirectly, to see if any are golden rectangles.

Activity B Read "Penrose and the Golden Rectangle." Follow the author's instructions on page 46 to make a golden rectangle without computing the proportions. Start with a cutout square. Draw around it. Fold the square in half. Align the half-square with the drawn square. Draw around it. The square plus the half-square is a golden rectangle. Check the measurements with a ruler and compute the ratio with a calculator.

Activity C Solve this puzzle:

> Artists often use the golden rectangle because it is considered to be pleasing to the eye. The length of a golden rectangle is about 1.62 times its width. Suppose you are making a picture frame in the shape of a golden rectangle. You have a 46-inch piece of wood. What are the length and width of the largest frame you can make? [From *Algebra: Tools for a Changing World* (Upper Saddle River, NJ: Prentice Hall, 1997), 193; quoted in Yvelyne Germain-McCarthy, *Bringing the NCTM Standards to Life* (Larchmont, NY: Eye on Education, 2001), 63.]

Activity D Use a tape measure to look for golden rectangles in body proportions. "Measure two distances, the first being the measure of the distance from the head to the navel, and the second being the measure of the distance from the navel to the feet. . . . Use the first result for the numerator of the fraction, and the second for the denominator. Determine how close the result is to 1.62 or to having a *divinely proportional body*" (Germain-McCarthy 2001, 66).

*What strategies might students **invent** or construct?*

Some students will use a trial-and-error approach as they search for and construct golden rectangles. Others will compute first and then construct. Students may work individually or in groups. Problem solving might be represented with drawings, models, or calculations.

*What insights, connections, or applications might students **discover**?*

- Golden rectangles are everywhere—in art, architecture, nature, and everyday objects.
- A golden rectangle is one and a half squares.
- To solve the problem in Activity C, you need to work with the idea of a perimeter of 46 inches.
- Proportion can be shown as a decimal or a fraction.
- The exact measurements can change in a golden rectangle, but the proportion stays the same.

Working with Data

68 Mini Gardens*

Grade Levels K–2

NCTM Standards	
Content	Process
■ Number and Operations	■ Problem Solving
□ Algebra	□ Reasoning and Proof
□ Geometry	■ Communication
■ Measurement	■ Connections
■ Data Analysis and Probability	■ Representation

Overview

Growing things have a special fascination for children. Even a small garden lets them discover the magic of planting seeds and watching tiny seedlings break through the soil. This activity provides some structure for their observations. Students learn the importance of mathematics in gardening as they count seeds, make schedules for watering, and assess and represent results.

Activity

What ideas or concepts will students explore?

- Collecting and recording data
- Reading and recording time and temperature
- Displaying data with drawings and graphs

What materials will you need?

packets of garden seeds • trays with planting soil • water, sunlight • garden journals (construction paper for cover, split pages for illustrating and writing) • crayons, markers, pencils • chart with pictures of seeds in packet • toothpicks with labels for each type of seed

What questions could you ask?

How many seeds do you think there are in your packet? How many different kinds?

How many days do you think it will take for your seeds to grow? Do you think they will grow all at once or come up at different times? Why?

What should you look for as you wait for your seeds to grow?

How can you keep track of their progress?

What effect do you think the temperature will have on your seeds?

*Adapted from a lesson taught by Mary Speer

What will students do? Estimate the number of seeds in the packet; then count the seeds and compare the total to the estimate. Organize the seeds by kind. Record the number of each kind of seed.

Make a garden journal. Use construction paper for the cover and decorate with designs or drawings. Use split sheets (half blank, half lined) for journal pages. Draw a plan for the mini garden on the first page of the journal. Then plant the seeds. Mark the seeds with toothpick signs showing the names of the seeds.

Plant and water the garden. Keep the soil moist until the seeds sprout. In the journal, record the date, temperature, and your estimates of which seeds will sprout first. Draw the seeds to show progress. When all of the seeds have sprouted, make a graph to show how many days each type of seed took to grow. (See illustration below.)

Shanyn's garden log.

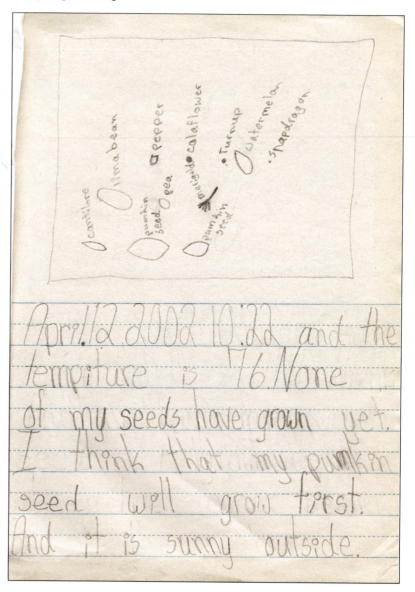

*What strategies might students **invent** or construct?*

Some students will plant in clusters; others will organize in rows. A few will want to dig up their seeds to check on their progress. Reading and recording temperatures and dates may be a challenge at first, but, once modeled, most will follow the examples consistently. Most will also base their estimate of the seeds that will sprout first on size, assuming that the bigger the seed, the greater its headstart on sprouting.

*What insights, connections, or applications might students **discover**?*

- Having an organizational plan helps us keep track of subjects and structure data collection.
- Data needs to be collected every day. Collecting data, such as temperatures, at the same time gives a better basis for comparison.

69 Collecting Data in Our Worlds

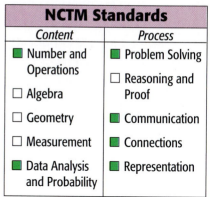

Grade Levels K–4

NCTM Standards	
Content	*Process*
■ Number and Operations	■ Problem Solving
□ Algebra	□ Reasoning and Proof
□ Geometry	■ Communication
□ Measurement	■ Connections
■ Data Analysis and Probability	■ Representation

Overview

Students discover that there are data everywhere in their worlds. They take the first steps toward being junior statisticians as they pose a research question and then do frequency counts. They take the next steps as they explore ways to represent the data they collected and then look for ways to sum up and interpret their findings.

Activity

What ideas or concepts will students *explore*?
- Collecting, organizing, and counting data
- Displaying data in graphs and drawings
- Finding patterns and drawing conclusions from data

What materials will you need?
tally sheets • counters or "Pattern: Counters" in the Making Manipulatives section of the CD-ROM that accompanies this text • paper, pencils • crayons or markers

What questions could you ask?
What do you see that can you count?
What kinds of things can you count?
Are there any kinds of things that you cannot count? Is there some other way that you can describe those things with numbers?
How about opinions? Is there some way you can count them? Or actions—things people do?
How many different ways can you think of to show something you have counted and collected data for?

What will students do? **Activity A** Choose something countable that you see every day and would like to collect data about (for example, trees, flowers, clothes classmates wear, backpacks, street signs, cars). Use a tally sheet to organize and tally information about what you see. Count and show the results in a bar graph.

165

Activity B Explore favorite things. Compose a question such as "What is your favorite pet? Food? Song? Cartoon character? Holiday?" Make a tally sheet with categories and columns for numbers. Then survey people you know, tallying their responses. Count the tally marks and graph the results.

*What strategies might students **invent** or construct?*

Students often discover the importance of exclusive categories when they find overlapping data. Tallying one person or thing more than once (for example, marking a person once for hair color and again for gender) will give a total tally that is larger than the number surveyed. Students solve the problem by either eliminating the overlapping categories from their data or by making more than one graph. Some will leave categories up to those surveyed (for example, letting them name their favorite pets); others will make a list and ask specifically about items on that list.

*What insights, connections, or applications might students **discover**?*

- Data are everywhere, and we can collect data about almost anything.
- Data need to be organized to be understood.
- A good plan for collecting data avoids overlapping categories and double counting.
- Displaying data is important to helping people understand it.

70

Pigs Will Be Pigs:
Collecting Data
and Money*

Mathematics in Literature

Grade Levels 3–5

NCTM Standards	
Content	*Process*
■ Number and Operations	■ Problem Solving
☐ Algebra	■ Reasoning and Proof
☐ Geometry	■ Communication
☐ Measurement	■ Connections
■ Data Analysis and Probability	■ Representation

Overview

Amy Axelrod's story *Pigs Will Be Pigs* provides an engaging context for developing an important life skill: managing money. Students learn about budgeting, comparison shopping, and making monetary choices that affect the group. Operations include manipulating numbers and working with decimals in a base-10 money system.

Activity

What ideas or concepts will students explore?

- Adding lists of numbers
- Decimals in money numbers
- Computations with money
- Collecting data about money
- Using money to buy something

What materials will you need?

Amy Axelrod's story *Pigs Will Be Pigs* (New York: Harcourt Brace, 1994) • calculators • tally sheets • pencils • copies of Enchanted Enchilada menu (included in *Pigs Will Be Pigs*)

What will you do?

Lead a brainstorming session about the need for money to purchase necessities such as food. Read *Pigs Will Be Pigs* aloud. Go slowly, page by page, to give students time to make calculations and write down data.

What questions could you ask?

Have you ever needed or wanted something and didn't have money to pay for it? What did you do?

What is your favorite restaurant? How do you think the prices compare to those at the Enchanted Enchilada? Why might it be important to compare prices?

What's the best way to keep track of lists of coins and bills?

How would you design a tally chart to keep what the pigs find organized?

---

*Adapted from a lesson taught by Karen Elton

What will students do?

Activity A Develop a tally sheet to help the pigs organize and record the money they find. Make different vertical columns for each coin and each denomination of bill. As the story is read, tally the money found. You may also want to make horizontal columns to have a record of each place money is found. At the end of the book, figure out the amount of money in each vertical column. Then add to find the total amount the pigs have to spend.

Activity B Help the pigs spend their money. Study the Enchanted Enchilada menu. Figure out the cost if the pigs order four specials or order four different meals. Subtract the cost of the meal from the total amount the pigs found to discover how much they had left.

Activity C The pigs' refrigerator is still empty. With the money left from their meal, how much take-out can the pigs order to eat later at home?

*What strategies might students **invent** or construct?*

Some students will write actual amounts in the tally-sheet columns to create a money ledger. Later they will add the columns. Others will use tally marks and then multiply to find the amount for each coin and add those results. In helping the pigs order their meals, students often focus on economy, choosing the least expensive meal for all four pigs; others follow taste and vary the orders.

*What insights, connections, or applications might students **discover**?*

- Lack of money can be a serious problem when you are hungry.
- Sometimes people (and pigs) have to go without.
- In a group you should consider what's best for everyone, perhaps choosing something that is not your favorite in order to be sure everyone has a share.
- Misplacing a decimal when adding money has a major impact on the total.
- Lining up the columns for dollars and cents is also important.

What extensions can you make?

Extend the idea of comparison shopping. Use grocery ads or a trip to a market as an opportunity to collect data about food prices. Make lists of all the food the pigs could have bought if they had shopped at the grocery store instead of eating at the Enchanted Enchilada. Discuss the difference in costs between eating at a restaurant and buying and cooking your own food.

71 Waste Collection and Graphing*

Grade Levels 3–5

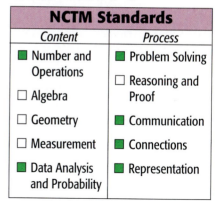

NCTM Standards	
Content	*Process*
■ Number and Operations	■ Problem Solving
☐ Algebra	☐ Reasoning and Proof
☐ Geometry	■ Communication
☐ Measurement	■ Connections
■ Data Analysis and Probability	■ Representation

Overview

Students explore the science, social issues, and mathematics of garbage. They take a hands-on approach to discovering the dimensions of the problem with litter—what is thrown as litter, what individuals can do about litter, and how litter impacts our immediate environment and the people and creatures who live there.

Activity

What ideas or concepts will students explore?

- Working with data (collecting, organizing, analyzing, displaying, interpreting, using)
- Connections with environmental science and social studies
- Graphing

What materials will you need?

pencils • tally sheets • graph paper • crayons or markers • trash bags • trash

What will you do?

Begin with a demonstration. Pick up pieces of paper, wad them up, and throw them on the floor. In other words, litter the classroom. Do this several times to see if you get a reaction. Ask the students if they know what you are doing. Take responses and explain that you are littering and that littering can be a bad habit like biting your nails—something done automatically without even thinking about it. Explain how litter can hurt the environment. Show the plastic rings from a pack of soft drinks. Demonstrate how birds and other animals can get tangled in the plastic. Brainstorm with the class and make a list of all the types of litter they have seen.

What questions could you ask?

Have you ever seen someone litter?
Have you ever littered?
What would happen if everyone littered and no one picked up the trash?

---

*Adapted from a lesson taught by Janie Gallegos

What kinds of litter do you think we might find on the playground or in areas around the school?

What will students do?

Working in teams, take a garbage bag outside and see how much trash you can collect in 30 minutes. Make this a clean-up activity as well as a data-collection project, and try to clear the playground and surrounding area of litter.

Back in the classroom, sort the waste by types identified earlier in the brainstorming session: plastic, paper/paperboard, food waste, yard waste, metal, glass, cloth, wood, and other. Make a chart to show types of litter and tallies of the litter of each type collected in your trash bag. Then graph your findings. Share graphs and findings with the class. Discuss what can be done about the litter problem at your school and in your community.

What strategies might students *invent* or construct?

On the trash-collection task, students will divide up the work, each clearing an area, or work together and move in circles around the trash bag. Some will see the project as a contest and try to collect more trash than any of the other groups. On sorting and quantifying the trash, some will work from a chart, listing types of trash and making tally marks; others will sort first and then list categories and count and record numbers for each category.

What insights, connections, or applications might students *discover*?

- Data help define and describe a problem (one or two items of litter are unimpressive; but dozens constitute a problem).
- The categories also help identify a solution since most of the litter found is probably recyclable.
- It is everyone's responsibility to do something about litter in the environment—not just the responsibility of custodians or teachers.
- Everyone working together can make a difference.

What extensions can you make?

Pool the results of all the teams, and make a graph for the entire class's data. Discuss whether the results show a serious or a minor problem and who might be able to help. Compose a letter or a petition to call the problem to the attention of the custodial staff or other responsible authorities and perhaps ask for recycling bins to be placed on the playground. Form litter-pick-up teams to collect trash during recess or lunch hour.

As a class, do some research about the growing problem of waste in the world (barges stacked with garbage roaming the seas, beaches closed because of toxic waste, difficulties with disposal of nuclear waste, and so forth). Discuss the implications of these problems for the future and the various solutions being tried or suggested (such as dumping garbage on the moon).

72 Exploring Data in the Bigger World

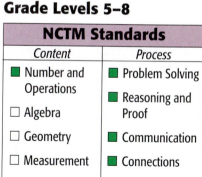

Grade Levels 5–8

NCTM Standards	
Content	*Process*
☑ Number and Operations	☑ Problem Solving
☐ Algebra	☑ Reasoning and Proof
☐ Geometry	☑ Communication
☐ Measurement	☑ Connections
☑ Data Analysis and Probability	☑ Representation

Overview

Data are everywhere. Decisions about major issues of the day—global warming, energy consumption, taxes, minimum-wage laws—begin with data. Collecting and understanding issue-related numbers can start with something as simple as a person-to-person survey. When students generate their own data, they get inside the issues and become more actively engaged in looking for solutions.

Activity

What ideas or concepts will students *explore*?

- Frequency counts
- Collecting, organizing, analyzing, displaying, interpreting, and using data
- Research and observation skills
- Finding mean, median, and mode

What materials will you need?

survey or data-collection log • graph paper • crayons, markers, pencils • calculators • Internet connection

What questions could you ask?

What issue or problem in the bigger world (society, the nation, the environment, and so forth) is important to you?
What do you know about this issue or problem?
What don't you know that you can find out?
How could you collect data to tell you more?
How could you use data you collect to impact this issue or problem?

What will students do?

Brainstorm in small groups about issues or problems in the world. Select one of mutual interest. Compose research questions, such as "Are most people trying to save energy, and, if so, how are they doing it?" or "What issues concern people the most?" or "Are people in our city carpooling to save energy?"

Do some research on the Internet, and use that information to help develop a data-collection plan. Develop a survey or data-collection log for recording data. Make a copy of the log for each member of the group. Collect data for a week; then pool information. Use a calculator to total numbers and help find means, medians, and modes if appropriate. Display the information in charts and graphs and present it to the entire class.

*What strategies might students **invent** or construct?*

Some students may focus on opinions, conducting surveys to find out what people think about issues. Others will emphasize actions, making frequency counts of what people are doing about problems. Some will count objects; others, people. Organization of data will sometimes be split between yes/no responses (Do you carpool?) and frequency data (1, 2, 3, 4 people in a car).

*What insights, connections, or applications might students **discover**?*

- Grouping and classification can change numbers into meaningful data.
- Data sets can point toward solutions.
- Measures of central value (mean, median, and mode) help make sense of numbers.
- Data are everywhere, but they have to be analyzed and understood to make a difference.

73 Rolling the Dice

NCTM Standards	
Content	*Process*
☐ Number and Operations	🟩 Problem Solving
☐ Algebra	🟩 Reasoning and Proof
☐ Geometry	☐ Communication
☐ Measurement	🟩 Connections
🟩 Data Analysis and Probability	🟩 Representation

Overview

With casinos appearing in so many states, the importance of gambling responsibly is becoming a national issue. Exploring the concepts of probability can prepare students to make informed decisions about gambling as early as elementary and middle school. In this activity students begin to understand the elements of chance involved in a popular form of gambling—rolling dice.

Activity

What ideas or concepts will students explore?

- Collecting and organizing data
- Probability
- Estimation
- Patterns

What materials will you need?

dice • tally sheets with combinations for one die and two dice • colored pencils

What questions could you ask?

How many possibilities are there if you roll one die? If you roll two dice? What does it mean if something is probably going to happen or not going to happen?
Do you believe in luck? Why or why not?
Have you ever played a game where you rolled dice? What happened?

What will students do?

Explore the possibilities of rolling dice. Identify all of the possibilities for rolling one die and then two dice. Use those possibilities to create two tally sheets. Use the possibilities to divide the sheets into columns. In teams, take turns rolling dice and tallying the results. Add the tallies. Then draw a horizontal line through the tally sheet and try guessing the numbers you will roll. Mark the estimates in a different color. Compare your guesses to the actual results. Look for patterns or lack of patterns. Display the results in a graph.

*What strategies might students **invent** or construct?*

Some students may try to influence the roll by throwing the dice hard or hardly at all. Some with a knowledge of dice games might look for certain patterns or combinations.

*What insights, connections, or applications might students **discover**?*

- There is no foolproof way to predict how the dice will fall.
- You have a better chance of predicting how one die rather than two dice will fall.
- The more throws you make, the more even the chances and the less likely predictions will be accurate.

What extensions can you make?

Discuss the implications of what you found for games of chance. What do your findings tell you about the chances of winning big at the casino or developing a system to "beat the house"?

74 A Slice of the Pie:
Percents and Pie Charts

Grade Levels 5–6

NCTM Standards	
Content	*Process*
■ Number and Operations	■ Problem Solving
□ Algebra	□ Reasoning and Proof
■ Geometry	□ Communication
■ Measurement	□ Connections
■ Data Analysis and Probability	■ Representation

Overview

One of the most common ways to represent data expressed as percents is to use a pie chart. Reading a pie chart begins the process of understanding the relationship of the visual image and the numbers; constructing a pie chart from scratch continues the process. Once students have used the hands-on approach, they will be better prepared to use computer programs that construct the charts for them.

Activity

*What ideas or concepts will students **explore**?*

- Organizing frequency counts into percents
- Representing percents with pie charts
- Measuring degrees of a circle

What materials will you need?

graph paper • colored pencils or markers • calculators, protractors, compasses • tally sheets

What questions could you ask?

What does the name "pie chart" suggest about its shape and the shape of its segments?

What does it mean literally to take a slice of the pie? Are there any other ways to use that expression?

When might you need to convert frequencies into percents? How would you do it?

How do you convert percents into degrees on a circle?

What will students do?

Survey 25 people to find out which kind of pie they prefer: apple, peach, coconut cream, pecan, lemon meringue, pumpkin, or other. Collect the data with a tally sheet; then add the tallies. Find totals and percentages of the total. Work in pairs to plan and collect data, calculate percents, convert percents to degrees, and develop pie charts.

What strategies might students *invent* or construct?

Some students will work percentages out with manipulatives before writing them in numbers. Some may forget that the percentages may not exceed 100%, while some will confuse percentage points and degrees. Frequently students do a halving process to estimate the segments of the pie; others make a model of angles and transfer from the model rather than measure directly on the circle.

What insights, connections, or applications might students *discover*?

- There is no one way to work with data; multiple methods can lead to broader understanding of the information.
- Organization of data can be demonstrated by conversions: frequencies to percents and percents to degrees.
- The slices of the pie cannot add up to more than 100%.

75

Are You Hot? Are You Cold?
Finding Mean, Median, and Mode

Grade Levels 6–8

NCTM Standards	
Content	*Process*
■ Number and Operations	■ Problem Solving
☐ Algebra	■ Reasoning and Proof
☐ Geometry	■ Communication
■ Measurement	■ Connections
■ Data Analysis and Probability	■ Representation

Overview

Mean, median, and mode are important mathematical concepts that help us make sense of descriptive statistics. In this activity students explore the use of these concepts as well as their limits in helping us understand the weather. The activity is also multidisciplinary, providing crossovers for science units and for social studies topics such as global warming.

Activity

What ideas or concepts will students explore?

- Applying descriptive statistics
- Interpreting descriptive statistics
- Mean, median, and mode
- Numbers operations

What materials will you need?

paper, pencils • calculators • weather data • videotape of day's weather forecast • Internet access • thermometer, barometer, tools to measure wind speed or precipitation as appropriate

What will you do?

Take the class outside. Brainstorm all of the descriptive terms you can think of to describe the weather. Estimate temperature, wind speed, pollution, pollen levels, and other data covered by weather reports. Use a thermometer and any other equipment available to take readings. Back in the classroom, watch the videotape of the day's forecast. Compare the forecast to the weather you experienced. Compare the forecast with the readings you were able to take. Talk about applying "measures of central value"—mean, median, and mode—to weather data. Use lists of figures from the Internet or other media to illustrate.

What questions could you ask?

Why is everyone always talking about the weather?
How high must the temperature go for you to consider it hot? How low to consider it cold?

What does it mean to be average? Is that idea useful in describing temperature? Might it be useful in describing any other weather data?
What about median and mode? Are they useful when analyzing weather data? Do we ever hear those terms used in a weather report?

What will students do?

Collect data about high and low temperatures for two places of interest. Organize the data in a chart or list. Then compute the mean, the median, and the mode for the high temperatures and the low temperatures for each place. Display the results in a graph or chart. Discuss the significance of the information.

Select other available data for the location, such as barometric pressure, humidity, wind speed, pollution, ultraviolet levels, or pollen counts. Collect and organize the data in a list or chart. Compute means, medians, and modes. Decide which measures are most important and create a graph to display that information.

What strategies might students *invent* or construct?

Instead of tallies, most students work with lists of actual numbers, rearranging data so that numbers are in ascending or descending order. Most arrange numbers by hand and then use a calculator for actual computations of means. Medians and modes they eyeball, although mode seems to be a difficult concept for many students. When working with long or multiple lists, some add smaller sections at a time and then add totals.

What insights, connections, or applications might students *discover*?

- Supposedly simple frequency counts may not be so simple or easy to understand.
- Different kinds of analysis can be applied to find interesting and relatively complex relationships and patterns.
- A set of data can be analyzed multiple times using different mathematical tools to reveal different perspectives and meanings.

76 $10,000 Stock Market Contest*

Grade Levels 5–8

NCTM Standards	
Content	*Process*
■ Number and Operations	■ Problem Solving
☐ Algebra	☐ Reasoning and Proof
☐ Geometry	■ Communication
☐ Measurement	■ Connections
■ Data Analysis and Probability	■ Representation

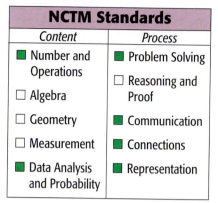

Overview

"Playing" the stock market can be a game or a class project. In areas where local newspapers participate in Newspapers for Education programs, classes can often participate in city-wide contests that may even include actual stock market professionals.

Activity

What ideas or concepts will students explore?
- Working with data, especially interpreting and predicting
- Decimals and percentages
- Patterns and relationships

What materials will you need?
stock market reports in newspapers or on the Internet • logs for recording data • pens or pencils • calculators • graph paper • markers or crayons

What will you do?
Introduce the idea of the stock market, making connections with economics and history. Talk about the various stock market crashes and their effect on the nation and the world. Discuss the idea of investing money for the future.

What questions could you ask?
What do you know about the stock market?
What does it mean to buy a share of a company?
What do the numbers in the stock market report mean?
How do you know if a stock has gone up or down and by how much?
What does a stockbroker do?
What does it mean to lose or to gain money in the stock market?

What will students do?
In teams of three or four make a plan for investing $10,000 in the stock market. Talk about companies that you know and your perceptions of their success. Research those companies and others on the Internet. Be sure to look at stock reports over a period of time to get an idea of the stocks' performance.

---

*Adapted from Stock Market Made Easy, a Newspapers-in-Education game described by Winthrop Quigley, "Youngsters Beat New York Stock Exchange Index." Albuquerque Journal, 15 May 2003, http://www.abqjournal.com.

Compile a portfolio of stocks. Research and keep a log of your portfolio's performance over eight weeks. At the end of the period, compare results with those of other teams. The team whose portfolio is worth the most wins.

*What strategies might students **invent** or construct?*

Students often select their stocks by familiarity, choosing companies such as The Gap or Toyota that they know and whose products they would buy. A few will base choices on research, taking into account market trends and the performance of the stock in the weeks before the game begins. During the game some teams take a stand-pat approach, selecting a set of stocks at the beginning and sticking with them throughout the eight weeks. Others "manage" their portfolios, buying and selling throughout the period.

*What insights, connections, or applications might students **discover**?*

- It is hard to predict which stocks will go up and which stocks will go down.
- Popular companies may have unpopular stocks for reasons that are not related to their product.
- Size of company is no guarantee that the stock is safe.
- It's important to know whether a stock is already rising or falling when you buy; you want to buy low and sell high.
- The market can plunge for reasons outside the business world, such as world events or weather.

77 Probability: Coin Tossing

Math
Manipulatives

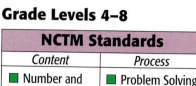

Grade Levels 4–8

NCTM Standards	
Content	*Process*
☑ Number and Operations	☑ Problem Solving
☐ Algebra	☐ Reasoning and Proof
☐ Geometry	☑ Communication
☐ Measurement	☐ Connections
☑ Data Analysis and Probability	☑ Representation

Overview

Computing probabilities often changes students' ideas about chance and luck. The numbers involved rob the process of an aura of magic that can make taking chances appealing. Coin tosses provide a good beginning place since the possibilities are more limited—heads or tails for one coin; heads-heads, tails-tails, heads-tails for two coins. Once students have experimented with one and two coins, they can move on to throwing dice in the extension activity.

Activity

What ideas or concepts will students *explore*?
- Probability and chance
- Data and prediction
- Patterns and relationships

What materials will you need? pennies • pencils • "Tally Sheet for 1 Coin, 10 Tosses," "Tally Sheet for 2 Coins, 30 Tosses," and "Tally Sheet for 2 Coins, 40 Tosses" in the Worksheets & Handouts section of the CD-ROM that accompanies this text.

What questions could you ask? Which side of a coin do we call heads? Tails? Why?
If you flip a coin in the air, what are the possibilities?
If you flip two coins in the air, what are the possibilities?
Can you predict how the coin or coins will fall?
If you have a 1 in 2 chance that a coin will land heads up, what is the percentage of chance that it will land tails up?
What is the chance that two coins tossed in the air will both land heads up? Tails up? One head and one tail?

What will students do? **Activity A** Working individually, throw a penny in the air 10 times and record heads or tails on the tally sheet after each throw. Describe your findings. Did you record more heads? More tails? Or an equal number of heads and tails?

Activity B Working in teams of two, throw a penny in the air 10 times, then 20 times, then 30 times, recording results after each throw. Record and graph results for each increase of 10. Describe and discuss findings.

Activity C Working in small groups, toss two pennies in the air at the same times for 40 throws. Before each throw, write the group's prediction at the side of the tally-sheet column. Then toss the coins and record and graph the results. Compare the predictions to the actual toss. How many times was the prediction correct? Discuss the results.

*What strategies might students **invent** or construct?*

Students might begin the exercise believing they can use tricks and skill to make the coins turn up the way they predict. As the number of tosses increases, this belief is usually exchanged for a better understanding of chance. Some students might explore the idea that two heads or two tails in a row makes the chances of the toss resulting in the opposite greater.

*What insights, connections, or applications might students **discover**?*

- There is an equal likelihood that a single coin will come up heads or tails.
- With each toss the probability does not change; it remains 50/50.
- A few tosses probably won't show the 50/50 outcomes, but the more the tosses, the more the results tend toward 50/50.

What extensions can you make?

Have students compute probabilities for the coin tosses. Then extend the exercise to throwing one and two dice, computing the likelihood of each combination throughout a series of tosses. (See "Tally Sheet for 30 Tosses of Dice" in the Worksheets & Handouts section of the CD-ROM that accompanies this text.)

Understanding Fractions

78 Tortilla Fractions

Grade Levels K–2

NCTM Standards	
Content	*Process*
■ Number and Operations	■ Problem Solving
□ Algebra	□ Reasoning and Proof
■ Geometry	■ Communication
■ Measurement	■ Connections
□ Data Analysis and Probability	■ Representation

Overview

Although most curriculums emphasize whole numbers, even very young students will find themselves working with parts of wholes. In this activity tortillas are both a motivational device and a manipulative. Students develop strategies for dividing the tortilla into parts for sharing and then enjoy the tortilla as a wholesome treat. They explore basic fractions such as $1/2$, $1/3$, and $1/4$, and they discover that a real-world activity such as eating a tortilla can have math applications.

Activity

What ideas or concepts will students explore?

- Basic fractions in numbers and words
- Equal-sharing strategies
- Comparing fractions (equal, more, less)

What materials will you need?

tortillas for each student • plastic knives • unlined paper • pencils, erasers • napkins • jam

What questions could you ask?

What can we do if we have one tortilla and two friends to share it with? How about four friends? Three friends? Six friends?
What does it mean when we say each friend should have an equal amount? What if one friend wants more of the tortilla and another wants less? Can you show what you would do by drawing a picture?

What will you do?

Talk about equal sharing. Use a circle of paper to show how you could divide a cookie or a tortilla to have two pieces, four pieces, and so forth.

What will students do?

Each of you will receive a tortilla, a plastic knife, and a napkin. Put the tortilla on the napkin and then work with pencils and unlined paper to make plans to divide the tortilla among different numbers of friends—two, four, three, six, and so forth. Share and discuss your plans in small groups. Then use the knife to cut the tortilla, spread the pieces with jam, and eat them as a treat.

What strategies might students *invent* or construct?

Students might draw circles and use rulers to divide them into halves, fourths, and so forth; or they might draw the circle, cut it out, and fold the circle to get a more accurate division. Thirds and sixths will be more difficult than halves, fourths, and eighths. One strategy for dividing into thirds will probably be estimation; another, reconstructing the circle from circle pieces, cutting and fitting until they have a circle.

What insights, connections, or applications might students *discover*?

- Equal sharing means everyone gets exactly the same amount.
- Fractions are less than one.
- Increasing the number of people to share decreases the portion each person gets.
- A half is more than a fourth, and a third is more than a sixth.

What extensions can you make?

Have students write a story about equal sharing. They could illustrate the story with their own drawings or with cutouts from magazines or newspapers. They can share the stories by reading them aloud or by trading and reading silently.

79 Hershey Bar Fractions*

Overview

Grade Levels 2–3

NCTM Standards	
Content	*Process*
■ Number and Operations	■ Problem Solving
☐ Algebra	☐ Reasoning and Proof
■ Geometry	■ Communication
■ Measurement	■ Connections
☐ Data Analysis and Probability	■ Representation

This activity is a favorite with students and teachers. The way the giant candy bars are segmented makes them a natural manipulative for fractions. Jerry Palotta's book *The Hershey's Milk Chocolate Fractions Book* provides many engaging activities and useful worksheets.

Activity

What ideas or concepts will students explore?
- Terms: *fracture, fraction, part, whole, half*
- Writing number sentences with fractions
- Identifying and representing fractions
- Difference between top and bottom numbers (numerator and denominator) in fractions

What materials will you need?
large Hershey bars (12 sections each) for each group of students ● Jerry Palotta's *The Hershey's Milk Chocolate Fractions Book* (New York: Scholastic, 1999) ● "Fractions Worksheet" in the Worksheets & Handouts section of the CD-ROM that accompanies this text. ● pencils, paper, scissors, rulers

What questions could you ask?
How many children can share a large Hershey bar? How do you know? How much of the bar will each student receive?
How many children can share half of a large Hershey bar? A third? A fourth? Is it important for each share to be equal? Why?

What will you do?
Read aloud *The Hershey's Milk Chocolate Fractions Book*. Discuss and explain as you go along. With a Hershey bar, demonstrate beginning fractions. Show examples of representing the fractions with drawings and numbers.

What will students do?
Explore the meaning of fractions with equal-sharing situations involving a 12-section Hershey bar. Divide the Hershey bar into halves, fourths, eighths, twelfths, and so forth. (Since too much handling of the candy can make the chocolate melt and cause it to become too dirty to eat, you will work first with drawings or cutouts).

---

*Adapted from an activity taught by Connie Wattenburger.

Learn and use basic fraction vocabulary for working with fractions, including *part* and *whole,* names of different fractions, and so forth.

Show and explain fractions of a Hershey bar with numbers. Write a number sentence to show the number of parts in the Hershey bar.

What strategies might students *invent* or construct?

Students might use a ruler to draw a rectangle with 12 parts or draw around the Hershey bar, fold the paper into parts, and then cut along the creases. Some will divide the bar one way to make a half; others will discover more than one way to make the division.

What insights, connections, or applications might students *discover*?

- Equal parts means all of the fractions are the same size.
- Equal sharing means dividing something into equal parts.
- When you write a fraction, the number on the bottom is the name of the fraction; the number on the top tells you how many of that fraction you have.

What extensions can you make?

Have students explore what happens when they combine or separate parts of the Hershey bar in various ways—such as putting 2 of the 12 parts together or taking away 2 parts from 4.

80 Writing and Identifying Fractions*

Overview

Connecting fractions to common objects such as packs of gum or cartons of soda makes the mathematical notation seem real and meaningful to students. In this activity students discover fractional relationship in familiar things and then translate what they find into mathematical language and symbols. Students begin the process of generalizing by modeling the fractions with counters and by discovering and representing equivalencies.

Grade Levels 2–3

NCTM Standards	
Content	*Process*
■ Number and Operations	■ Problem Solving
☐ Algebra	■ Reasoning and Proof
☐ Geometry	■ Communication
■ Measurement	■ Connections
☐ Data Analysis and Probability	■ Representation

Activity

*What ideas or concepts will students **explore**?*

- Fractional notation
- Equivalence
- Fractions as parts of sets
- Fractions as parts of wholes

What materials will you need?

12 counters of two different colors (for example, some red and some white beans) for each student ● sixpack of soda ● bunch of 4 bananas ● pack of 5 sticks of gum ● other concrete examples ● "Fractions with Counters Worksheet" in the Worksheets & Handouts section of the CD-ROM that accompanies this text ● pencils, paper

What questions could you ask?

What do you think the 6 refers to in $\frac{1}{6}$? The 1?

How could you write the fractional part of the sixpack of soda that you did not drink? (Continue for different concrete examples and different fractions.)

What fraction of a group are boys (vary size and composition of group)? Girls? Have brown hair? Blond hair? Have glasses?

What fractional part of the whole set of counters is represented by each group?

How many counters are in $\frac{1}{3}$? Flip the counters in one group. What fractional part of the whole set is red? White?

---

*Adapted from an activity taught by Lisa Mueller.

What will students do?

Explore fractions as parts of sets. Work with a sixpack of soda, a bunch of 4 bananas, a pack of 5 sticks of gum, and examples using students (ones with blond hair as part of the whole, ones with glasses, and so forth) as real-life subjects to relate to fractions. As the teacher writes fractions on the board, discuss how the fractions apply to the objects—for example, $\frac{1}{6}$ for the cans in the soda pack. Discuss the meanings of each fraction—that $\frac{1}{6}$ means one-sixth, or one of six parts. Continue the process with every group of objects, discussing what each part of the fraction means and why it applies to the set of objects.

Model objects examined in group discussion individually with counters and then represent findings on worksheets with drawings, words, and numbers. Use the counters of two different colors to explore various combinations of objects, creating different sets and different fractions of the sets. Look for fraction equivalencies—such as the relationship of $\frac{1}{6}$ and $\frac{1}{6}$ to $\frac{1}{3}$. Continue to represent manipulative work on your worksheets.

*What strategies might students **invent** or construct?*

Students will represent fractions by drawing objects on paper, naming them with words, and writing number sentences. On the worksheet, some will draw pictures of the actual counters; others will represent the counters with circles or other marks.

*What insights, connections, or applications might students **discover**?*

- Different arrangements do not necessarily mean different fractions.
- The activities in this lesson connect to real-life applications involving two-color differences.
- Dividing a set of objects results in a number we can count with whole numbers as well as a fraction to show the relationship of a part of the set to the whole set.

What extensions can you make?

Using two colors of counters is just the beginning for exploring fractions. Have students continue the explorations with counters of three, four, and more colors for a deeper understanding of the concepts.

81 Fraction Kits*

Grade Levels 1–5

NCTM Standards	
Content	*Process*
■ Number and Operations	■ Problem Solving
□ Algebra	□ Reasoning and Proof
■ Geometry	■ Communication
■ Measurement	■ Connections
□ Data Analysis and Probability	■ Representation

Overview

Making their own manipulatives gives students a feeling of control as they tackle fraction concepts. The fraction strips and later the circles they make can be put into envelopes with students' names and used again. Both strips and circles work well for showing equivalence. Using different colors of construction paper for each fraction (green for $\frac{1}{2}$ and so forth) makes relationships easier to test and identify.

Activity

What ideas or concepts will students explore?
- Parts of a whole
- Equivalent fractions
- Ordering and comparing fractions
- Writing fractions

What materials will you need? for each student: one $11'' \times 1''$ purple strip of construction paper, one $11'' \times 1''$ yellow strip of construction paper, one $11'' \times 1''$ red strip of construction paper, one $11'' \times 1''$ green strip of construction paper, strips of other colors depending on the number of fractions to be studied ● one letter size envelope ● scissors, pencils or markers ● fraction die

What questions could you ask? Which strip is the longest?
Why would we call the longest strip a "whole?"
Which is greater, $\frac{1}{2}$ or $\frac{1}{4}$? Is $\frac{1}{8}$ greater than $\frac{1}{4}$? Is $\frac{1}{8}$ greater than $\frac{1}{2}$?
How could you use the fraction strips to test your answers?

What will you do? Review concepts of $\frac{1}{2}$, $\frac{1}{4}$, $\frac{1}{8}$, and other parts of a whole in order to prepare the students to make fraction kits and use them to better understand the concept of parts of a whole.

Draw a circle on the board. Draw lines to cut the circle into fourths. Ask students to volunteer to color $\frac{1}{4}$ of the circle green. Ask for another volunteer to color $\frac{1}{2}$ of the circle red. Draw a line to cut the remaining $\frac{1}{4}$ in half. Ask for another volunteer to color $\frac{1}{8}$ of the circle yellow. Ask for a volunteer to tell what part of the whole is remaining. Continue for other fractions.

---

*Adapted from a lesson taught by Amy Johnston.

What will students do?

Look at a completed sample fraction kit. Understand that you will be making kits to help you throughout your study of fractions.

Collect one strip of construction paper in each color. Hold a red strip of paper up in the air to make sure that everyone has the right color. Write $\frac{1}{1}$ on the red strip to show that the strip represents 1 part of 1 part, or 1 whole.

Hold the green strip of paper up in the air to make sure that everyone has the right color. Fold the green strip of paper in half at the middle to make a crease. Unfold the strip and cut along the crease. Label each piece $\frac{1}{2}$ to show that each piece represents 1 part of 2 parts, or 1 half of the whole. Continue with each strip of paper.

Store completed kits in envelope.

In groups of two to four students, play the game Cover-up.* Roll die to select fraction strip. Put fraction strip on whole strip. Continue until a player covers the whole strip with fractions.

What strategies might students *invent* or construct?

Students might rely on folding to divide strips and focus on relationships among strips or use a ruler and quantify sizes. They should also be able to construct other materials to compare $\frac{1}{2}, \frac{1}{4}, \frac{1}{8}$, and other fractions.

What insights, connections, or applications might students *discover*?

- You can make a whole from strips of a single color.
- You can also make a whole by combining strips of different colors.
- The smaller the bottom number in a fraction, the larger the fraction.

What extensions can you make?

Have students add fraction circles to their kits. Start with circles in different colors. Then, as a group, fold and cut them in halves, fourths, and so on.

———————————

*Game created by Marilyn Burns.

82 Introduction to Fractions*

Mathematics in Literature

Grade Levels 3–4

NCTM Standards	
Content	*Process*
■ Number and Operations	■ Problem Solving
□ Algebra	■ Reasoning and Proof
■ Geometry	■ Communication
■ Measurement	■ Connections
□ Data Analysis and Probability	■ Representation

Overview

Both the cooking applications and the story make this a highly engaging activity. Students hear, see, and do, in the process discovering basic fractions both as mathematical concepts and as real-world applications. You may want to use cutouts of giant cookies as an additional manipulative as well as actual cookies as a treat.

Activity

*What ideas or concepts will students **explore**?*

- Identifying basic fractions
- Representing basic fractions
- Writing basic fractions
- Real-world applications and uses of fractions

What materials will you need?

overhead projector and transparencies • Pat Hutchins's story *The Doorbell Rang* (New York: Mulberry Books, 1989) • fraction manipulatives, fraction circles, or "Pattern: Fraction Circles" (on the CD-ROM that accompanies this text) • paper, markers, crayons • measuring spoons and cups • optional: giant cookie cutouts and actual cookies

What questions could you ask?

What is a fraction?
What is the difference between a whole and a fraction?
How many ways can you think of that we use fractions in real life?
Have you ever made a cake or baked cookies?
What fractions does cooking involve?
How do you measure a fraction in cooking?

What will you do?

Read *The Doorbell Rang* aloud. Use fraction circles to demonstrate ideas in the story. Then use the measuring spoons to talk about fractions and cooking and to demonstrate the difference between whole and fraction measurements.

Use the overhead projector to show what happens when something is divided into halves, fourths, thirds, and so forth. Show how to represent a fraction with drawings, how to write it in words, and how to write

---

*Adapted from an activity taught by Mark Johnston.

it in numbers. Discuss the relationships shown by fractions—comparing sizes and place on a number line. Describe the fraction $\frac{1}{2}$. Ask, "Is $\frac{1}{2}$ larger than $\frac{1}{3}$? Why or why not? Is the fraction $\frac{1}{3}$ larger or smaller than the fraction $\frac{1}{4}$? Which size of cookie would you prefer: $\frac{1}{2}$ of a cookie, $\frac{1}{3}$ of a cookie, or $\frac{1}{4}$ of a cookie? Why?

What will students do?

Use the fraction manipulatives to explore fraction relationships. Put parts of fraction circles in ascending and descending order. Combine fraction pieces in various ways to make whole circles. Write number sentences to represent the result.

Discuss ways fractions are used in everyday life. Listen to *The Doorbell Rang.* Draw a picture to represent the number of people who divided the cookies and their equal shares.

Use manipulatives to develop an understanding of numerators and denominators. Work in different groups to find different fraction pieces that make $\frac{1}{2}$, $\frac{1}{3}$, or $\frac{1}{4}$. In math journals explain what a fraction is to a student who was absent.

*What strategies might students **invent** or construct?*

Students might be able to construct a mini plan for working with one or all of the target fractions—$\frac{1}{2}$, $\frac{1}{3}$, or $\frac{1}{4}$. Students might invent another visual or manipulative for representing these fractions. Students might opt to work with fraction rectangles as an alternative to the fraction circles.

*What insights, connections, or applications might students **discover**?*

- Working with fractions such as $\frac{1}{2}$, $\frac{1}{3}$, and $\frac{1}{4}$ means that you are working with common, everyday fractions that are everywhere.
- Fractions have a lot to do with measurement.
- A fraction is a way to show division of something.
- A fraction can mean dividing one object into pieces or a group of objects into smaller groups.

83 Learning Fractions with Pictures*

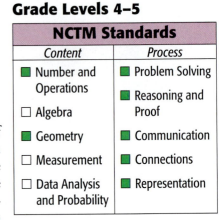

Grade Levels 4–5

NCTM Standards	
Content	*Process*
☑ Number and Operations	☑ Problem Solving
☐ Algebra	☑ Reasoning and Proof
☑ Geometry	☑ Communication
☐ Measurement	☑ Connections
☐ Data Analysis and Probability	☑ Representation

Overview

Grounding understanding of fractions and fractional notation in visual images helps make the concepts concrete. Once these images are established as reference points, students can begin to develop mental tools for dealing with fractions in a variety of contexts. The activity uses simple images to illustrate fractions. Students might also draw their own pictures.

Activity

What ideas or concepts will students explore?

- Representing fractions in equivalent forms
- Using concrete materials and fraction equivalents to represent and compare halves, thirds, fourths, eighths, and tenths.
- Identifying a model that is divided into equal fractional parts (halves, thirds, and fourths).

What materials will you need?

manipulatives: egg cartons, tennis balls, ice-cube trays, colored balls • white board and two different-colored markers. • "Fractions with Shapes" on the CD-ROM that accompanies this text • pencils

What questions could you ask?

What is the difference between the numerator of a fraction and its denominator? Is this difference important? Why or why not?
Is there a difference between the fraction $\frac{2}{4}$ and the fraction $\frac{3}{6}$? Why or why not?
Is there a difference between $\frac{2}{5}$ and $\frac{1}{3}$? How could we find out?

What will you do?

Draw pictures on the board (such as circles) and ask, "How many objects are on the board?" Write the number on the board. Shade in some of the objects and ask the class, "How many objects are shaded in?" Record the number on the board above the first number. Explain how to read the fraction, introducing the terms *numerator* and *denominator*. Repeat the process by drawing different objects and then shading them in. Demonstrate simple fractions such as $\frac{1}{2}$, $\frac{1}{4}$, $\frac{1}{3}$, and $\frac{3}{5}$.

Ask for volunteers to go up to the board to write the fraction for each example. Then draw boxes on the board and shade in certain areas to represent fractions. Ask students how the fraction would be written in each

---

*Adapted from an activity taught by Mark Johnson.

case. Afterwards, use objects such as different colored balls, cans of tennis balls, ice-cube trays, and egg cartons to demonstrate fractions in model form. (Example: 4 red balls and 8 blue balls can be placed in an egg carton. What fraction of the balls are red?)

What will students do?

Through the use of pictures and manipulative materials, learn to identify and represent fractions. Construct fractions to show parts of whole objects and parts of whole sets. Explore the relationship between the numerator and the denominator in fraction notation.

In small groups, work on fraction worksheets. Model and discuss each fraction situation. Use fraction vocabulary to explain the problem, the problem-solving process, and the answers.

Create, represent, and share additional fraction situations.

What strategies might students ***invent*** *or construct?*

Students will begin with manipulatives and then move to drawings and numbers. Some might generalize from pictures to numbers quickly and shift from images to fractional notation; others will feel more comfortable working through the entire process for each situation: concrete objects, drawings, numbers. They might also extend their explorations to include other fractions such as $\frac{1}{6}, \frac{1}{7}, \frac{1}{9}$, and $\frac{1}{11}$.

What insights, connections, or applications might students ***discover***?

- Fractions represent relationships.
- Half of a big circle and half of a small circle are still both halves.
- You can have a half or a fourth or a third of any shape or kind of object.
- Fractions are numbers that have more than one part—a top number that gives a count of the number of pieces and a bottom number that shows the relationship of the part to the whole.

84 M&Ms Fractions, Data, and Prediction

Mathematical Thinking

Grade Levels 4–5

NCTM Standards	
Content	*Process*
■ Number and Operations	■ Problem Solving
□ Algebra	■ Reasoning and Proof
□ Geometry	□ Communication
□ Measurement	■ Connections
■ Data Analysis and Probability	■ Representation

Overview

Many students count and sort M&Ms by color in the early grades and then make a graph of their findings. This activity builds on those familiar tasks, taking them a step further to use the data collected to predict the contents of bags of M&Ms.

Activity

What ideas or concepts will students explore?

- Collecting and analyzing data
- Representing data with fractions and graphs
- Using data to predict

What materials will you need?

small, individual-serving-size bags of M&Ms for each student ● paper for graphing ● rulers ● markers, crayons, or colored pencils ● compass ● protractor

What questions could you ask?

Before opening bags:

What do you know about M&Ms?
How many different colors do you remember?
How many M&Ms do you think there are in a bag?
Can you estimate how many of those will be green, red, and so forth?

After opening bags:

How do the contents differ from your estimate?
Are there more or less candies?
Are there more, fewer, or different colors?
Are the portions of different colors the same as what you expected?
Are all the bags the same? How do they differ?
What would a graph of your counts look like?
Would the bars in a graph be the same or nearly the same height? Why or why not?

What will students do?

Work in pairs. Open the M&M bags. Count and divide the M&Ms by color. Write total numbers and fractions of the whole set for each color. Graph and explain the results. Share and interpret the results. Make and test predictions for other bags.

What strategies might students *invent* or construct?

Some students will approach the activity in terms of whole-number operations; others may focus on fractions and relationships of parts of the whole set. The former might create bar graphs based on the total number of different-colored candies; the latter might try their hands at a pie chart and explore converting fractions to percentages.

What insights, connections, or applications might students *discover*?

- Not all M&M bags are created equal.
- Even though the number of M&Ms in a bag may differ, each bag can still be represented by 1 to indicate a whole.
- It is difficult to predict exactly, but predicting from data can be more reliable than simply guessing.
- It can be helpful in predicting to work with averages or means — the average number of M&Ms in a package, the average fraction of each color.
- When making a pie chart, the fractions should add up to 1 and the percents to 100.

85 Pi as a Fraction

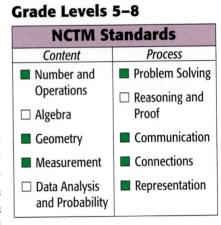

NCTM Standards	
Content	*Process*
■ Number and Operations	■ Problem Solving
☐ Algebra	☐ Reasoning and Proof
■ Geometry	■ Communication
■ Measurement	■ Connections
☐ Data Analysis and Probability	■ Representation

Overview

For many students pi is just a number to be memorized. To make pi more meaningful to students and connect it to real things in the real world, this activity puts pi in a dramatic context and applies it to common, hands-on measurement problems. Students have a chance to role-play and to develop their own problems using pi.

Activity

What ideas or concepts will students explore?

- Circumferences of different tortillas (or any circular flat bread)
- Finding areas of different tortillas
- Pi in fractional form
- Diameter and radius

What materials will you need?

tortillas with 8-inch, 10-inch, and 12-inch diameters for each pair of students • measuring tape, rulers • paper, graph paper, pencils • calculators

What questions could you ask?

What is the circumference, diameter, and radius of a circle?
What is pi?
Does pi change when the size of the circle changes?
How might you show your answer mathematically?

What will you do? Present a scenario for role playing:

Tom and Pete, brothers in competition, find themselves disagreeing on the answer to the question: "Which piece of tortilla is largest: 1/2 of the tortilla with an 8-inch diameter, 1/3 of the tortilla with a 10-inch diameter, or 1/4 of the tortilla with a 12-inch diameter?"

Tom says, "Clearly 1/4 of the largest tortilla is larger than the fractions of the smallest and the middle-sized one."

Pete responds, "I don't know about that. Let's use the area of a circle to find out if your statement is correct. And let's use 22/7 as our measure of pi."

Tom responded, "Whatever!"

What will students do? Working in pairs, choose one partner to play the role of Tom, the other Pete. Measure the circumference and diameter and calculate the total area of each of the three different-sized tortillas; Then discover other measurements that will help you resolve the problem confronting Tom and Pete. Develop your own measurement problems using pi.

What strategies might students *invent* or construct?

Each student will work with a variety of concepts: measurement, pi, the fraction $\frac{22}{7}$, area of a circle, comparisons of different areas of the three different-sized tortillas, and interpretation of results. Some might use a grid or centimeter paper to approximate area (in the making Manipulative section of the CD-ROM that accompanies this text). Others might use what they know about finding the area of rectangles to make an estimate.

What insights, connections, or applications might students *discover*?

- The same method works to find the area of any size of circle.
- Working with the fractional estimate of pi, $\frac{22}{7}$ can be easier than working with a decimal form.
- Pi is the same whatever the circumference and area of the circle.
- It is harder to measure a circular object accurately than it is to measure a straight line.
- The area of a circle is the space inside it, the circumference is the distance around it, the diameter is the distance across, and the radius is the distance from the edge to the center.

What extensions can you make?

Have students research the origins and use of pi. Discuss the comparative value of $\frac{22}{7}$ as a fractional form of pi and the decimal form, which has been extended to billions of places.

86 The Fractions of Time

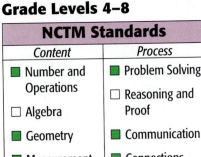

Grade Levels 4–8

NCTM Standards	
Content	*Process*
☒ Number and Operations	☒ Problem Solving
☐ Algebra	☐ Reasoning and Proof
☒ Geometry	☒ Communication
☒ Measurement	☒ Connections
☐ Data Analysis and Probability	☒ Representation

Overview

The conventions of time measurement have strong cultural connections, but there are also geometric and scientific foundations for our measures of time. Students explore the number systems behind our 12-hour clocks and 60-minute hours. They also study the relationships between units of time, the rotation of the earth on its axis, and its revolutions around the sun, as well as the role of the moon in measuring time.

Activity

What ideas or concepts will students explore?

- Measures of time: seconds, minutes, hours, days, weeks, months, years
- Base-12 and base-60 concepts involved in time measurement
- Science and geometry connections

What materials will you need?

clock • globe • model of solar system • paper, pencils • calculators, protractors, compasses

What questions could you ask?

How many measures of time can you think of?
What fractions do we use in measuring time?
How does a round clock help you read fractions of an hour or a minute?
What does a half hour or a quarter of an hour really mean?
How do we measure years and months? Centuries and millennia?
What fraction of a year is a month?
What fraction of a century is a year?
Imagine you will live to the age of 80. What fraction of your life have you already lived?
If your father is twice as old as you are today, what fraction of his age will you be in 20 years?

What will students do?

Use clocks, globes, and models of the solar system to create geometric representations of units of time, including hours and minutes, years and months. Use the representations and calculators as tools to identify ways to divide the units into fractions and to find common fractions ($\frac{1}{2}$, $\frac{1}{4}$, $\frac{1}{3}$, etc.) of the whole. Discuss the importance of fractions in dealing with time. Make a list of the vocabulary and common expressions that use fractions in time measurement. Identify base-12 and base-60 elements in measurements of time.

What strategies might students *invent* or construct?

Students might create clock fraction circles, cut the hours into 12ths, and then use the pieces as manipulatives to explore different time fractions. Some will want to do the same with years and months but will discover that the earth's oval orbit doesn't lend itself to the strategy as well as a circle does. Students could use the calculators to divide segments of time and then convert to fractions, an approach that prepares them for other fraction conversions.

What insights, connections, or applications might students *discover*?

- Measurements of time are both conventions and science-based units related to the earth's movement on its axis, the moon's rotation around the earth, and the earth's rotation around the sun.
- We talk about a quarter of an hour and half an hour but not about a 12th or a 6th of an hour.
- Most clocks actually only measure half a day, 12 hours; military time, based on the full 24 hours, may be more accurate but is less common than the 12-plus-12 system.

What extensions can you make?

Research the Babylonian base-60 number system and its connections with contemporary time measurement. Take explorations of time and geometry a step further and look for relationships between the 360 degrees in a circle and the 60 minutes in an hour and so forth.

87 Fractions and Space/Distance*

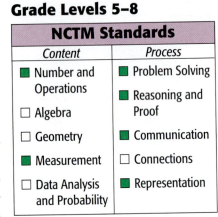

Overview

Students develop flexibility in mathematical thinking as they find and represent multiple answers to problems. They also work toward discriminating between mathematical situations in which multiple answers are appropriate and those in which a single answer is appropriate.

Grade Levels 5–8

NCTM Standards	
Content	*Process*
■ Number and Operations	■ Problem Solving
☐ Algebra	■ Reasoning and Proof
☐ Geometry	■ Communication
■ Measurement	☐ Connections
☐ Data Analysis and Probability	■ Representation

Activity

What ideas or concepts will students explore?
- Distance and space related to fractions
- Using and interpreting measurement tools
- Convergent and divergent thinking

What materials will you need? calculators • paper, pencils • rulers, yard- or metersticks

What questions could you ask? How many different ways is a standard ruler divided?
What fractions of the length do the different lines on the ruler represent?
How do those fractions relate to multiples of the basic measurements—as in metersticks and yardsticks.
Why might there be multiple answers to some measurement problems but only one answer to others?

What will students do? Read and discuss the following story context for exploring distance and fractions:

> Greeny the Frog is playing a game called "Tag, You're It" with his frog playmate, Croaky. Greeny can leap in increments of 8 inches to 12 inches. How many leaps will he need to make and what are their respective lengths as he tags Croaky from a distance of 5 feet? Develop 5 different answers. How many fractions are involved in solving this problem?
>
> If Greeny had to leap up a 4-foot-high and 2-foot-wide mud bank to get to Croaky, who was on the other side of the bank but still 5 feet away from Greeny, how much distance will Greeny have to travel to tag Croaky? What fraction of the entire distance traveled does Greeny leap up and down?

Use rulers to represent the problems on paper; then measure distances and make calculations on calculators. Convert results to fractions. Discuss the results, including the multiple answers in the first situation and the single answer in the second situation.

What strategies might students *invent* or construct?

Some students will emphasize visual representation and physical measurement in the problem-solving process. Others will focus on manipulating numbers, creating a formula and plugging in the numbers to find answers. Generally those who work with images will be more comfortable with multiple answers, while those who focus on numbers are more comfortable with a single answer. Discussing this difference may help each group to better understand diversity in perspective and problem-solving styles.

What insights, connections, or applications might students *discover*?

- What goes up must come down—even a frog.
- For some problems there may be multiple answers; for others, a single answer.
- Fractions of measurements are difficult to work with in the standard system of inches and feet.
- Because the metric system uses base 10 instead of base 12 or base 60, fractions are measured in 10ths and are easy to calculate and work with.

88 Finding Fractions in Your Life

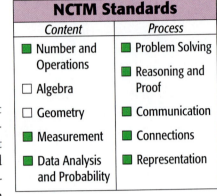

Grade Levels 4–8

NCTM Standards	
Content	*Process*
■ Number and Operations	■ Problem Solving
☐ Algebra	■ Reasoning and Proof
☐ Geometry	■ Communication
■ Measurement	■ Connections
■ Data Analysis and Probability	■ Representation

Overview

Step one in making learning about fractions meaningful is for students to discover meanings that relate to their own lives and worlds. Instead of studying fractions as abstract, textbook-math topics, students find fractions in the world around them and discover how important understanding and being able to work with fractions can be to daily living.

Activity

*What ideas or concepts will students **explore**?*

- Fractions in everyday life
- Fractions in society
- Fractions as necessary in common situations

What materials will you need?

drawing paper, construction paper ● colored markers, crayons, pencils ● rulers, compasses ● log sheets

What questions could you ask?

What do fractions say about you?
What fractions are important to you?
Are there any fractions that you strongly like or dislike?
Can you describe yourself with fractions?
Can you describe yourself with mathematical ideas?

What will students do?

Activity A: Fractions Self-Portrait Draw a picture of yourself. Then label different parts of the picture with words and numbers. For example, label fingers and give the number of fingers. Label feet and give shoe size or length. Label and count buttons, pockets, hair braids, freckles.

Identify at least 7 fractions from your numbers. For example, what is the fraction between the height and the length of your arm or leg? Develop fractions that seem to make sense to you and explain why you chose certain measurements to relate to other measurements.

Activity B: Numbers Idea Web Draw an idea web with you in the center. Then, in circles like balloons, write in the important fractions in your life (see your responses to Activity A).

Are any of your fractions important for more than one reason? Draw more balloons to show the different ways a fraction is important to you. Use straight lines to connect fractions to you in the center or to other balloons. Explain the numbers web to a classmate.

Activity C: Fractions Graph Keep a record for what you do for two or three days. Put your activities in categories such as sleeping, eating, studying, working, goofing off.

Make a log sheet with the activities at the top and lines between the activities. Whenever you do something, determine how long you spend doing it and record it on your log sheet. At the end of the two or three days, calculate the fraction of time you spent doing each activity for each individual day. Then do an overall calculation for all days.

What do your fractions say about you? Write a brief description.

*What strategies might students **invent** or construct?*

For some students the activities become a math-in-art project; for others, a mapping project, connecting numbers and dots to form an idea rather than an image map. Many describe in their discussion papers a preconception that fractions are "school math," unrelated to real life or their daily lives. They say that the activities encouraged them to approach fractions in different ways and that making fractions personal helped them understand the concepts.

*What insights, connections, or applications might students **discover**?*

- Fractions are everywhere.
- Fractions can describe relationships between measurements.
- Knowing fractions and how to calculate them can be important in observing, analyzing, and understanding the world around us.
- Fractions are more than abstract ideas in school math; they are useful and part of many simple, everyday activities.

What extensions can you make?

In small groups, students can survey an edition of a daily newspaper for fractions. Each member of the group can work with a different section and compile a list of stories and quotations. If the groups use the same edition, they might compare and discuss their lists.

89 Jazz and Math: Rhythmic Innovations*

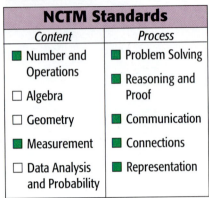

Overview

Students are often surprised to discover the connections between math and music and even more surprised to discover the role that fractions play in musical notation and performance. This activity will take several class periods and can form the basis for class projects relating other types of music to mathematics.

Grade Levels 7–8

NCTM Standards	
Content	*Process*
■ Number and Operations	■ Problem Solving
□ Algebra	■ Reasoning and Proof
□ Geometry	■ Communication
■ Measurement	■ Connections
□ Data Analysis and Probability	■ Representation

Activity

*What ideas or concepts will students **explore**?*

- Connections between fractions and musical notation
- Comparisons of jazz and straight rhythms
- Representations of notes and fractions with bar and pie graphs

What materials will you need?

episode 1 of *Jazz*, a PBS Ken Burns documentary • computer with Internet access • white board with colored markers • CDs of jazz and marches, CD player • chart of fractions and musical notes • fraction manipulatives • "Musical Notes and Fractions Worksheet" in the Worksheets & Handout section of the CD-ROM that accompanies this text

What questions could you ask?

When you listen to music, what kinds of differences can you hear in the rhythms?
How would you represent the rhythm of a march with your hands and feet? Of a jazz piece? Of other types of music?
What does the "big four" refer to in jazz?
What is a measure of music?
Why do you think some notes are called half notes, others eighth notes, others sixteenth notes?

What will you do?

Show the Jazz video about Buddy Bolden. Discuss Bolden's contributions to jazz rhythms. Demonstrate rhythms with dance steps or clapping. Use a chart to show different musical notes and fraction equivalents. Show how a measure of notes becomes a rhythm by clapping in $4/4$ time, $3/4$ time, and so forth.

---

*Adapted from a lesson by Amy Lein http://www.pbs.org/jazz/classroom/ rhythmic-innovations.htm.

What will students do?

Watch and discuss the Buddy Bolden video. Then listen to different rhythms on CDs. Stand and use body movements to duplicate the rhythms (clapping, dancing, waving hands, and so forth).

Invent ways to show the rhythms with fraction manipulatives and on paper. Use fraction circles and strips, other geometric shapes, wavy lines, and other images. Compare the results with a written measure of music.

Use the Fractions and Musical Notation chart to identify note and fraction equivalents. Fill out the "Musical Notes and Fractions Worksheet." Create a pie graph and a bar graph to represent the relationship of notes and fractions. Compare graphs with those at the PBS website (www.pbs.org/jazz/classroom/rhythmicinnovations.htm//procedures).

What strategies might students *invent* or construct?

Students might approach rhythms in terms of words and sounds ("boom chick, boom chick"), or they might use colors and shapes (red for long beat, yellow for short; square for long, triangle for short). Some will prefer to start with manipulatives, choosing $\frac{1}{16}$ strips to show 16th notes and so forth. Others might turn a measure into a numbers sentence: $\frac{1}{4} + \frac{1}{4} + \frac{1}{4} + \frac{1}{4} = 1$ whole note.

What insights, connections, or applications might students *discover*?

- Musical notes have two purposes: they show a note on a scale and the duration of the sound the note makes.
- Music is written in measures.
- Each measure is like a numbers sentence, with the fraction equivalents of each measure in the piece adding up to the same amount.
- March rhythms are straight and even.
- Jazz rhythms are uneven and lilting.

What extensions can you make?

Have students listen to other types of music and study the musical notation. Write a measure or more of each type of music in fractions and represent them with manipulatives. Discuss the differences in sound and rhythms of the different types of music.

Exploring Part-Whole Relationships: Decimals and Percents

90 Decimals and Percents in the Newspaper

Grade Levels 4–6

NCTM Standards	
Content	*Process*
■ Number and Operations	□ Problem Solving
□ Algebra	■ Reasoning and Proof
□ Geometry	■ Communication
□ Measurement	■ Connections
□ Data Analysis and Probability	■ Representation

Overview

The newspaper offers meaningful contexts for identifying and interpreting decimals and percents. Students survey the different sections of the newspaper to find examples and to discover how important decimals and percents are to the various messages in the different types of entries—news stories, advertisements, and so forth.

Activity

What ideas or concepts will students explore?
- Identifying decimals and percents
- Understanding decimals and percents in context
- Place-value concepts

What materials will you need?
copies of a newspaper ● pens or pencils ● scissors ● decimals/percent log sheets: large sheets of lined paper divided into columns headed "Decimals," "Percents," "Location," "Meaning"

What questions could you ask?
Where might you expect to find decimals and percents in the newspaper? Did you find them where you expected to? Any surprises?
Where do you find the most decimals and percents? The fewest?
Are decimals and percents easy to understand? Why or why not?

What will students do?
In groups or pairs, look for decimals and percents in a section of the newspaper. Circle each decimal and percent. Cut out paragraphs, articles, and ads. Attach them to the large log sheets. Write down where you found the examples. In the "Meaning" column, explain what they mean.

What strategies might students invent or construct?
Students might read the numbers literally, relying on their understanding of the number system for explanations. Some will go a step further and use contexts to interpret. To explain meaning, many will rewrite in their own words and also use verbal equivalents for numbers.

*What insights, connections, or applications might students **discover**?*

- Newspapers use decimals and percents in most sections—in news stories, sports, business, health, classifieds, and advertisements.
- Many of the numbers are rounded rather than exact.
- Decimals and percents are used to show money, trends, studies, sports scores, and other data.

91 Shopping by the Numbers

Grade Levels 5–7

NCTM Standards	
Content	*Process*
▣ Number and Operations	▣ Problem Solving
☐ Algebra	▣ Reasoning and Proof
☐ Geometry	▣ Communication
☐ Measurement	▣ Connections
☐ Data Analysis and Probability	▣ Representation

Overview

Shopping for and planning a party generate high levels of student interest. In this activity students make shopping lists, budget money, and comparison-shop. They deal with the specifics of becoming smart shoppers—understanding retail and sale prices, interpreting the percentages in discounts accurately, and matching purchases to money available.

Activity

What ideas or concepts will students *explore*?
- Exchanging money for things
- Decimals in money notation
- Discounts, deductions, and percent off
- Decimals and percents on the calculator

What materials will you need?
calculator • advertisements • money (real or make-believe) • shopping lists • pencils, paper • "Planning a Party Worksheet" in the Worksheets & Handouts section of the CD-ROM that accompanies this text

What questions could you ask?
What do the numbers in the advertisements mean?
What does the decimal mean when we write the numbers for money?
What does it mean if something is on sale?
What does it mean to pay retail price?
Who is a smart shopper? How many different things do you have to consider in smart shopping?

What will students do?
Activity A Find 20 food prices in the advertisements. Put them in order from most expensive to least expensive. Add up the prices on the calculator.

Activity B Find five advertisements with percentages in them. Explain what the percents mean. Compute the cost of the items with the percent discount.

Activity C Plan a party for yourself and 25 friends. Make a list of the things you would like to have for your party. Estimate how much of each item you will need for 25 friends and yourself. Take a trip to a grocery store or other place where you might buy the party items. Write down the cost of each item. Use the calculator to figure out the total cost for your party.

What strategies might students *invent* or construct?

Students will discover the importance of making lists to shop and figure costs. After some trial-and-error with entering items on the calculator, they might also discover the importance of placing the decimal properly. Some will find that estimating is a useful preliminary step in shopping; others, that estimation can be helpful in finding errors when entering numbers on the calculator.

What insights, connections, or applications might students *discover*?

- Money enables us to purchase things, but the amount of money available influences what we can purchase.
- How much something costs can vary with the store you are shopping at and with advertised sales.
- Smart shopping means getting the most for your money—best quality and the greatest amount of products for the least amount of money.

92 Modeling Decimal Numbers with Base-10 Blocks

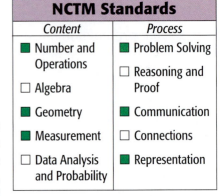

Math Manipulatives

Grade Levels 3–6

NCTM Standards	
Content	*Process*
■ Number and Operations	■ Problem Solving
□ Algebra	□ Reasoning and Proof
■ Geometry	■ Communication
■ Measurement	□ Connections
□ Data Analysis and Probability	■ Representation

Overview

Working with decimals presents a good opportunity to explain the connection between the word *decimal* and its root *decima*, Latin for "tithe" or "tenth," and the base-10 system. Base-10 blocks can be used to demonstrate place values to the right of the decimal point. Students can use cubes to model ones, flats to model tenths, rods to model hundredths and units to model thousandths.

Activity

*What ideas or concepts will students **explore**?*

- Parts-whole relationships
- Decimal notation
- Base-10 number system
- Place value and face value

What materials will you need?

base-10 blocks or "Pattern: Base-10 Blocks" in the Make Manipulatives section of the CD-ROM that accompanies this text • place-value and face-value charts for whole and decimal numbers • pencils, paper

What questions could you ask?

What do we mean by place value when we read numbers?
What is face value?
Why do numbers have both place value and face value?
What value do we assign to each type of block when we model whole numbers?
If we changed the value of a cube to 1, what would be the value of a flat, a rod, and a unit?
How would you write the equivalents of each block in numbers?

What will students do?

Activity A Review working with whole numbers and base-10 blocks by modeling small and large numbers. Use the blocks to build and solve addition, subtraction, multiplication, and division problems. Represent problems and answers with drawings, words, and numbers. Share and discuss results.

Activity B Model decimal numbers using base-10 blocks. Assign a value of 1 to the cube, $\frac{1}{10}$ to the flat, $\frac{1}{100}$ to the rod, and $\frac{1}{1,000}$ to the unit. Explain the values in terms of the parts-whole relationship. Represent numbers you build with drawings, words, and numbers.

Activity C Model addition and subtraction of decimal numbers using base-10 blocks. Use the values for blocks from Activity B. In pairs, take turns writing and modeling problems. Represent solutions with drawings, words, and numbers.

Activity D Use base-10 blocks to model multiplication and division problems. In pairs, take turns writing and modeling problems. Represent solutions with drawings, words, and numbers.

*What strategies might students **invent** or construct?*

Initially, students will build models and work out problems in detail. After a while, some may mix models and operations, building some numbers and using notation for others. Once students understand the 10 for 1 relationship of place values, they could vary the blocks used; for example, if a problem has 1s and 10ths, they might find it easier to work with rods for 1s and units for 10ths. Typically, multiplication and division require more block building than students may have time, space, and blocks for; then they might build initial numbers but use repeated addition or subtraction and mental calculations to complete patterns.

*What insights, connections, or applications might students **discover**?*

- Moving to the left of the decimal point, numbers increase by powers of 10; to the right, they decrease by powers of 10.
- It is important to line up decimal places in addition and subtraction and to count decimal places in multiplication and division.
- Multiplying and dividing with decimals are like multiplying and dividing with fractions; the results may be the opposite of what we expect from experiences with whole numbers.

What extensions can you make?

Follow up the modeled problems by making the same calculations with a calculator. Verbalize what you enter and see on the display. Try to visualize the quantities involved.

93 Connecting Fractions, Decimals, and Percents with Virtual Manipulatives

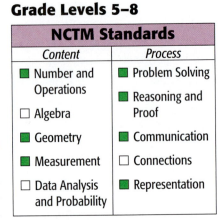

Math and Technology

Grade Levels 5–8

NCTM Standards	
Content	*Process*
☑ Number and Operations	☑ Problem Solving
☐ Algebra	☑ Reasoning and Proof
☑ Geometry	☑ Communication
☑ Measurement	☐ Connections
☐ Data Analysis and Probability	☑ Representation

Overview

The National Library of Virtual Manipulatives is a valuable resource for interactive activities for exploring mathematics. Topics include work suitable for students at different grade levels and use visual representations that can be altered to show related mathematical situations. The work for *parts of wholes* uses charts and graphs to show relationships that are then written in fractional notation, decimals, and percents.

Activity

What ideas or concepts will students *explore*?
- Fractions, decimals, and percents
- Equivalent expressions
- Visual representations
- Strategies for conversion

What materials will you need?
- computers with Internet access

What questions could you ask?
What do we mean by a part of a whole?
How many different ways can we show a part?
How many different ways can we show the part-whole relationship?
What do we mean by a fraction, a decimal, a percent?

What will students do?
In small groups, explore the idea of equivalent expressions by creating visuals and equivalent expressions for benchmark quantities such as halves, fourths, and thirds.

Then, individually, use the equivalent expressions manipulative at the National Library of Virtual Manipulatives (http://matti.usu.edu) to extend and expand the study. Fill in numbers for two of the three: decimals, percents, wholes. The display then fills in the third number and represents the relationship with two visuals, a bar and a circle that are shaded to show the part of the whole. The relationships are also represented with numbers and conversion formulas. Continue with different number combinations until you feel you understand the concepts and processes thoroughly.

What strategies might students *invent* or construct?

Working with the virtual manipulatives allows students to pair numbers and images effectively, but they may feel more involved if they can apply what they see. This could mean writing out the numbers before observing those on the screen or even marking drawings before observing the graphs. Verbalizing and explaining what they are seeing can also be helpful, especially when students work in pairs or groups.

What insights, connections, or applications might students *discover*?

- Every fraction can be represented with a decimal and a percent.
- Fractions, decimals, and percents show relationships to a whole rather than a specific quantity.
- Formulas show how to get from one from to the other, but the graphs show what the forms really mean.

94 Rounding

Grade Levels 4–5

NCTM Standards	
Content	*Process*
■ Number and Operations	■ Problem Solving
	□ Reasoning and Proof
□ Algebra	
□ Geometry	■ Communication
□ Measurement	■ Connections
□ Data Analysis and Probability	■ Representation

Overview

The concept of rounding is a particularly big idea for everyday use of numbers. It helps with estimation and in communicating quantities when exact numbers are less important than a general impression is (as in many newspaper stories). Students explore the usefulness of rounding by using rounded numbers and by interpreting and evaluating rounded numbers used by others.

Activity

What ideas or concepts will students explore?
- Rounded numbers
- Place and face value
- Whole numbers, decimals, and percents

What materials will you need? pencils, paper • calculators • newspapers

What questions could you ask?
What does it mean to round a number?
How can you tell if a number has been rounded off?
When might it be useful to round whole numbers? Decimals? Percents?
Where have you seen rounded numbers?
Who uses them? Do you?

What will you do? Use a number line to demonstrate the concept of rounding. Mark the halfway point; then introduce the rules of thumb: (1) If the number to the right is 5 or more, round up; (2) if the number to the right is 4 or less, round down.

Round up and down a series of numbers; then compare total of rounded numbers with total of exact numbers. The longer the list, usually the closer the totals will be.

What will students do?

Compose and then round numbers to the nearest 10, 100, and 1,000. Then, working with decimals and percents, round to the nearest 1,000th, 100th, 10th, whole, and percent.

Find five examples in the daily newspaper of numbers that have been rounded off. In writing, describe each number in terms of the place value of the rounding; also describe the context (the story, the situation) where the number was found.

What strategies might students ***invent*** *or construct?*

To make practice more meaningful and to stay focused, students can verbalize or write numbers in words. Some find it helpful to draw arrows or cross out the number rounded. Rounding to specific places encourages students to think in terms not only of face value of numbers but also place value.

What insights, connections, or applications might students ***discover***?

- Rounding may occur in different contexts.
- The degree of accuracy needed determines whether rounding is appropriate or whether it detracts from meaning.
- Rounding may work in long lists of items such as amounts of money because differences tend to average out.

95 Playing Concentration with Parts of Wholes*

Grade Levels 6–8

NCTM Standards	
Content	*Process*
■ Number and Operations	■ Problem Solving
□ Algebra	□ Reasoning and Proof
□ Geometry	□ Communication
□ Measurement	□ Connections
□ Data Analysis and Probability	■ Representation

Overview

Developing a sense for equivalent expressions and for converting fractions into percents and decimals and vice versa requires practice. Putting that practice into the context of a game keeps interest and engagement high. Having students make the actual playing materials requires a deeper level of understanding than do simple recognition skills.

Activity

What ideas or concepts will students explore?
- Equivalent expressions
- Visual representation for parts of wholes
- Relationship of parts to wholes

What materials will you need?
blank 3″ × 5″ index cards • compasses, protractors • charts with circle graphs showing typical fractions, decimals, percents • calculators • colored pencils or markers

What questions could you ask?
How can we know that a fraction and decimal or percent refer to the same segment of a whole?
How can we show it?

What will you do?
Make and use charts to show what benchmark fractions, decimals, percents look like. Show students how to make a circle graph with a compass and how to measure degrees of the circle. Have students figure out degrees of a circle for benchmark fractions, decimals, and percents.

What will students do?
Work in groups of four with assigned numbers in fraction, decimal, or percent form. Work together to find equivalent values. Use the blank index cards to make a set of four cards for each assigned number—one

---

*Adapted from Elizabeth S. Sweeney and Robert J. Quinn, "Concentration: Connecting Fractions, Decimals, and Percents," *Mathematics Teaching in the Middle School* 5 (January 2000): 324–28.

each for decimal, percent, fraction, and circle graph. As a group, create a deck of eight sets (32 cards) or combine your four-card sets with those from other groups.

To play, the cards are shuffled and placed face down on the table in a four-by-eight rectangular array. You can play as individuals or as groups. Each player turns two cards face up. If the cards show equivalent expressions, they form a match and are removed from play. If they do not match, they are returned to the table face down. Play continues until all of the cards have been matched. The player matching the most cards wins.

What strategies might students *invent* or construct?

Some students will prepare each playing card individually, carefully drawing circles with compasses and using the calculator to figure out equivalent expressions. Others will classify and create an assembly line—one process for decimals, one for percents, one for fractions, one for graphs. For making the circle graphs, some will prefer to work with fractions—half of a half of a circle for 25% instead of $.25 \times 360°$; they might use rulers instead of the protractor to measure.

What insights, connections, or applications might students *discover*?

- Having a visual image of a segment helps you estimate equivalent expressions more accurately (for example, knowing that a segment of more than half of a circle cannot be represented by an expression of less than 50%, .5, or $\frac{1}{2}$).
- Decimals, fractions, and percents are different ways of representing the same thing.
- Being able to convert from one expression to the other gives you a clearer picture of what "parts of a whole" means and also gives you greater flexibility for working with the numbers.

What extensions can you make?

Increase the difficulty of the numbers used to create the decks of cards. Have groups exchange cards to encourage working with as many different sets of expressions as possible.

96 Finding Decimals and Percents in Your World

Grade Levels 4–8

NCTM Standards	
Content	*Process*
☑ Number and Operations	☑ Problem Solving
☐ Algebra	☑ Reasoning and Proof
☐ Geometry	☑ Communication
☐ Measurement	☑ Connections
☑ Data Analysis and Probability	☑ Representation

Overview

Students become math prospectors, looking for decimals and percents in their own worlds. Because the activity emphasizes personal connections with the concepts, students come to see decimals and percents as meaningful and important. Keeping a log of their findings provides a record of the process of discovering and understanding the personal importance of the concepts.

Activity

What ideas or concepts will students explore?
- Identifying decimals and percents
- Understanding decimals and percents in context
- Classifying and organizing
- Representing data with graphs

What materials will you need?
decimal/percent log sheets: construction paper cover and lined sheets for writing • colored pencils or markers • "Graph and Pie Chart Worksheet" in theWorksheets & Handouts section of the CD-ROM that accompanies this text

What questions could you ask?
What do decimals and percents mean to you personally?
Do you use them?
Do the people around you use them?
Do you see them regularly?
Do you use them regularly?
Are they helpful tools?

What will students do?
Search and find decimals and percents in the world around you—in newspapers, magazines, books you find at home; on signs or banners you see on the street and in stores; in cash register receipts; in the mail. Make log sheets and write down, describe, and make a visual representation of examples you find over a set period, such as a week. Once the collection period is complete, develop different categories and organize the examples into those categories. You may need to set up different categories for decimals and percents.

*What strategies might students **invent** or construct?*

Students will find decimals and percents everywhere. They might find them in contexts related to the family budget, shopping lists, mad money, investments for college education, vacation plans, and mortgage and car payments.

*What insights, connections, or applications might students **discover**?*

- Decimals and percents are not just school-math topics; they are important to the everyday functioning of the family and serve as tools in planning for the future.
- Most people know a lot more about decimals and percents than they realize, but understanding them as math topics helps us to interpret uses in context and to consult them in planning and decision making.

What extensions can you make?

Have students represent their decimal and percent data with both a bar graph and a pie chart. They will need to do different graphs and charts for the different sets of data. Have them explain their findings, their categories, and their representations to the group or class.

97 Fractions to Decimals and Percents with Fraction Strips

Grade Levels 3–5

NCTM Standards	
Content	*Process*
■ Number and Operations	■ Problem Solving
☐ Algebra	☐ Reasoning and Proof
☐ Geometry	☐ Communication
■ Measurement	☐ Connections
☐ Data Analysis and Probability	■ Representation

Overview

Although fractions are fairly easy to visualize, some students have difficulty creating mental images of the corresponding decimals and percents. The activity builds visual bridges by starting with a traditional fraction-strips activity and then adds work with equivalent percents and decimals.

Activity

*What ideas or concepts will students **explore**?*
- Equivalent expressions, fractions, decimals, and percents
- Parts-of-whole relationships
- Visual representations

What materials will you need?
fraction tiles or "Pattern: Fraction Strips" in the Making Manipulatives section of the CD-ROM that accompanies this text • rulers, scissors • different colored paper for each different fraction • calculators • pencils, paper

What questions could you ask?
What does it mean when we say something represents a part of a whole? What would a whole look like?
What would half of a whole look like? A fourth? A third? A sixth? An eighth? How would you work out those images in your head?

What will you do?
Use fraction tiles or fraction strip patterns to demonstrate parts-of-whole relationships. Have students name the fractions for each tile; then figure out equivalent expressions in decimals and percents. Combine the tiles in different ways to create wholes, halves, and so on.

What will students do?
Begin by making your own fraction tiles from different colors of construction paper. Choose a different colored paper for each different fraction and measure in inches and then in centimeters. Label and cut out $\frac{1}{2}$, $\frac{1}{4}$, $\frac{1}{5}$, $\frac{1}{8}$, $\frac{1}{10}$, $\frac{1}{12}$ and $\frac{1}{16}$ lengths.

Using calculator or paper and pencil, convert each fraction to its decimal and percent equivalents; then measure the tiles in inches and in centimeters, and label the fraction tiles with decimals and equivalents.

What strategies might students *invent* or construct?

Some students will prefer measuring with the ruler before they cut the tiles; others might use folding to make the cuts and then measure to find equivalents.

What insights, connections, or applications might students *discover*?

- Each fraction can be represented with a decimal and a percent.
- You can figure out measurements by measuring each strip or by finding the fraction, decimal, or percent of the length of the whole.

What extensions can you make?

Add more fractions to explore. Combine, compare, and order fractions in a variety of ways.

98 Fractions to Decimals: Repeating Decimals and Rounding

Grade Levels 5–8

NCTM Standards	
Content	*Process*
■ Number and Operations	■ Problem Solving
□ Algebra	□ Reasoning and Proof
□ Geometry	■ Communication
■ Measurement	□ Connections
□ Data Analysis and Probability	■ Representation

Overview

This is a follow-up activity for Activity 97. The materials are essentially the same; students go a step further in applications to deal with decimals with repeating decimals and decimal numbers that have been rounded.

Activity

What ideas or concepts will students *explore*?
- Conversions from fractions to decimals
- Decimals with repeating digits
- Representing fractions and decimals visually

What materials will you need?
pencils, paper • rulers • different colored paper for each different fraction • calculators

What questions could you ask?
What do you know about these fractions: $\frac{1}{3}, \frac{1}{6}, \frac{1}{7}, \frac{1}{9}, \frac{1}{11}, \frac{1}{13}, \frac{1}{17}, \frac{1}{19}$?
What do they look like?
What equivalent expressions do you already know?
How would you find equivalent expressions for the others?
What problems might you encounter with these fractions that you did not encounter with halves and fourths?

What will students do?
Use different colors of construction paper to make fraction strips for $\frac{1}{3}, \frac{1}{6}, \frac{1}{7}, \frac{1}{9}, \frac{1}{11}, \frac{1}{13}, \frac{1}{17}, \frac{1}{19}$. Measure in inches, then in centimeters; then label and cut out the tiles. (Some estimation and approximation can be expected.)

Use calculators or paper and pencil to convert each fraction to its decimal equivalent in inches and centimeters. For each decimal equivalent, add a label to the matching fraction tiles. For each repeating decimal, round off to the nearest thousandth, hundredth, and tenth and explain which rounded number is closest in equivalence to the fraction and should be added to the tile labels.

*What strategies might students **invent** or construct?*

Students soon find that making strips for basic fractions such as $\frac{1}{3}$ or $\frac{1}{6}$ is much easier than making strips for $\frac{1}{11}$ or $\frac{1}{19}$. To simplify the process, some will measure $\frac{1}{10}$, then subtract a little to make the $\frac{1}{11}$ strip; also, they might measure half of $\frac{1}{10}$ and add a little to make the $\frac{1}{19}$ strip.

*What insights, connections, or applications might students **discover**?*

- Working with repeating decimals differs from working with nonrepeating decimals in terms of accuracy. Similarly, working with rounded decimals differs from working with nonrounded decimals.
- Converting fractions to decimals can be more complicated with fractions that, when transformed to decimals, produce rounded decimals.
- It is easier to model simple fractions like $\frac{1}{2}$ or $\frac{1}{8}$.
- The fraction from a rounded decimal is not quite equivalent or as accurate as the decimal.

99 Percents, Decimals, and the Dream Vacation

Grade Levels 3–8

NCTM Standards	
Content	*Process*
■ Number and Operations	■ Problem Solving
☐ Algebra	☐ Reasoning and Proof
☐ Geometry	■ Communication
■ Measurement	■ Connections
■ Data Analysis and Probability	■ Representation

Overview

This activity is a good way to involve families in students' study of mathematics. Often students will hold a family meeting to select a destination and then include family members in the specific details of planning the vacation, including setting a budget.

Activity

What ideas or concepts will students explore?
- Itinerary, cost, and time
- Map making and reading
- Budgeting
- Operations with decimals and percents

What materials will you need? calculators • pens or pencils, paper • maps, travel brochures, or access to Internet information on travel

What questions could you ask? Where would you go for your dream vacation?
How many people would you want to take with you?
How much money and time would you like to spend?
How would you plan your vacation so that you get the most enjoyment for your money?
What restrictions would you place on your plan—for example, the amount of time spent getting to and from a vacation spot?

What will students do? Plan a trip for several people. Determine the destination in terms of the following questions: What total distance will be traveled? What is the cost of transportation, food, entertainment, lodging, side trips, spending money, tips? How long will the trip last?

Then determine the totals and percent for the following: equal shares of cost for each person for the different categories; time spent on the different categories.

*What strategies might students **invent** or construct?*

Students might create planning logs and ledgers to help them keep track of costs. They could use maps to plot and record distances. For finding totals and percents they might multiply or use repeated addition; for dividing costs they could use repeated subtraction, estimating and rounding, or simply divide with the calculator and then convert.

*What insights, connections, or applications might students **discover**?*

- The longer the trip, the greater the time and money expended.
- Decimals and percents can be applied to measurements as well as money.
- Equal sharing means the same percent and decimal amount of the total.

What extensions can you make?

Add a survivor game element to the plan. Choose one or more of the original vacationers to leave behind. Explain the reasons in detail and calculate the effect on trip costs of dumping that person or persons. Then extend the vacation plan in time or destinations to spend the extra money saved by dumping some of the vacationers.

100

Do Women and Men Work for Equal Pay in Sports?

Mathematics Across the Curriculum

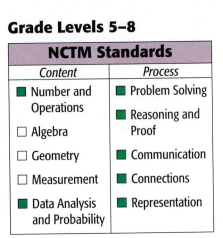

Grade Levels 5–8

NCTM Standards	
Content	*Process*
■ Number and Operations	■ Problem Solving
☐ Algebra	■ Reasoning and Proof
☐ Geometry	■ Communication
☐ Measurement	■ Connections
■ Data Analysis and Probability	■ Representation

Overview

This activity connects decimals and percents with a social issue: gender inequity in the salaries of athletes. Students research, interpret, and discuss data. They use their findings to try to understand and perhaps take a stand on the social issue.

Activity

What ideas or concepts will students *explore*?
- Issues about gender equity and inequity in professional athletes' salaries
- Decimal and percent applications in the context of salaries

What materials will you need?
several different sports pages or sports interviews from local newspapers and national magazines • pens or pencils, paper • calculators

What questions could you ask?
Is there gender equity in the salaries of professional athletes? Both women and men compete in such sports as tennis, basketball, race driving, and golf. Do they get paid equally? Why or why not?
If men, on average, receive more pay in a given sport, what percent of the men's earnings do the women earn?

What will students do?
Working in small groups of three or four students, dig out information from several media sources to find out how men and women compare in either salaries or earnings in two or three sports. For each sport, compute means and medians for both men and women and answer the questions posed in "What questions could you ask?"

What strategies might students *invent* or construct?
Some students will research a question by looking for others' calculations and conclusions. They might compare figures in published comments with their own findings. Most will focus on *what*—the facts of the situation. Some will focus on *why*—the reasons for as well as the effects of the situation.

*What insights, connections, or applications might students **discover**?*

- Means and other statistics can be used to help determine and measure fairness: for example, a gap of 75% means a greater level of unfairness than a gap of 10% does.
- The principle *equal pay for equal work* does not seem to be operative in most professional sports.
- Gender gaps may be narrowing in sports such as tennis and golf.

What extensions can you make?

Have students look at similar issues in amateur sports—for example, the amount of money budgeted for men's and women's sports in college or high school athletics.

101 Population Percentages

Overview

Students work with percents within the context of a social-studies project. They do research, compile and interpret data, and represent their findings with maps.

NCTM Standards	
Content	*Process*
■ Number and Operations	■ Problem Solving
□ Algebra	■ Reasoning and Proof
□ Geometry	■ Communication
□ Measurement	■ Connections
■ Data Analysis and Probability	■ Representation

Activity

What ideas or concepts will students explore?

- Human populations by geographic area
- Percentages of human populations in different geographic areas
- Data collection, analysis, representation, interpretation

What materials will you need?

calculators • pens or pencils, paper • access to encyclopedias, magazines, world maps and gazettes, the Internet • worksheets with nations and continents drawn in but with space for adding data

What questions could you ask?

Where is the largest concentration of humans?
Where would one find the fewest humans?
By geographic area where do the top 10 populations live?
What hemisphere contains the most people?
What continent contains the most people?

What will students do?

In groups of three or four, explore these questions by doing research in printed resources or on the Internet. Each student in your group might focus on one or two questions. Once individuals have found some answers, you can compile the results and create maps to show percentages and other data.

What strategies might students invent or construct?

Students might work with total populations and figure percents from those numbers, or look for percentages in reference works. Some will decide to work with rounded numbers for estimates; others, with the most exact numbers they can find. Students might discover at first that their percentages exceed or fall below 100%. They may need to rework estimates and use more exact numbers.

What insights, connections, or applications might students *discover*?

- Most people live in one part of the world.
- No matter whether we are dealing with billions or thousands, the total percent should add up to 100%.
- To use the calculator to compute extremely large numbers, we may need to use knowledge of the base-10 number system and work with millions and 10ths of millions (for example, 10.5 for 10,500,000).

What extensions can you make?

Compare percentages for world's population and percentages for land mass, resources, wealth, food, health care, and so forth. Discuss the distribution of essential materials and available resources in terms of continents as well as population numbers.

Building Bridges

102 Real Numbers in the Workplace

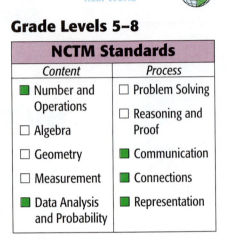

Grade Levels 5–8

NCTM Standards	
Content	*Process*
☑ Number and Operations	☐ Problem Solving
☐ Algebra	☐ Reasoning and Proof
☐ Geometry	☑ Communication
☐ Measurement	☑ Connections
☑ Data Analysis and Probability	☑ Representation

Overview

This is a discovery activity. Students find for themselves the meanings and importance of real numbers in the workplace. In the process, they collect and organize data, interpret and represent findings. They share and discuss outcomes to broaden understanding and develop multiple perspectives.

Activity

What ideas or concepts will students *explore*?
- Identifying real numbers in the workplace
- Finding different kinds of real numbers
- Understanding real numbers

What materials will you need?   pens, pencils • writing pads

What questions could you ask?

What is a real number?
What kinds of real numbers exist?
Who works with real numbers? For example, what kinds of numbers do lawyers work with? Does a criminal lawyer work with different kinds of numbers than a corporate lawyer does? Explain.

What will you do?

Use yourself as an example and describe the kinds of real numbers you work with in your different roles in life—as a teacher, a counselor, a parent, and so forth. Convey to your class that all professionals work with real numbers on a daily basis as part of their work, as part of their livelihood.

What will students do?

Identify a place of work; identify and categorize the kinds of duties associated with the place of work. Identify and categorize the kinds of real numbers dealt with in that type of work. Interview one to three people at the worksite and determine time and/or frequency with which they work with the real numbers previously identified. Keep a log of their answers. Develop a bar chart or other visual that represents the information gathered.

*What strategies might students **invent** or construct?*

Students could begin with a web search to determine what kinds of real numbers are associated with different types of work. They might choose a profession they are interested in pursuing or one that people they know work in. To gather specific information, they might telephone or e-mail the interviewees. They might work in small groups to help each other interpret the information they gathered.

*What insights, connections, or applications might students **discover**?*

- Real numbers play an important role in the workplace.
- Real numbers do not exist in a vacuum in mathematics textbooks.
- Real numbers are used by real people all the time.

103 Real Numbers at the Zoo

Grade Levels 5–8

NCTM Standards	
Content	*Process*
■ Number and Operations	■ Problem Solving
☐ Algebra	■ Reasoning and Proof
☐ Geometry	■ Communication
☐ Measurement	■ Connections
■ Data Analysis and Probability	■ Representation

Overview

In this multidisciplinary activity, students combine mathematics and life sciences. They take a field trip to a zoo or animal park to observe and record animal behaviors.

Activity

What ideas or concepts will students explore?

- Real numbers and zoo animals
- Observing behavior
- Recording observations
- Representing and interpreting data
- Frequency counts
- Basic statistics

What materials will you need?

paper, pencils ● "Numbers at the Zoo Worksheet" in the Worksheets & Handout section of the CD-ROM that accompanies this text ● markers and graph paper for constructing bar charts

What questions could you ask?

Do real numbers have anything to do with the zoo?
How can we find out?
Does mathematics mix with animals? How can we tell?
What is your favorite zoo animal? Why?
What animal behaviors do you enjoy watching? Why?

What will students do?

Select one kind of animal to observe at the zoo for a period of about two hours. Take notes on and keep a log of the behavior of all participants. What do they do? How often do they do whatever it is that they do? Do all participants participate in the same way? If so, count the similarities. If not, count the differences. Develop a frequency bar chart of your findings. Interpret your findings. Share your findings with your class.

What strategies might students *invent* or construct?

Some students will choose a popular subject like the monkeys to observe; others will look for less-active animals like the elephants or lions. Student teams might divide the observations, with one student recording one or two types of behavior; the other, one or two other types. To interpret and represent findings, some may work with straight number counts; others could apply some type of statistical analysis to the data—for example, finding means or medians.

What insights connections, or applications might students *discover*?

- Real numbers can provide a world of information about animals, both large and small.
- This information can be invaluable in one's attempt to understand the animal kingdom.
- Frequency counts can be graphed to show patterns and relationships.
- Typically, frequency counts are shown on a bar graph: the vertical axis shows the frequency; the horizontal axis can show qualitative data.
- If the information on the horizontal axis is quantitative, then the result is a frequency polygon.

104

Irrational Numbers, a Pattern Activity:
π, Φ, $\sqrt{2}$

Grade Levels 6–8

NCTM Standards	
Content	*Process*
■ Number and Operations	■ Problem Solving
☐ Algebra	■ Reasoning and Proof
☐ Geometry	☐ Communication
☐ Measurement	☐ Connections
☐ Data Analysis and Probability	☐ Representation

Overview

Students use square roots and calculators to explore rational and irrational numbers.

Activity

*What ideas or concepts will students **explore**?*

- Rational numbers
- Irrational numbers
- Using calculators to find square roots

What materials will you need?

pencils, paper • calculators with square-root keys

What questions could you ask?

What is a rational number?
What is an irrational number?
What makes an irrational number *irrational?*
How do irrational numbers differ from rational numbers?
What happens when you multiply a number by itself?
Why is that number called a square?
What is a square root?
How can you use the calculator to compute a square root?

What will students do?

Answer the questions in "What questions could you ask?" first from previous experiences and speculation and then by investigation and discovery. Remember that real numbers that are irrational can be represented in decimal form and not fractional form. When in decimal form, irrational numbers are nonterminating and nonrepeating. Bring out your calculators and do the following activity:

Discover which of the following are irrational, and explain why:

$$\sqrt{2} \quad \sqrt{4} \quad \sqrt{3} \quad \sqrt{5} \quad \sqrt{6}$$
$$\sqrt{7} \quad \sqrt{8} \quad \sqrt{9} \quad \sqrt{10} \quad \sqrt{11}$$

What kind of pattern emerges from this activity that would enable you to know which quantities are irrational without having to do any calculations?

*What strategies might students **invent** or construct?*

Some students will do all of the calculations and then answer the questions. Others will first eliminate numbers like 4 and 9 that their knowledge of math facts tells them will not result in an irrational number.

*What insights, connections, or applications might students **discover**?*

- A rational number can be named by a ratio, such as $\frac{1}{2}$ or $\frac{3}{4}$.
- An irrational number cannot be named by a ratio.
- In decimal form, an irrational number neither repeats nor shows a pattern.
- The square root of a nonperfect square such as 3 is an irrational number.

105 Is Pi Measurable?

Grade Levels 7–8

NCTM Standards	
Content	*Process*
■ Number and Operations	■ Problem Solving
☐ Algebra	■ Reasoning and Proof
■ Geometry	■ Communication
■ Measurement	■ Connections
■ Data Analysis and Probability	■ Representation

Overview

This activity can be used as a follow-up to Activity 104. Students measure circles to find circumferences and diameters and then use their findings to try to compute pi. The activity demonstrates the value and the difficulty of precise measurements.

Activity

What ideas or concepts will students explore?

- Pi as an irrational number
- Finding pi by dividing circumference by diameter of a circle
- Measuring circles
- Estimation
- Variations

What materials will you need?

10 circular objects that vary in size and ease of measurement (cups, basketballs, hula hoops, wall clocks, tires, and so forth) • pencils, paper • calculators • measuring tapes, yardsticks, rulers

What questions could you ask?

Is pi a number? Why or why not?
How do we arrive at pi?
Is pi a ratio? If so, what is it a ratio of? Is it the ratio between the radius of a circle and its diameter? Or the diameter of a circle and its area? Or the radius of a circle and its circumference? Or the circumference of a circle and its diameter? How can you demonstrate the answer to these questions?

What will students do?

In pairs, measure each of the 10 circular objects. Apply the *C/d* formula (circumference divided by diameter) for each object, and use calculators to compute ratios to four or five decimal places. Then compute an average of the 10 estimates of pi. Discuss the problems you had in measuring the different objects. Write an explanation of why your team's measurements varied, and explain why you think there is such a discrepancy between your calculations of pi and what mathematicians say that pi equals: 3.14159. . . .

What strategies might students _invent_ or construct?

Students will use the measuring tapes to find the circumferences and diameters of smaller round objects, wrapping the tape around the outside and then across the middle. For spheres, some will estimate the diameter by holding the measuring tape flat; others will use their pencils to mark the far points of the sphere on paper, then measure the distance between the markings. A few will try to cut the sphere in half and measure across the center.

What insights, connections, or applications might students _discover_?

- Actually measuring pi is more difficult than most people expect.
- The variations in estimates of pi can be unexpected.
- Obtaining an estimate even remotely close to 3.14159 is highly improbable.
- Variations can be influenced by the accuracy of the measurer and the measuring tools.
- Computing pi accurately requires more than simply measuring a few circles.

What extensions can you make?

Research Archimedes' and Chinese mathematicians' methods of computing pi by measuring multiple-sided polygons. Use the Internet to find information or read books about pi such as Alfred S. Posamentier and Ingmar Lehmann's π: _A Biography of the World's Most Mysterious Number_ (Amherst, New York: Prometheus, 2004).

106 The Golden Ratio, Phi (Φ), and Physical Beauty

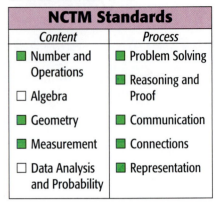

Grade Levels 7–8

NCTM Standards	
Content	*Process*
☑ Number and Operations	☑ Problem Solving
☐ Algebra	☑ Reasoning and Proof
☑ Geometry	☑ Communication
☑ Measurement	☑ Connections
☐ Data Analysis and Probability	☑ Representation

Overview

Beauty and attractiveness are often preoccupations among young people. Finding and exploring a mathematical dimension of the topic makes a connection with student interests and engages them in the task. Mathematical concepts explored include symmetry, ratio and proportion, spatial relationships, and equations. Students can also connect the mathematics of the golden ratio with culture and history, architecture, life sciences, and art.

Activity

What ideas or concepts will students *explore*?
- The golden ratio, ratio and proportion
- Measuring objects and people to find golden ratios
- Physical beauty and attractiveness

What materials will you need?
pencils, writing pads • calculators • measuring tapes and sticks • computers with Internet access, encyclopedias, and other reference sources

What questions could you ask?
What is beauty?
What do you see when you describe an object or a person as attractive?
What is the golden ratio?
Is this number relevant to us? Why or why not?
Do you think that you can make calculations that are relevant to the golden ratio?

What will you do?
Explain to your students the concept of the golden ratio and its symbol phi, or Φ. (For more background, see Huntley, H. E. (1970). *The divine proportion.* New York: Dover.) Phi is an irrational number with the value of $(1 + \sqrt{5})/2$, or 1.6180340 to an accuracy of seven decimal places.

Explain that, historically, this ratio shows up in many contexts—from such manmade edifices as the Parthenon to objects found in nature, like the seashell. More recently, a number of researchers have studied connections between the physical proportions of the human body and the golden ratio. The thinking of this research is that the closer a measured physical ratio matches the golden ratio, the more "attractive" and symmetrical that proportion is.

Pose some additional questions: "What do you think? Is physical beauty 'in the eye of the beholder,' or can it be measured and defined with a ruler and numbers? And what does this idea have to do with the measurement of physical beauty?"

What will students do? **Activity A** Working in pairs, use the Internet and other resources to explore the questions raised in your class discussion about beauty and measurements. Arrive at some conclusions based on your findings; then present your findings to the class.

Activity B Working in pairs, use measurements to look for golden ratios:

1. Measure a picture or a volunteer's physical height (in centimeters for all measurements).
2. Measure the distance from foot to navel.
3. Calculate the ratio of physical height divided by navel height.
4. Measure from the top of the head to the navel.
5. Calculate the ratio of navel height divided by top-of-the-head-to-navel height.
6. The closer a calculation is to 1.618, the closer the measurements are to the golden ratio.

What strategies might students ***invent*** *or construct?* Some students will approach the activities looking for affirmation—for evidence that their perceptions of beauty can be "proven," as it were, with measurements. Others will be skeptical and look for evidence that measurements have nothing to do with beauty. Many will look for additional material on the Internet, including images of architecture and artwork that fit the golden ratio ideal of beauty. Some may prefer to measure pictures rather than people and use the activity to test their perceptions of beauty as they relate to various celebrities.

What insights, connections, or applications might students ***discover***?
- Physical beauty may not have much to do with the golden ratio.
- Physical attractiveness seems to transcend mathematical measurements.
- The golden ratio defines a very classical and rigid idea of beauty as regularity and symmetry.

Real Numbers, Math Games, and Alphanumeric Puzzles

Grade Level 8

NCTM Standards	
Content	*Process*
■ Number and Operations	■ Problem Solving
☐ Algebra	■ Reasoning and Proof
☐ Geometry	☐ Communication
☐ Measurement	☐ Connections
☐ Data Analysis and Probability	■ Representation

Overview

In this activity students work with the concepts of codes, puzzles, and code breaking. They experiment with alphanumeric codes and try to solve codes in which numbers substitute for letters in a sentence of words and letters substitute for numbers in a number sentence.

Activity

*What ideas or concepts will students **explore**?*

- Puzzles as mathematical tasks
- Alphanumerics
- Making and breaking codes
- Logical patterns

What materials will you need?

pencils, writing pads • calculators

What questions could you ask?

Do you enjoy solving puzzles? Why or why not?
What do you know about codes?
Have you ever made up a secret code to communicate with your friends?
If so, did you use numbers or letters or both in your code?
How would you go about making up a very difficult code?
How would you go about cracking a difficult code?
How is cracking a code like solving a puzzle?

What will you do?

Introduce the concept of codes by talking about some of codes of the past. You might mention the Navajo code talkers, the Japanese red and blue code books, and the German Enigma machine. Then present a series of numerical and letter codes to be solved as a class. Discuss the idea of an alphanumeric code or puzzle (numbers for letters and letters for numbers), and ask for suggestions on cracking the code.

What will students do?

Work together in pairs or small groups to solve these puzzles:

8 5 12 12 15!   8 15 23   1 18 5   25 15 21?

XZM   DV YV   UIRVMWH?

*What strategies might students **invent** or construct?*

Most students will work by trial-and-error, substituting letters for numbers and numbers for letters. Some will look for patterns such as one-to-one correspondence between the number sequence and the alphabet or a reverse relationship with *z* standing for *1* and so forth.

*What insights, connections, or applications might students **discover**?*

- Numbers can be substituted for letters and letters for numbers to create a code.
- To break a code, you need to discover the pattern of substitution.
- To make a code difficult to break, you might use a random rather than a regular relationship between the letters and the numbers.
- Using both letters and numbers in a code adds a greater degree of difficulty.
- Code breaking is part logic and part trial-and-error.

108 Functions and Straight Lines

Grade Levels 6–8

NCTM Standards	
Content	*Process*
■ Number and Operations	■ Problem Solving
■ Algebra	■ Reasoning and Proof
■ Geometry	☐ Communication
■ Measurement	☐ Connections
☐ Data Analysis and Probability	■ Representation

Overview

As preparation for graphing linear equations, students explore the properties of straight lines.

Activity

What ideas or concepts will students *explore*?

- Properties of straight lines
- Straight lines of physical objects
- Ordering lines by length
- Categorizing straight lines as vertical lines, horizontal lines, neither vertical nor horizontal lines

What materials will you need?

pencils, paper • straight-edged physical objects: books, shelves, doors, cabinets, bulletin boards, and so on • measuring tools with straight edges such as rulers and yard- or metersticks

What questions could you ask?

What objects around you contain straight lines?
Do doors have straight lines?
Do the shelves and cabinets in your home consist of straight lines?
Are these straight lines measurable in terms of length?
What percentage of the straight lines around you are vertical? Horizontal? Neither vertical nor horizontal?

What will students do?

Describe 10 objects that have straight lines. Measure the length of the straight lines of each object. Keep a record of your measurements. Order the different lengths of your measurements from shortest to longest. Categorize straight lines by percentages into one of three categories: vertical, horizontal, and neither vertical nor horizontal.

What strategies might students *invent* or construct?

Some students will find and measure lines one at a time and then group the lines by type later. Others will use the categories to structure their investigation—looking first for vertical lines, then horizontal, and then for lines that are neither vertical nor horizontal.

What insights, connections, or applications might students ***discover****?*

- Lines can be organized into three categories: vertical, horizontal, or neither vertical nor horizontal.
- There are straight lines everywhere.
- Ordering lines by length is less effective than ordering by orientation since there are too many specific lengths to group the lines.

109 Functions: Straight Line, Graphing Linear Equations Using Intercepts

BIG IDEAS
in Mathematics

Grade Levels 7–8

NCTM Standards	
Content	*Process*
■ Number and Operations	■ Problem Solving
■ Algebra	■ Reasoning and Proof
■ Geometry	☐ Communication
■ Measurement	☐ Connections
☐ Data Analysis and Probability	■ Representation

Overview

Students explore graphing linear equations. They discover the minimal number of points needed to graph a straight line and the use of a third point to test their accuracy.

Activity

*What ideas or concepts will students **explore**?*
- Straight lines and linear equations
- Slopes of straight lines
- Points on a line
- Graphing linear equations using intercepts

What materials will you need?
pencils • graph paper • graphing calculators

What questions could you ask?
What is a linear equation?
How would you find the y-intercept in a linear equation?
What about the x-intercept?
What is the Cartesian coordinate system?
How does the Cartesian coordinate system apply to graphing linear equations?

What will you do?
Demonstrate and explain key ideas:

- To find the y-intercept, let $x = 0$; meaning if $x = 0$, notice that whatever the value for y, the line will go through the y-axis.
- To find the x-intercept, set $y = 0$, using the same logic as before.
- By finding the y and the x intercepts, you have two points; if you have two points, you can graph the linear equation.

Give example: Graph: $3x + 2y = 12$

To find the y-intercept, set $x = 0$, then solve for y.

$3x + 2y = 12$
$3(0) + 2y = 12$
$2y = 12$
$2y/2 = 12/2$
$y = 6$ Therefore, the y-intercept is (0,6).

To find the *x*-intercept, set *y* = 0, then solve for *x*.

$3x + 2y = 12$
$3x + 2(0) = 12$
$3x = 12$
$3x/3 = 12/3$
$x = 4$ Therefore, the *x*-intercept is (4,0).

On graph paper, graph the two points, (0,6) and (4,0), and then draw a straight line through both points. This graph is the graph of the linear function, $3x + 2y = 12$. (See the illustration that follows.)

Graphing a linear equation.

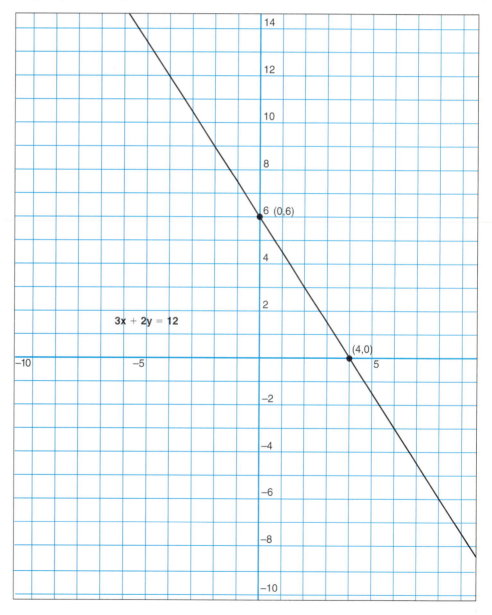

What will students do?   First, follow the directions for graphing the linear equation in your teacher's example. Then apply the same method for graphing the following equations:

$$y + 4 = 6 \qquad 2x - 2y = 14 \qquad 3x + 12y = 2y \qquad y - x = 2$$
$$4y + 4 = 16 \qquad 2x + 2y = 14 \qquad 3x + 12y = -y \qquad -y - x = 2$$

What strategies might students invent or construct?   At first students might plot many points until they find that they really need only two points on a straight line in order to graph it. Then some will discover they can check their calculations by determining a third point. If the third point fits on the line, the initial figuring is correct; if not, check all calculations.

What insights, connections, or applications might students discover?

- A linear function has all of its points on a straight line.
- A linear equation gives us the algebraic representation of the graph.

110 Trail Mix Ratios

Grade Levels 5–6

NCTM Standards	
Content	*Process*
■ Number and Operations	■ Problem Solving
☐ Algebra	■ Reasoning and Proof
☐ Geometry	☐ Communication
■ Measurement	■ Connections
■ Data Analysis and Probability	■ Representation

Overview

Students develop a visual and concrete foundation for understanding ratios. They begin with the familiar, estimating and counting various items found in handfuls of trail mix. Then they work with the totals to find multiples and then ratios of various items. One outcome might be a recipe for their own version of trail mix.

Activity

*What ideas or concepts will students **explore**?*

■ Counting and estimating numbers in a three-dimensional context
■ Relationship between counting and finding ratios
■ Ratios
■ Comparing ratios

What materials will you need?

paper, pencils • calculators • "Counting Sheets" in the Worksheets & Handout section of the CD-ROM that accompanies this text • packages of trail mix with various kinds of nuts, sunflower seeds, raisins, dates, and so on • plastic bags for each student

What questions could you ask?

How many _____ do you think you will find in a handful of trail mix?
Do you think that you will have more of the smaller items like sunflower seeds or larger items like nuts? Why?
Do you think that, with different trail mix items, you have twice as many of one kind as another? Or even three or four times as many?

What will you do?

Demonstrate ratios of 2 to 1, 3 to 1, 4 to 1. Ask students if they see the following relationships on their counting sheets—that they counted twice (or almost twice) as many of one kind of food as another or three times as many of one as another or even four times as many. If students find even one of these situations to be true, they should make note of it in the space provided on their counting sheets.

What will students do?

Pick up two handfuls of trail mix and put each handful in a plastic bag. Working in pairs, spread out the trail mix items on the table one bag at a time. Identify and list the different items and count each item. Write down the totals for each item count on the "Counting Sheets."

Compare counts and decide whether any of the food-item counts double, triple, or even quadruple exactly or almost any of the other food items. Show any multiple relationships on the "Counting Sheets."

*What strategies might students **invent** or construct?*

Some students will cluster items and count one cluster at a time; others will show number correspondence with parallel lines of items. Students who have studied the concepts of rounding might work with rounded numbers to make comparisons easier. Since there will probably be few exact multiples, students will need to work with approximates to demonstrate various ratios.

*What insights, connections, or applications might students **discover**?*

- The size of food items affects the count since it helps determine how many fit in a handful.
- Different counts can be understood in terms of twice as many or three times as many.
- Multiples form the basis of ratios: multiples of 2 making 2 to 1 ratios, multiples of 3 making 3 to 1 ratios, and so forth.

What extensions could you make?

Compile class information to create an approximate recipe for the trail mix you provided. Discuss the various items included to determine which ingredients students liked best, least, and so forth. Then, starting with ratios (for example, 2 to 1 ratio of sunflower seeds to pumpkin seeds), come up with a class recipe for enough trail mix for a snack for everyone.

111 M&M Count and Crunch: Fractions and Ratios with M&Ms*

Math Manipulatives

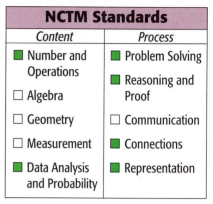

Overview

Students predict the numbers of M&Ms of different colors and then count and compare the actual numbers. They organize data in a table with whole numbers, fractions, and percentages and represent their findings with a graph.

Grade Levels 5–6

NCTM Standards	
Content	*Process*
■ Number and Operations	■ Problem Solving
☐ Algebra	■ Reasoning and Proof
☐ Geometry	☐ Communication
☐ Measurement	■ Connections
■ Data Analysis and Probability	■ Representation

Activity

What ideas or concepts will students *explore*?

- Fractions and ratios
- Relationship between counting and finding ratios
- Percents
- Predictions
- Graphing
- Categorizing

What materials will you need?

"M&M Count and Crunch Worksheet" on the CD-ROM that accompanies this text • individual bags of M&Ms • pencils, crayons, or colored pencils • paper

What questions could you ask?

How do we make predictions about numbers and quantities?
What is an example of a ratio?
What are the different ways to express a ratio?
What do we do to turn a ratio into a percent?

What will students do?

Working in teams of three or more, make predictions on your worksheet for questions 1–9, filling in the prediction column of the chart. Open bags of M&Ms and answer those questions, filling in the "actual" column of the chart. Complete the M&M data table, converting both predictions and actual numbers into ratios and percents. Design a graph to display results.

---

*Adapted from an activity taught by Bernadette Garcia

*What strategies might students **invent** or construct?*

Although students work in groups, each student has a bag of M&Ms to explore. Many will quickly find that there are differences between bags that can affect outcomes. To show the differences, many will do different worksheets for each bag. Students who have studied averages might work with an average for two or more bags.

*What insights, connections, or applications might students **discover**?*

- Ratios are equal to percents.
- Not all bags of M&Ms are equal in count.
- Ratios can be turned into percents, and percents can be reversed into ratios.
- Ratios can be expressed in three different ways.
- There are different ways to graph your results.
- Multiplication and division are the key to ratios, fractions, and percents.

What extensions could you make?

Have students write ratio and proportion statements for other sets of data. You might use "Ratio Worksheets 1 and 2" (in the Worksheets & Handout section of the CD-ROM that accompanies this text) or assign students to collect their own data.